Cross–Industry Applications of Cyber Security Frameworks

Sukanta Kumar Baral
Indira Gandhi National Tribal University, India

Richa Goel
Amity University, India

Md Mashiur Rahman
Bank Asia Ltd., Bangladesh

Jahangir Sultan
Bentley University, USA

Sarkar Jahan
Royal Bank of Canada, Canada

A volume in the Advances in
Information Security, Privacy, and
Ethics (AISPE) Book Series

Published in the United States of America by
   IGI Global
   Information Science Reference (an imprint of IGI Global)
   701 E. Chocolate Avenue
   Hershey PA, USA 17033
   Tel: 717-533-8845
   Fax: 717-533-8661
   E-mail: cust@igi-global.com
   Web site: http://www.igi-global.com

Library of Congress Cataloging-in-Publication Data

Names: Baral, Sukanta Kumar, 1966- editor. | Goel, Richa, 1980- editor. |
   Rahman, Md. Mashiur, 1980- editor. | Sultan, Jahangir, 1956- editor. |
   Jahan, Sarkar, 1979- editor.
Title: Cross-industry applications of cyber security frameworks / Sukanta
   Kumar Baral, Richa Goel, Md Mashiur Rahman, Jahangir Sultan, and Sarkar
   Jahan, editors.
Description: Hershey, PA : Information Science Reference, an imprint of IGI
   Global, [2022] | Includes bibliographical references and index. |
   Summary: "This book posits that rather than cybersecurity being simply
   an issue of securing systems and networks, corporate leaders need to
   think in terms of assuring the integrity and durability of the
   interconnected business and social structures that sit on top of an
   increasingly complex technology landscape"-- Provided by publisher.
Identifiers: LCCN 2022013979 (print) | LCCN 2022013980 (ebook) | ISBN
   9781668434482 (h/c) | ISBN 9781668434499 (s/c) | ISBN 9781668434505
   (ebook)
Subjects: LCSH: Computer networks--Security measures. | Computer security.
   | Industries--Data processing--Security measures.
Classification: LCC TK5105.59 .C758 2022 (print) | LCC TK5105.59 (ebook)
   | DDC 005.8--dc23/eng/20220525
LC record available at https://lccn.loc.gov/2022013979
LC ebook record available at https://lccn.loc.gov/2022013980

This book is published in the IGI Global book series Advances in Information Security, Privacy,
and Ethics (AISPE) (ISSN: 1948-9730; eISSN: 1948-9749)

British Cataloguing in Publication Data
A Cataloguing in Publication record for this book is available from the British Library.

All work contributed to this book is new, previously-unpublished material.
The views expressed in this book are those of the authors, but not necessarily of the publisher.

For electronic access to this publication, please contact: eresources@igi-global.com.

Advances in Information Security, Privacy, and Ethics (AISPE) Book Series

ISSN:1948-9730
EISSN:1948-9749

Editor-in-Chief: Manish Gupta State University of New York, USA

MISSION

As digital technologies become more pervasive in everyday life and the Internet is utilized in ever increasing ways by both private and public entities, concern over digital threats becomes more prevalent.

The **Advances in Information Security, Privacy, & Ethics (AISPE) Book Series** provides cutting-edge research on the protection and misuse of information and technology across various industries and settings. Comprised of scholarly research on topics such as identity management, cryptography, system security, authentication, and data protection, this book series is ideal for reference by IT professionals, academicians, and upper-level students.

COVERAGE

- Internet Governance
- Security Information Management
- Cyberethics
- Computer ethics
- Device Fingerprinting
- Security Classifications
- Access Control
- IT Risk
- CIA Triad of Information Security
- Cookies

IGI Global is currently accepting manuscripts for publication within this series. To submit a proposal for a volume in this series, please contact our Acquisition Editors at Acquisitions@igi-global.com or visit: http://www.igi-global.com/publish/.

Titles in this Series

For a list of additional titles in this series, please visit:
www.igi-global.com/book-series/advances-information-security-privacy-ethics/37157

Information Security Practices for the Internet of Things, 5G, and Next-Generation Wireless Networks
Biswa Mohan Sahoo (Amity University, India) and Suman Avdhesh Yadav (Amity University, India)
Information Science Reference • © 2022 • 325pp • H/C (ISBN: 9781668439210) • US $250.00

Global Perspectives on Information Security Regulations Compliance, Controls, and Assurance
Guillermo A. Francia III (University of West Florida, USA) and Jeffrey S. Zanzig (Jacksonville State University, USA)
Information Science Reference • © 2022 • 309pp • H/C (ISBN: 9781799883906) • US $240.00

Handbook of Research on Cyber Law, Data Protection, and Privacy
Nisha Dhanraj Dewani (Maharaja Agrasen Institute of Management Studies, Guru Gobind Singh Indraprastha University, India) Zubair Ahmed Khan (University School of Law and Legal Studies, Guru Gobind Singh Indraprastha University, India) Aarushi Agarwal (Maharaja Agrasen Institute of Management Studies, India) Mamta Sharma (Gautam Buddha University, India) and Shaharyar Asaf Khan (Manav Rachna University, India)
Information Science Reference • © 2022 • 390pp • H/C (ISBN: 9781799886419) • US $305.00

Cybersecurity Crisis Management and Lessons Learned From the COVID-19 Pandemic
Ryma Abassi (Sup'Com, University of Carthage, Tunisia) and Aida Ben Chehida Douss (Sup'Com, University of Carthage, Tunisia)
Information Science Reference • © 2022 • 276pp • H/C (ISBN: 9781799891642) • US $240.00

Applications of Machine Learning and Deep Learning for Privacy and Cybersecurity
Anacleto Correia (CINAV, Portuguese Naval Academy, Portugal) and Victor Lobo (Nova-IMS, Naval Academy, Portugal)
Information Science Reference • © 2022 • 315pp • H/C (ISBN: 9781799894308) • US $250.00

IGI Global
PUBLISHER of TIMELY KNOWLEDGE

701 East Chocolate Avenue, Hershey, PA 17033, USA
Tel: 717-533-8845 x100 • Fax: 717-533-8661
E-Mail: cust@igi-global.com • www.igi-global.com

Table of Contents

Detailed Table of Contents

Chapter 1
Saurabh Tiwari, University of Petroleum and Energy Studies, India
Rajeev Srivastava, University of Petroleum and Energy Studies, India

The last few years are known as the era of digitization, which also focuses on Industry 4.0. On one side, these latest tools and techniques like IoT, big data analytics, blockchain help the organizations to make better decision making and better future predictions in terms of processes and services; on the other hand, it also leads to the new problem known as cybercrime. Keeping data on the cloud and processing it using cloud-based technology gives more opportunities to hackers to misuse things. Many governments and organizations invest in huge amounts to train their employees and save their data from such cybercrimes. These cybercrimes not only impact organizations but also the females and children of the countries. The purpose of this study is to know the current state of cybercrime in India and to identify the impact of cybercrime on females and children.

Chapter 2
Ramesh Chandra Rath, Jharkhand University of Technology, India
Sukanta Kumar Baral, Indira Gandhi National Tribal University, India
Richa Goel, Amity University, India

Cyber security is paramount in all aspects of life, particularly in digital technology. Stories of artificial intelligence and data breaches, ID theft, cracking the security code, operating machines with remote sensors, and other such incidents abound, affecting millions of individuals and organizations. The problems in developing appropriate controls and processes and applying them with utmost precision to combat cyber-attacks and crimes have always been unending. With recent advances in artificial intelligence, the ever-increasing danger of cyber-attacks and crimes has grown tremendously. It has been used in nearly every branch of research and engineering. AI has sparked a revolution in everything from healthcare to robotics. This ball of fire could not be kept away from cyber thieves, and therefore, "normal" cyber-attacks have evolved into "intelligent" cyber-attacks. The authors of this chapter attempt to discuss prospective artificial intelligence approaches to use such strategies in cyber security for expecting outcome-based conclusions related to future research work.

Chapter 3

Aswani Kumar Aswani Cherukuri, Vellore Institute of Technology, India
Sushant Sinha, Vellore Institute of Technology, India

The rapid development in telecommunication technologies in the last decade gave rise to a new set of sophisticated security threats. Software-defined networking (SDN) is a new network paradigm that isolates the network control plane from the data plane. This provides network programmability, which reduces operating costs and enables business growth. However, this new technology has several security threats, which is a major concern in its adaptation. This chapter presents a comprehensive review of the security issues of SDN and mitigation strategies.

Chapter 4

Saila Sarmin Rapti, Bangladesh Bank, Bangladesh
Nabila Fahria, Bangladesh Bank, Bangladesh
Sunita Rani Das, Bangladesh Bank, Bangladesh

Following the COVID-19 outbreak, the world has seen another rising challenge of accessing financial services. By limiting the transmission of COVID-19, fintech accelerated access to financial services for all aspects of society, allowing individuals to become more flexible and comfortable with fintech. However, cyber-attacks can hinder the progress of this evolution by attacking any type of banking channel, including traditional banking, internet banking, credit cards, ATMs, agent banking, and mobile banking. From the standpoint of central bank risk management, this chapter investigates fintech and the associated field of cybersecurity.

Chapter 5

Diptirekha Mohapatra, Sambalpur University, India

Cybercrimes have become a global phenomenon due to the digital world. Cybercrimes in India are no exception. Because of this, it becomes very difficult to ensure cyber security. This adversely affects not only individuals but also companies, government, and society at large. As huge data is lost as a result of such crime, a law in India was enacted called the Information Technology Act, 2000 with an objective to prevent all types of crime relating to cyber security. Accordingly, other laws were amended like Indian Penal Code, 1860; The Negotiable Instrument Act, 1881; and the Indian Evidence Act, 1882. But, in spite of these stringent laws, the data of National Crimes Bureau shows an upward trend in every head relating to cybercrimes, thereby ensuring cyber security.

Data privacy (also known as information privacy or data protection) refers to the legal right of the data subject to access, use, and collection of data. For the development of a digital economy, privacy protection and identity management are critical. The current regulatory framework's efficiency has been called into consideration from a legal standpoint. In both industry and academia, big data has become a hot issue for research. This chapter presents a succinct but comprehensive examination of data security and privacy issues at all phases of the data life cycle. The chapter then goes over some of the current solutions. Finally, this chapter discusses future research projects related to data security and privacy protection. It further explores other facets of the privacy problem that turn out to be critical for the broad adoption of privacy-enhancing technology, giving a more holistic picture of the situation.

The study focuses on some technological cyber security challenges that are prevailing. It covers the technologies that are used in healthcare and how digitalization has given a new regime to it. The challenges from the perspective of cybersecurity that are poised to digitalized healthcare have been covered in the study as cyber threats and security vulnerabilities can jeopardize patient protected health information and distract healthcare professionals. At the end, the study covered solutions to handle the technical and cyber-related problems, which can be considered one of the possible solutions.

Ayon Dutta, University of Dhaka, Bangladesh
Partho Ghosh, North South University, Bangladesh
Avishak Bala, North South University, Bangladesh

The internet is part and parcel of our everyday lives. Internet banking is playing a major role. But the risk is always there: malpractitioners always ready with their unethical and illegal ways of making crimes. Internet banking is the updated medium of communication to serve customers. Recently, the use of the internet in the banking sector of Bangladesh has increased rapidly. Through the internet banking system, banks have made a consequential growth and the number of frauds also has increased. Like other countries, Bangladesh is facing security problems. It is not totally free form risk and fraudulent activities. This chapter unveils internet banking crimes methodology and the limitations of existing security systems. To mitigate the internet security problems, manifold-layered security systems should be ensured among the clients and the banks. The internet banking security structure and its manifold-layered security systems have been developed and evaluated through an expert evaluation method.

Rabinarayan Patnaik, Institute of Management and Information Science,
India

In an era dominated by technology and trade, the business processes have started looking forward to innovations and ever-changing applications. This paradigm shift in the thought processes is not limited to any industry per se. Thus, the cyber practices have developed various tools, practices, as well as avenues for applications in real-time situations. With the advancement of these technological platforms, various gadgets in the form of smart phone, etc. have also complimented to the use of the same. Retail processes like any other business practices have also seen the changes due to these technological interventions. As a process responsible for creating direct customer touch points, retail at its operational level needs to be vigilant about the threats, insecurity, loss of privacy, and challenges coming because of the technological adoptions. Therefore, a systematic and well-designed data privacy policy with all possible components incorporated can lead to a secure environment.

Chapter 10
Lopamudra Hota, National Institute of Technology, Rourkela, India
Dhruba Charan Hota, Maharaja Bir Bikram College, India

During the last year, the pandemic prompted a heavier reliance on technology, as well as the adoption of interconnected devices and hybrid work settings. As a result, we are more vulnerable to cyber-attacks than ever before. The chapter introduces open banking and cyber security concepts briefly, presenting the reasons for rising of open banking. An insight to open banking in India is also presented. In India, the non-banking financial companies are intermediaries responsible for open banking and customer consent management. The trend of open banking systems is depicted from recent years. A short description of various threats and key security measures are discussed. Further, the need and implementation of cyber security in open banking are elaborated. Finally, future perspectives and research challenges are described to extend work on cyber security mechanisms in open banking.

Chapter 11
Shivani Choudhary, Amity School of Economics, Amity University, India
Neeru Sidana, Amity School of Economics, Amity University, India
Richa Goel, Amity International Business School, Amity University,
India

The study aims to examine internet users' perceptions of information sensitivity, as well as to assess individuals' privacy attitudes, experiences with privacy violations, and risk factors that can influence internet users' privacy concerns. The topic of whether the information is considered sensitive by an individual and what influences this perception of sensitivity emerges since each person perceives information sensitivity differently. This study used an online survey method to collect data utilizing a structured questionnaire, and 385 internet users of Delhi participated in the study to assess their perceived sensitivity through 39 different categories of data. The findings of this research can contribute to a better understanding of how online websites can construct their privacy policies without infringing on individuals' rights to privacy and additionally develop innovative communication strategies to educate customers about the importance of responsible data sharing on websites.

Preface

Data is the most important commodity, dubbed "the money of the twenty-first century," which is why data protection has become a global priority. Data breaches and security flaws can jeopardize the global economy. Organizations face a greater risk of failing to achieve strategy and business goals as cyber threat behaviour grows in frequency, sophistication, and destructiveness. A breach can result in data loss, business interruption, brand, and reputation harm, as well as regulatory and legal consequences. Furthermore, cyber security has evolved into a critical component of national defence. Its sphere of control encompasses all facets of a country's government, economy, and health, in addition to military realms. Companies of all sizes, markets, and market environments face the task of securing their vital systems and data on daily basis. A company needs a strategic, well-thought-out cybersecurity strategy to secure its critical infrastructure and information systems to overcome these challenges. As a result, businesses should seek guidance from cybersecurity frameworks.

This book examines alternative solutions thoroughly, beginning with an awareness of ICS security advancements in terms of cyber threats, vulnerabilities, assaults and patterns, agents, risks, and the impact of all of these on the industrial environment and the companies that rely on it. Such an episteme will improve security knowledge, competency, and the execution of effective security measures, as well as stakeholder acceptance of suggestions. Many security vulnerabilities and hazards have evolved, particularly in the manufacturing sector, and are rapidly being abused. To address this issue, sophisticated and comprehensive security strategies and solutions (combining people, technique, and technology perspectives) are required to improve ICS security.

This Book will really prove to be an insight for future readers as compared to other books as it tries to touch the most sensitive area of cybersecurity. This book will target selected high-quality research papers on Cyber Security Framework with Cataclysmic issues. The book shall be equipped with Cybersecurity framework best practices for common practices and suggestions which may be highly relevant or appropriate in every case. This best practice framework book is intended to cater various industries and institutions as a living document and will continue to be updated and improved as industry provides feedback on implementation. The book aids in that effort by providing a readable guide for security professionals, business executives, and stakeholders of various industries to understand the cybersecurity threat to their businesses and to develop an effective program to guard against cyber-threats.

Many academic areas are reflected in this book which includes

- Cybersecurity Challenges
- Cybersecurity in FinTech
- Data Privacy Policy
- Digitalization
- Legal Framework
- Legal Implications
- Mitigation Strategies
- Open Banking
- Smart Healthcare
- Software-Defined Networks
- Banking Safety

This book of Research on *Cross-Industry Applications of Cyber Security Frameworks* provides an understanding of the specific, standards-based security controls that make up a best practice cybersecurity program. It is a comprehensive assimilation of contemporary development in the current scenario of industry 5.0.

It talks about the enlisted chapters:

Chapter 1 talks about cyber security trend analysis in context to the indian perspective. The last few years are known to be the era of digitization, which also focuses on Industry 4.0. On one side these latest tools and techniques like IoT, big data analytics, blockchain help the organizations to make better decision making and better future predictions in terms of processes and services, on the other hand, it also leads to the new problem known as cyber-crime. Keeping data on the cloud and processing it using cloud-based technology gives more opportunities to hackers to misuse things. Many governments and organizations invest in huge amounts to train their employees and save their data from such cyber-crimes. These cybercrimes not only impact organizations but also the female and children of the countries. The purpose of this study is to know the current state of cyber-crime in India along with to identify the impact of cybercrime on females and children.

Chapter 2 talks about the role of artificial intelligence on cybersecurity and its control. Nowadays, cyber security is paramount in all aspects of life, particularly in digital technology. Stories of artificial intelligence and data breaches, ID theft, cracking the security code, operating machines with remote sensors, and other such incidents abound, affecting millions of individuals and organizations. The problems in developing appropriate controls and processes and applying them with utmost precision to combat cyber-attacks & crimes have always been unending. With recent advances in artificial intelligence, the ever-increasing danger of cyber-attacks and crimes has grown tremendously. It has been used in nearly every branch of research and engineering. AI has sparked a revolution in everything from health care to robotics. This ball of fire could not be kept away from cyber thieves, and therefore "normal" cyber-attacks have evolved into "intelligent" cyber-attacks. The authors of this paper attempt to discuss prospective artificial intelligence approaches to use such strategies in cyber security for expecting outcome-based conclusions related to future research work.

Chapter 3 talks about Analysis and Mitigation Strategies of Security Issues of Software Defined Networks. The rapid development in telecommunication technologies in the last decade gave rise to a new set of sophisticated security threats. Software-Defined Networking (SDN) is a new network paradigm that isolates the network control plane from the data plane. This provides network programmability, which reduces operating costs and enables business growth. However, this new technology has several security threats, which is a major concern in its adaptation. This chapter presents a comprehensive review of the security issues of SDN and mitigation strategies.

Chapter 4 talks about the role of Bangladesh Bank on cybersecurity in fintech. Following the COVID-19 outbreak, the world has seen another rising challenge of accessing to financial services. By limiting the transmission of the virus of the Covid-19, Fintech accelerated access to financial services for all aspects of society, allowing individuals to become more flexible and comfortable with fintech. However, Cyber-attacks can hinder the progress of this evolution by attacking any type of banking channel, including traditional banking, internet banking, credit cards, ATMs, agent banking and mobile banking. From the standpoint of central bank risk management, this article investigates fintech and the associated field of cybersecurity.

Chapter 5 talks about an appraisal of India's cyber security legal framework. Cyber-crimes have become global phenomenon due to digital world. Because of this, it becomes very difficult to ensure cyber security. This adversely affects not only individuals but also companies, Government, and society at large. As huge data is lost as a result of such crime, a law in India was enacted called the Information Technology Act, 2000 with an objective to prevent all types of crime relating to cyber security. Accordingly other laws were amended like, Indian Penal Code, 1860, The Negotiable Instrument Act, 1881 and the Indian Evidence Act, 1882. But, to the utter surprise, in spite of these stringent laws the data of National Crimes Bureau shows upward trend in every head relating to cyber-crimes thereby ensuring cyber security.

Chapter 6 talks about the Big Data Privacy in Cross Industrial Challenges and Legal Implications. Data privacy (also known as information privacy or data protection) refers to the legal right of the data subject to access, use, and collection of data. For the development of a digital economy, privacy protection and identity management are critical. The current regulatory framework's efficiency has been called into consideration from a legal standpoint. In both industry and academia, big data has become a hot issue for research. This paper presents a succinct but comprehensive examination of data security and privacy issues at all phases of the data life cycle. The paper then goes over some of the current solutions. Finally, this paper discusses future research projects related to data security and privacy protection. It further explores other facets of the privacy problem that turn out to be critical for the broad adoption of privacy-enhancing technology, giving us a more holistic picture of the situation.

Chapter 7 talks about the Smart Healthcare and Digitalization. The study focuses on some of technological cyber security challenges that are prevailing. It covers the technologies that are used in healthcare, how digitalization has given a new regime to it. The challenges from the perspective of cybersecurity that are poised to digitalized healthcare have been covered in the study as Cyber threats and security vulnerabilities can jeopardize patient protected health information and distract healthcare professionals. At the end, the study has covered solutions to handle the technical and cyber related problem which can be considered as one of the possible solutions.

Chapter 8 talks about the internet banking safety framework an evaluation of banking industry in Bangladesh. Nowadays internet is the part and parcel of our everyday life. Internet banking is playing a major role. But the risk is always there: malpractitioners always ready with their unethical and illegal ways of making crimes. Internet banking is the updated medium of communication to serve customers. Recently the use of the internet in the banking sector of Bangladesh has increased rapidly. Through the internet banking system, banks have made a consequential growth and the number of frauds also has increased. Like other countries, Bangladesh is also facing security problems. It is not totally free form risk and fraudulent activities. This research paper unveils internet banking crimes methodology and the limitations of existing security system. To mitigate the internet security problems, manifold-layered security system should be ensured among the clients and the banks. The Internet Banking security structure and its manifold-layered security systems have been developed and evaluated through an expert evaluation method.

Chapter 9 talks about data privacy policy with an insight to cyber security implications on retail operations. In an era dominated by technology and trade, the business processes have started looking forward to innovations and ever-changing applications. This paradigm shift in the thought processes is not limited to any industry per se. Thus, the cyber practices have developed various tools, practices as well as avenues for applications in real time situations. With the advancement of these technological platforms, various gadgets in the form of smart phone etc. have also complimented to the use of the same. Retail processes like any other business practices have also seen the changes due to these technological interventions. As a process responsible for creating direct customer touch points, retail at its operational level needs to be vigilant about the threats, insecurity, loss of privacy and challenges coming because of the technological adoptions. Therefore, a systematic and well-designed data privacy policy with all possible components incorporated can lead to a secure environment.

Chapter 10 talks about cyber-security-heart of open banking in an insight to existing and futuristic approach. During the last year, the pandemic prompted a heavier reliance on technology, as well as the adoption of interconnected devices and hybrid work settings. As a result, we are more vulnerable to cyber-attacks than ever before. The chapter introduces open banking and cyber security concepts briefly, presenting the reasons for rising of open banking. An insight to open banking in India is also presented, In India, the Non-Banking Financial Companies are intermediaries responsible for open banking and customer consent management. The trend of open banking systems is depicted from past to recent years. A short description of various threats and key security measures are discussed. Further, the need and implementation of cyber security in open banking are elaborated. Finally, future perspectives and research challenges are described to extend work on cyber security mechanisms in open banking.

Chapter 11 talks about the perception of internet users with respect to privacy and information sensitivity in Delhi. The study aims to examine internet users' perceptions of information sensitivity, as well as to assess individuals' privacy attitudes, experiences with privacy violations, and risk factors that can influence Internet users' privacy concerns. The topic of whether the information is considered sensitive by an individual and what influences this perception of sensitivity emerges since each person perceives information sensitivity differently. The findings of this research can contribute to a better understanding of how online websites can construct their privacy policies without infringing on individuals' right to privacy, and additionally develop innovative communication strategies to educate customers about the importance of responsible data sharing on online websites.

Thus, this book intends to give a quality publication with unique insights and methods of application for current scholars and users.

Sukanta Kumar Baral
Indira Gandhi National Tribal University, India

Preface

Richa Goel
Amity University, India

Md. Mashiur Rahman
Bank Asia Ltd., Bangladesh

Jahangir Sultan
Bentley University, USA

Sarkar Jahan
Royal Bank of Canada, Canada

Acknowledgment

First and foremost, we would like to thank our Almighty God. In the process of putting this book together we realized how true this gift of writing is. You gave us the power to believe in our passion and pursue our dreams. We could never have done this without the faith in you.

Our Sincere and heartfelt thanks to our family members who were there supporting us throughout the arduous process of completing this book and has been a big pillar throughout

The editors would like to acknowledge the help of all the people involved in this project and, more specifically, to the authors and reviewers that took part in the review process. Without their support, this book would not have become a reality. First, the editors would like to thank each one of the authors for their contributions. Our sincere gratitude goes to the chapter's authors who contributed their time and expertise to this book. Second, the editors wish to acknowledge the valuable contributions of the reviewers regarding the improvement of quality, coherence, and content presentation of chapters. Most of the authors also served as referees; we highly appreciate their double task.

We owe an enormous debt of gratitude to those who gave us detailed and constructive comments on few chapters and pushed us to clarify concepts, explore, facets of insight work and explain the rationales for specific recommendations. We also like to thank many people who have helped us learn and practice both the art and science of networking throughout the years to complete this piece of research book titled *Cross-Industry Applications of Cyber Security Frameworks*.

Chapter 1
Cyber Security Trend Analysis:
An Indian Perspective

Saurabh Tiwari
 https://orcid.org/0000-0002-4278-0389
University of Petroleum and Energy Studies, India

Rajeev Srivastava
 https://orcid.org/0000-0002-8569-195X
University of Petroleum and Energy Studies, India

ABSTRACT

The last few years are known as the era of digitization, which also focuses on Industry 4.0. On one side, these latest tools and techniques like IoT, big data analytics, blockchain help the organizations to make better decision making and better future predictions in terms of processes and services; on the other hand, it also leads to the new problem known as cybercrime. Keeping data on the cloud and processing it using cloud-based technology gives more opportunities to hackers to misuse things. Many governments and organizations invest in huge amounts to train their employees and save their data from such cybercrimes. These cybercrimes not only impact organizations but also the females and children of the countries. The purpose of this study is to know the current state of cybercrime in India and to identify the impact of cybercrime on females and children.

INTRODUCTION

Cyber security is critical in the information technology industry, and protecting data has emerged as one of the most difficult challenges of our time. Cyber security is

DOI: 10.4018/978-1-6684-3448-2.ch001

a collection of tools, techniques, policies, security measures, security guidelines, risk mitigation strategies, actions, training, good practices, security assurance, and cutting-edge technologies that can be used to protect cyberspace and users' assets (Cheng et al., 2013). According to Techopedia cybercrime can be defined as a type of crime in which one used the computer as an object to do cybercrime. Cybercrimes are carried out against computers or devises directly to damage or disable them, spread malware and steel secret information. In the same way that computer technology and communication will inexorably permeate every facet of human life, cybercrime is evolving at an astounding rate. Mobile device usage is increasing at an exponential rate, which raises the corresponding number of security risks. The threat of cybercrime is increasing at an astronomical rate. Each new Smartphone, laptop, or other mobile device creates a new cyber-attack portal, providing an insecure network access point to the public network. Criminals waiting in the wings with targeted ransomware and attacks utilizing mobile apps are well aware of this depressing paradigm. These new and old innovations, which were once part of the cyber-security expected radar, will also be included in the ongoing problem of missing and compromised computers. As defined by the US Department of Justice, cybercrime now includes any illegal activity involving the use of a computer to store evidence. When we talk about cybercrime, we're referring to any illegal activity that involves computers in some way, shape, or form. While traditional crimes like theft, harassment, intimidation, and extremism are still a problem for individuals and nations, the growing list of cybercrimes includes offences with code-imposed penalties, like network intrusions and computer virus distribution. To put it simply, cybercrime is any criminal act carried out by means of a computer or the Internet, such as stealing a victim's personal information, selling pornography, or harassing them. As the use of technology in people's daily lives continues to grow, so will the incidence of cybercrime. The various types of cybercrimes are shown in figure 1.

Hackers are usually performed such types of unethical tasks by accessing unauthorized transactions and use them for malicious activities. However, the tech companies are updating their software to save their data and transaction to be hacked. But hackers are also making new targets and using the latest tools and techniques for doing different types of cybercrimes. These hackers are not only targeting organizations but also females and children. Many studies have been done related to threat intelligence (Fernandez et al., 2012; Jasper, 2017). The studies also focused on various types of cyber security threats (Tsai et al., 2007; Vande et al., 2014; Moran, 2020; Jaishankar, 2020). Keeping in view the above issues, the focus of this study to understand the status of cyber-crime from an Indian perspective is discussed. This study is focused to understand the trend of cybercrime in India from 2017 to 2019. To understand the scenario of different types of cyber-crimes like Cyber blackmailing/threatening, Fake profiling, Cyber pornography/hosting and

Figure 1. Various types of Cybercrimes

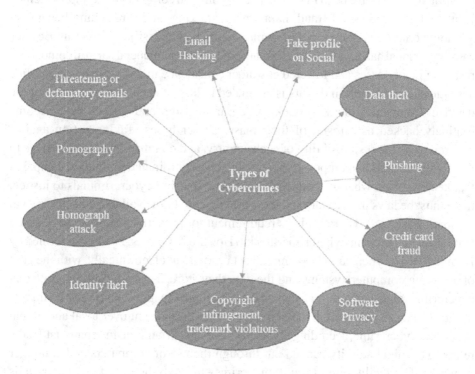

publishing obscene sexual materials depicting children, Cyber stalking /Bullying and Internet crimes through online games, etc. The study also discussed the status of the state-wise training to the different people against cyber-crime.

CYBERCRIME

The academic community has yet to come up with a consensus definition of cybercrime (Alsmadi, 2019). Other terms used to describe it include "computer-related crime" and "electronic crime." Different types of cybercrime have been classified, according to Krausz & Walker (2013), cybercrime occurs when a computer is used as the primary means of committing the crime, or when a computer is specifically targeted as a means of committing the crime. This type of classification isn't practical for this research, but it's critical for understanding the term. According to the severity of the crimes, cybercrimes can be divided into two types: Type I and Type II (Moore, 2016). There are two types of cybercrime: type I refers to technical crimes like hacking. When it comes to Type II, human interaction is more important than technology. Many traditional crimes have been made easier to commit on computers. Examples include identity theft, credit card fraud, harassment, stalking, and threatening behaviour. Without computers, these types of crimes would be impossible to commit. Besides causing personal harm, cybercrime has caused significant financial harm to companies, resulting in job losses and lowered customer confidence in an organization's online activities Over 2.8 billion dollars is estimated to be lost each year as a result of the damage. Companies like Facebook, Instagram, Twitter and TikTok have become routinely hacked as a result of their massive user bases. Taking action against cybercrime is the responsibility of each country, and countries should take steps to protect institutions and empower them to launch a coordinated mitigation campaign that keeps tabs on what happens in cyberspace. To bring cybercriminals to justice, there must be laws in place around the world that are both available and effective in combating the vice. There is also a requirement for proactive measures to be taken to monitor and prevent cybercrime attacks (Howard & Gulyas, 2014). As defined by Bernik (2014), cybercrime is a criminal act carried out electronically, with the goal of attacking computer systems and the data they store. These definitions state that cybercrime takes place in a virtual space where information about people, things, events, or facts is encoded in mathematical symbols and sent over local and global networks. Cybercrime, according to Canada's Foreign Affairs and International Trade, refers to criminal activity carried out through the use of computers and computer networks. The facilitation of traditional crimes through the use of computers falls under cybercrime. Child pornography and online fraud are two examples of more traditional forms of crime.

METHODOLOGY

This research employs a qualitative approach in order to compile comparable data on cybercrime and computer crime activities across the different states of India of cybercrime in the time range from 2017-2019. In order to better understand cybercrime and cybersecurity, this research was conducted with a specific goal in mind. Business intelligence tool Tableau is used to analyze the cybercrime data extracted from the India Statista database which is known to be the most authentic data shared by the government. The analysis includes the trend of cybercrime from 2017 to September 2019. The critical analysis is done to know the current status of cybercrime against the woman and children of India. The state-wise status cybercrime status is analyzed and presented using the different types of visualization.

		(R/s. in Crore)
Year	Funds Released	Funds utilized
2017-2018	86.48	78.62
2018-2019	141.33	137.38
2019-2020	135.75	122.04

RESULT AND DISCUSSION

The result received from the analysis of cybercrime data collected from the Statista database from the duration of 2017 to mid-2019 is presented and discussed in this section. In the first part, the detail of the funds released and utilized on cyber security by Ministry of Electronics and Information Technology in India during that duration is presented. The second section discusses the trend of Indian Computer Emergency Response Team (CERT-In) reported cyber security incidents month by month. In the third section, the detail of the different types of Cybercrime against the children is discussed. It includes the different types of Cybercrime like Cyber blackmailing/threatening, fake profiling, Cyber pornography/hosting and publishing obscene sexual materials depicting children, Cyber stalking /bullying, and Internet crimes through online games, etc. In section four the fact and figures of different types of these Cybercrime against the woman is presented. In the last and final section, the status of the different types of training programs across the various states is presented and discussed.

Utilization and Release of Funds

The detail of the funds released and Utilized on cyber security by Ministry of Electronics and Information Technology in India (2017 – 2020) is shown in Table 1. The figures are shown in the table (Table 1), clearly indicate that the release of the funds, as well as the utilization of the fund, is increasing continuously year by year.

Month-Wise Number of Cyber Security Incidents Reported

Cyber security incidents reported to Indian Computer Emergency Response Team (CERT-In) in India (2017 and 2018) and the trend of the month-wise number of is shown in figure 2. The trend shows that the number of cyber incidents down from January to February in 2017 and 2018. In 2017 there is a big jump in May and from

Figure 2. Month-wise number of cases (2017-2018)

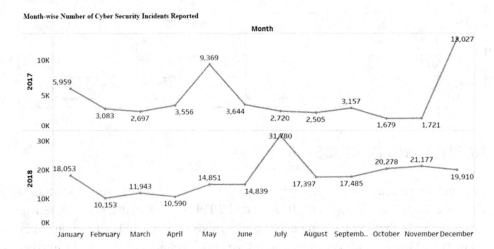

Month-wise Number of Cyber Security Incidents Reported

November to December also the number of cases increases from 1721 to 18027. Similarly, in July 2018 there was a huge jump in the number of cases.

Number of Cyber security incidents reported to Indian Computer Emergency Response Team (CERT-In) in India month-wise (2019-upto September) is shown in figure 3. The trend shows that the number of cases continuously increased from June onwards. The number of cases increased from 18,706 to 57,769. The total number of Cybercrime also increasing continuously from 2017 onwards, a total of 53117 cases found in 2017, 208456 cases in 2018, and 313649 cases till October 2019.

Cybercrime against Children

There are different types of Cybercrime against children. The details of the different types of Cybercrime like Cyber blackmailing/threatening (Sec. 506, 503, 384 IPC R/W IT Act), Fake profiling (IT Act R/W IPC/SLL), Cyber pornography/hosting, and publishing obscene sexual materials depicting children ((Sec. 67B of IT Act R/W other IPC/SLL), Cyber stalking /Bullying (Sec.354D IPC r/w IT Act) and Internet crimes through online games, etc. (Sec.305 IPCr/w IT Act) is shown in figure 4. This figure presents the state-wise comparative analysis of different types of Cybercrime against children.

The analysis depicts that the maximum number of cyber blackmailing/threatening cases were found in Maharashtra and Chhattisgarh. Maharashtra was found to be top in different types of crimes against children like cyber stalking /Bullying, fake profiles, and Internet crimes through online games, etc. While in cyber pornography/

hosting and publishing obscene sexual materials depicting children Himachal Pradesh was found to be at the top.

Figure 3. Cyber security incidents during 2019 (till October 2019)

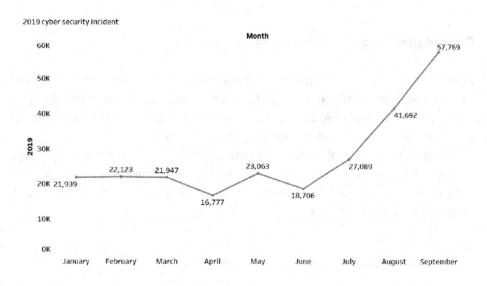

Figure 4. State-wise comparison of different types of Cybercrime against children

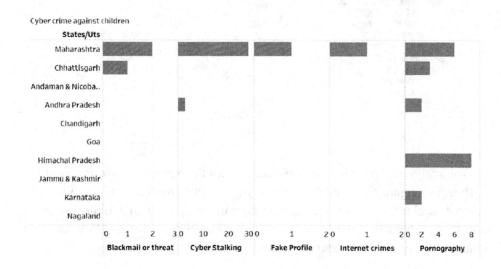

State/UTs	Blackmailing	Pornography	Cyber Stalking	Defamation	Fake profile	Other crimes	Total crimes
India	113	1158	791	61	289	5967	8379

Cybercrime against the Woman

Like Cybercrime against children, there are different types of Cybercrime found against women also. These different types of Cybercrime are blackmailing, pornography, cyber stalking, defamation, fake profile, and other crimes. The fact and figures of different types of these Cybercrime are shown in Table 2.

The state-wise status of blackmailing against the woman of India, which is a type of cybercrime is presented in figure 5. The top five states with the maximum number of blackmailing cases against women are Andhra Pradesh, Assam, Uttarakhand, Uttar Pradesh, and Maharashtra.

Figure 5. State-wise Cybercrime (blackmailing) against woman

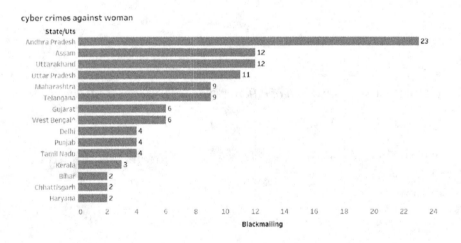

The analysis of the cyberstalking cases against the women of the different states is shown in figure 6. A per the analysis Maharashtra has the maximum number of cyber stalking cases (n=427) against the woman as compared to the rest of the states. The other four states with the maximum number of cases are Haryana, Uttar Pradesh, Andhra Pradesh, and Telangana.

Figure 6. State-wise cyberstalking cases against woman

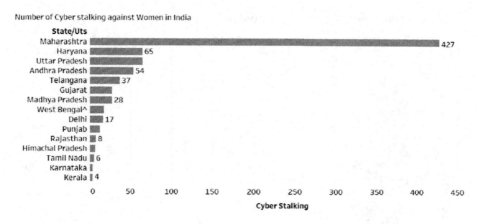

The detail of the number of defamation cases against the woman in India is shown in figure 7. It's very strange to find out that Odisha is the only state with the maximum number of cases (n= 49). Other states like Gujarat, Kerala, Maharashtra, and Rajasthan are having a very little few of cases.

As we know the Cybercrime using the fake profiles of other known people is keep growing now a days. Similarly, the number of fake profile cases against woman in India is also are growing. The analysis of these Cybercrime against the woman is shown in figure 8. The state Assam is found to be a maximum number of such cases (n=173). Other states like Maharashtra, Kerala, Uttar Pradesh, and Rajasthan also have such types of cases registered.

On one side the internet, smart devices, and social media platforms are considered as the revolution in the terms of information, but on the other side or bad side, the number of pornography cases against women is also increasing day by day. The detail of the number of pornography cases against children in India is shown in figure 9. As compared to the rest of the cybercrime types, pornography has the highest number of cases across many states. Odisha is at the top with the maximum number of cases (n= 341). Two more states Uttar Pradesh (n=178) and Assam (n = 148) have more than 100 cases. Karnataka, Telangana, and Madhya Pradesh also have more than 50 cases.

There are many other types of crimes against the woman except the major one mentioned in the above section. The detail of which is shown in figure 9. In this report, Karnataka is at the top with more than 2600 cases registered during that duration. Maharashtra also reported around 1000 cases. Many states reported such types of crimes against the woman, the top fifteen state status is shown in figure 10.

Figure 7. Number of defamation cases against woman

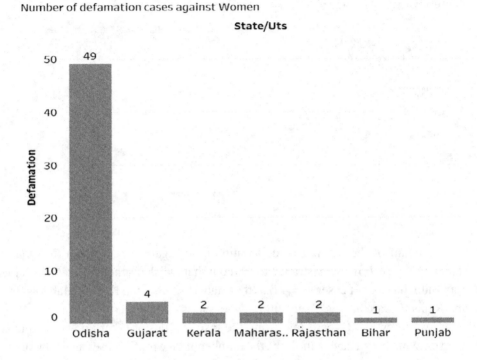

Number of defamation cases against Women

Figure 8. Number of fake profile cases against woman

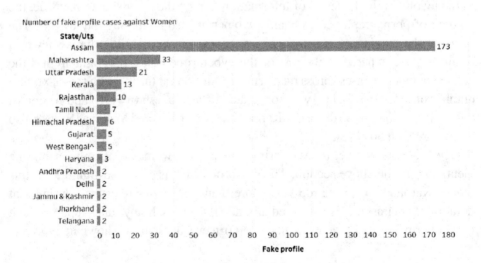

Figure 9. Number of pornography cases against woman

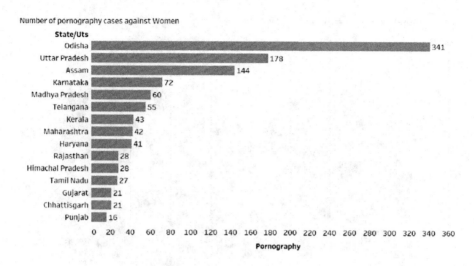

Number of pornography cases against Women

Training on Cyber Crime Investigation

Keeping in view the increase in the number of cybercrime cases in different states as mentioned in the above sections. The government is also organizing the different types of training programs across the various states. Law Enforcement Agencies in India have trained a total of 4559 people in cybercrime investigation (As of 31.03.2019). The word cloud based on the number of people trained in the various states is shown in figure 10. The more the number of people trained bigger will be the size of the circle. The analysis depicts that the maximum number of people trained

Figure 10. Number of other types of cyber crimes against woman

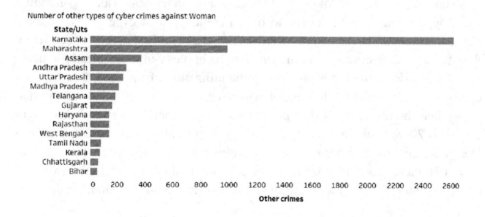

Number of other types of cyber crimes against Woman

Figure 11. State/ Type-wise cyber crime investigation training

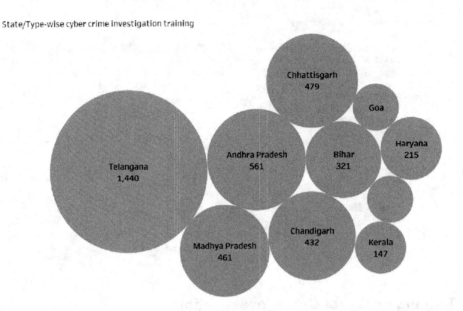

State/Type-wise cyber crime investigation training

in Telangana (n= 1440). Similarly in other states like Andhra Pradesh (n=561), Madya Pradesh (n=461), Chhattisgarh (n=479) people trained. The detail of the top ten states training status is shown in figure 11.

CONCLUSION

As the number of internet users, online payment, social networking websites, and App users are growing the number of cybercrimes are also increasing. On one side these online platforms making our life comfortable on the other side it's providing more opportunities to the hacker to do different types of cyber-crimes against women, children. The detail of the funds released and utilized on cyber security by the Ministry of Electronics and Information Technology in India, clearly indicate that the release of the funds, as well as the utilization of the fund, is increasing continuously year by year. The trend of month-wise cyber security incidents reported shows that the number of cyber incidents is down from January to February in 2017 and 2018, while in 2017 there is a big jump in May and from November to December also the number of cases increases from 1721 to 18027. Similarly, in July 2018 there was a huge jump and in 2019 the trend shows that the number of cases continuously increased from June onwards. In the third section, the detail of the different types of cybercrimes against the children is discussed. It includes the different types of cybercrimes like Cyber blackmailing/threatening, fake profiling, Cyber pornography/hosting and publishing obscene sexual materials depicting children, Cyber stalking /bullying and Internet crimes through online games, etc. The analysis depicts that the maximum number of cyber blackmailing/threatening cases were found in Maharashtra and Chhattisgarh. Maharashtra was found to be top in different types of crimes against children like cyber stalking /Bullying, fake profiles, and Internet crimes through online games, etc. Himachal Pradesh ranked first in cyber pornography/hosting and publishing obscene sexual materials depicting children. The analysis of different types of cybercrimes against the woman depicts that the top five states with the maximum number of blackmailing cases against the women are Andhra Pradesh, Assam, Uttarakhand, Uttar Pradesh, and Maharashtra. Maharashtra has also the maximum number of cyberstalking cases and the other four states with the maximum number of cases are Haryana, Uttar Pradesh, Andhra Pradesh, and Telangana. The maximum number of defamation cases against women are finding out in Odisha. The other types of cybercrimes against the woman are found in Assam followed by Maharashtra, Kerala, Uttar Pradesh, and Rajasthan. In pornography cases, Odisha is at the top and the two more states Uttar Pradesh and Assam have more than 100 cases. The status of the different types of training programs across the various states depicts that the maximum number of people trained in Telangana. Similarly in other states like Andhra Pradesh, Madya Pradesh, Chhattisgarh many people were trained.

REFERENCES

Alsmadi, I. (2019). *The NICE cyber security framework: Cyber security intelligence and analytics*. Springer. doi:10.1007/978-3-030-02360-7

Bernik, I. (2014). Cyberwarfare. *Cybercrime and Cyberwarfare*, 57-140.

Cheng, M., Crow, M., & Erbacher, R. F. (2013, January). Vulnerability analysis of a smart grid with monitoring and control system. In *Proceedings of the Eighth Annual Cyber Security and Information Intelligence Research Workshop* (pp. 1-4). 10.1145/2459976.2460042

Cybercrime. (2020). https://www.techopedia.com/definition/2387/cybercrime

HowardP. N.GulyasO. (2014). *Data breaches in Europe: Reported breaches of compromised personal records in europe, 2005-2014*. Available at SSRN 2554352. doi:10.2139/ssrn.2554352

Jaishankar, K. (2020). Cyber Victimology: A New Sub-Discipline of the Twenty-First Century Victimology. In An International Perspective on Contemporary Developments in Victimology (pp. 3-19). Springer.

Jasper, S. E. (2017). US cyber threat intelligence sharing frameworks. *International Journal of Intelligence and CounterIntelligence, 30*(1), 53–65. doi:10.1080/0885 0607.2016.1230701

Krausz, M., & Walker, J. (2013). *The true cost of information security breaches and cybercrime.* IT Governance Publishing.

Krausz, M., & Walker, J. (2013). *The true cost of information security breaches and cybercrime.* IT Governance Publishing.

Moran, A. (2020). Cyber security. In *International Security Studies* (pp. 299–311). Routledge.

Tsai, F. S., & Chan, K. L. (2007, April). Detecting cyber security threats in weblogs using probabilistic models. In *Pacific-Asia Workshop on Intelligence and Security Informatics* (pp. 46-57). Springer. 10.1007/978-3-540-71549-8_4

Vande Putte, D., & Verhelst, M. (2014). Cybercrime: Can a standard risk analysis help in the challenges facing business continuity managers? *Journal of Business Continuity & Emergency Planning, 7*(2), 126–137. PMID:24457324

Vázquez, D. F., Acosta, O. P., Spirito, C., Brown, S., & Reid, E. (2012, June). Conceptual framework for cyber defense information sharing within trust relationships. In *2012 4th International Conference on Cyber Conflict (CYCON 2012)* (pp. 1-17). IEEE.

Chapter 2
Role of Artificial Intelligence on Cybersecurity and Its Control

Ramesh Chandra Rath
Jharkhand University of Technology, India

Sukanta Kumar Baral
Indira Gandhi National Tribal University, India

Richa Goel
Amity University, India

ABSTRACT

Cyber security is paramount in all aspects of life, particularly in digital technology. Stories of artificial intelligence and data breaches, ID theft, cracking the security code, operating machines with remote sensors, and other such incidents abound, affecting millions of individuals and organizations. The problems in developing appropriate controls and processes and applying them with utmost precision to combat cyber-attacks and crimes have always been unending. With recent advances in artificial intelligence, the ever-increasing danger of cyber-attacks and crimes has grown tremendously. It has been used in nearly every branch of research and engineering. AI has sparked a revolution in everything from healthcare to robotics. This ball of fire could not be kept away from cyber thieves, and therefore, "normal" cyber-attacks have evolved into "intelligent" cyber-attacks. The authors of this chapter attempt to discuss prospective artificial intelligence approaches to use such strategies in cyber security for expecting outcome-based conclusions related to future research work.

DOI: 10.4018/978-1-6684-3448-2.ch002

INTRODUCTION

AI and system gaining knowledge of are fast turning into necessary in facts safety, because these technologies are capable of hastily comparing hundreds of thousands of facts units and detecting a wide range of cyber dangers, from malware threats to shady behavior which can result in a phishing assault. Those structures are always getting to know and enhancing, the use of information from beyond and gift encounters to perceive new varieties of attacks that would occur today or the next day. On this piece, we will have a look at the use of artificial intelligence in cyber protection (both right and awful), as well as what specialists and managers have to mention approximately it.

LITERATURE REVIEW

In the literature review segment, we researchers used both fact-gathering methods, but collected most facts from published resources and target 10 companies of India through an online Google forms survey to complete the above survey. Images were collected from 300 respondents from companies and workplaces. Cyber security is difficult with existing challenges that require the pursuit of integration and utilization of software and contemporary solutions through the deployment of related security measures. This was referenced by Mathew, 2021 in terms of artificial intelligence crime regarding the ability of cybercriminals to use intelligence to improve their attacks. Cyber security and AI can produce fruitful results when run in parallel. ML's current approach seems to be best suited to resolve violations of previous rule-based security structures. AI collects, sorts, and researches vast amounts of data, enabling businesses to add value from their data. These attributes are used in the field of cyber security.

The purpose of this study is to uncover ongoing trends and applications for achieving organizational-level cyber security using AI (Juneja, 2021), these attributes are used in the industry. The purpose of this study is to clarify current trends and applications to address cyber security is an ever-evolving industry that evolves and evolves to protect people and businesses from cyber- attacks. The Web of Things (Zeng, Song, and Cheng, 2011), faculty of computer science and engineering, affiliated with the University of Aizu conducted extensive research on cyber security and its control. It has also been published in another journal entitled "Restoring Decentralized Adaptive Cyber Defense Using Block-chain, Game Theory and Machine Learning in Cyber Security." and their book (Cybenko and Hallman, 2016) multi-component systems operating in competing environments are for learning while maintaining the same retention capabilities, found that and needed to use redundancy. This overview paper cites this paper, explaining visions, concepts, technologies, challenges, innovation directions, and different Internet applications.

According to the research paper of Misra, Kumar, and Agarwal, 2016, "Internet of Things (IoT) – Technical Analysis and Research on Vision" and is a wireless sensor network that supports energy management using web services and uses cyber security protection to fully manage security codes while avoiding the use of unauthorized calls (WSN) found to be a case study and fraudulent activity from a survey report on cloud computing research: an architecture (Dinh, 2013), enrolled in the Faculty of Computer Engineering. Gain basic knowledge of cyber security and its applications accepted in wireless communications and mobile computing and controlled by the use of cloud computing software created (Gubbi, 2013).

From this above said research article, the authors' gained complete step-by-step knowledge of architectural processes and elements to help prevent and protect cyber security in various sections of machine operation and control, and prevent cyber fraud and its activities at present time. Similarly, published a research article, "Created by the Definitions, Characteristics, Architecture, Realization Techniques, Applications and Future Challenges of the Internet of Things IOT:" (Patel and Patel, 2016), the basics of properties, architectural processes, and supporting technologies for applying different cyber security software's to different organizations for successful cyber protection. In this context, artificial intelligence (AI) is a key element of cyber protection on a regular basis, helping businesses of all sizes and industries to improve cyber security efficiency. The fastest and most mature industries in AI adoption strategies are information technology and telecommunications.

According to a research study of "Internet of Things (IoT), Architectures, Protocol and application (Sethi, Smruti and Sarangi, 2017), shows studies of great importance in order to control cyber security defences. According to the research article "A survey of internet things (IoT) based on smart systems" (Smys, 2020) refers to the abstract: Internet of Things (IoT) is a collection of networks, and objects related to cyber security, and its control which enhances the knowledge of cyber security networks and their application in future consequences. The research article "internet of things for supporting Marketing Activities" (Taylor, Reilly, and Wren, 2018), this article refers to the use of the internet and marketing activities related to cyber security and its control. The research paper "Internet of things Strategic Research Road Map" (Vermesan 2009), a strategic research road map for using IoT in a real application and reacting autonomously to the " real and physical world" events and influencing it. The research paper "Cyber Security and Artificial Intelligence Applications in the Future" (Sahay, Goel, Jadliwala, and Upadhyaya 2021), further evaluated the role of IoT and its applications in future information security protection technologies.

According to the research article "Edge Computing Architecture for the Internet of Things" written by Hamdan on the Industrial Internet of Things" (Salman, Elhajj,

Kayssi and Chehab, 2020), refers to edge computing that enables the Internet of Things and its control in relation to future applications will enrich more positive research in this area. According to the research article "Application of Artificial Intelligence in Cyber Security and Cyber Defence" (Sarma, Matheus, and Senaratne, 2021), examines advances in IoT as an approach. Economics, business practices, growth, and emerging market economic policies related to future applications of IoT and its software for prevention and control. In connection with the research study of "Internet of Things, Architectures, Protocol and application (Sethi, Smruti and Sarangi, 2017), shows studies of great importance in order to control cyber security defences. According to the research paper (Yan, Zhang, and Vasilakos, 2014) "Survey on Trust Management of the Internet of Things", focusing on network activities of computer applications and their future outcomes, we have acquired the basic knowledge related to the above research activities and activities.

Similarly, in this research paper, the researchers' have studied and reviewed more than 70 research papers as per the cited references and found that today, algorithmically knowledgeable AI and gadgets make inhumane speed decisions to significantly reduce cybercrime through activity automation, information processing, cyber security enhancements, and three research objectives.

The following studies goals had been taken by means of the researcher unanimously with a view to justify the aforesaid studies identify that

- To know the root purpose of cyber – security why hackers hacking the patron's non-public debts in addition to government. and personal organizations account,
- To find out, numerous methods of answer of cyber-crime and its manipulate
- To realize about the criminal rights and method of cyber- crime- and it's manipulate and attention.
- To look at the software of artificial Intelligence and virtual generation how it prevents to the cyber- crime and it's manipulated.

MEANING AND CONCEPT OF CYBER-SAFETY

Cyber: The phrase "Cyber- safety" has been derived from English phrases including 'Cyber' and 'protection' where as cyber way space on net using with a platform or software in illegally by using hackers for hacking the account or webpage or security code or robbery a few data form others account, that's treated as crook offence with the aid of Indian Penal code in addition to its far treated as crime even though out the world.

Security: We must protect our computers and statistics within the same manner that we comfortable the doors to our homes.

Safety: We must behave in ways that protect us towards dangers and threats that include era.

WHAT IS CYBER-ATTACK?

The cyber-attack surface in cutting-edge employer environments is big, and it's persevering with to develop unexpectedly. This means that analyzing and enhancing a business enterprise's cyber-security posture desires extra than mere human intervention.

WHY CYBER FOCUS IS NEEDED?

Due to fast incensement of population in world the agencies improved numerous sophisticated items for the intake of capacity buyers who are having plenty of cash the ones aren't having, a number of them may be tries for having it through unfair ways od use internet with the aid of hacking purchaser debts in order that the cybercrime expanded day –through-day and its manage we need cybercrime recognition like:

a)   Cyber- crime is a growing trend
b)   Improve focus of threats
c)   As with most crimes the police can't tackle this problem on my own
d)   To inspire reporting
e)   Promote government sponsored scheme 'Cyber necessities'
f)   Cyber- crime is massively below pronounced.

SIGNIFICANCE OF CYBER-SECURITY

The subsequent significance has appeared even as cyber –protection attacks due to

a)   The internet permits an attacker to work from anywhere on the planet
b)   Dangers due to negative security information and practice:
    1)   Identification robbery
    2)   Economic robbery
    3)   Felony Ramifications (for yourself and your organization)
    4)   Sanctions or termination if rules aren't observed

c)   In line with the SANS Institute, the top vectors for vulnerabilities to be had to
a cyber-crook are:
1)   Web Browser
2)   IM customers
3)   Internet programs
4)   Excessive consumer Rights

Figure 1. Models for user of cyber security awareness
Source: URL Link https://www.slideshare.net/BilmyRikas/usgsecurityawarenessprimerpptx

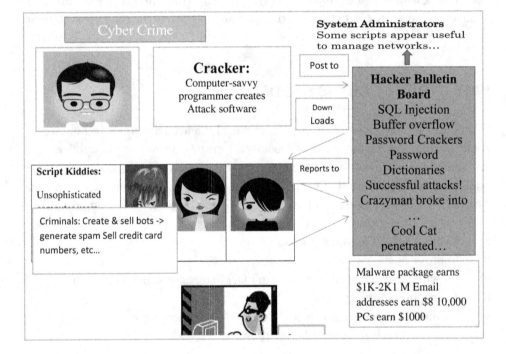

LEADING THREATS

a)   Viruses
b)   Worms
c)   Trojan Horses / logic Bombs
d)   Social Engineering
e)   Rootkits
f)   Botnets / Zombies

VIRUSES

a)   A virus attaches itself to a program, file, or disk.

b)   Whilst the program is accomplished, the virus activates and replicates itself.

c)   The virus may be benign or malignant however executes its payload in some unspecified time in the future (frequently upon touch).

d)   Viruses can cause laptop crashes and loss of facts.

e)   Which will get better or prevent virus attacks:

f)   Avoid potentially unreliable websites/emails.

g)   Device repair.

h)   Re-install running system.

i)   Use and keep anti-virus software program.

WORMS

a)   Unbiased software that replicates itself and sends copies from pc to computer across community connections.

b)   Upon arrival, the malicious program can be activated to duplicate

GOOD JUDGMENT BOMB

Malware logic executes upon positive conditions. This system is often used for otherwise legitimate reasons.

Examples

a)   Software which malfunctions if upkeep price isn't always paid.

b)   Employee triggers a database erase whilst he's fired.

Trojan Horses

a.   It maladies the data and control the program while quietly destroying data or damaging your computers system.

b.   **Trojan bug**: Masquerades as a benign application while quietly destroying records or unfavorable your gadget

Figure 2. Refers virus of Trojan Horses

Figure 3. Refers cyber security and control
Source: URL Link https://www.slideshare.net/BilmyRikas/usgsecurityawarenessprimerpptx

DOWNLOAD A GAME

It could be amusing however carries hidden code that gathers non-public information without your knowledge.

Social engineering manipulates humans into performing movements or divulging exclusive information. Much like a self-assurance trick or easy fraud, the time period applies to the use of deception to gain statistics, commit fraud, or get right of entry to computer structures

MODELS OF SOCIAL ENGINEERING

Figure 4. Social engineering and security awareness
Source: URL Link https://www.slideshare.net/BilmyRikas/usgsecurityawarenessprimerpptx

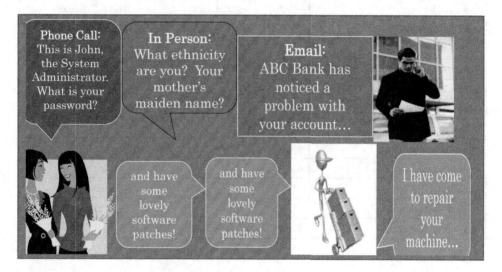

ROOT KITS

Upon penetrating a Personal computer, a hacker may deploy a set of packages, referred to as a rootkit.

- **May additionally enable:**
  a) Easy get entry to for the hacker (and others) into the corporation
  b) Keystroke logger
- Gets rid of evidence of wreck-in.
- Modifies the running gadget.

BOTNET

A botnet is a number of compromised computers used to create and send unsolicited mail or viruses or flood a network with messages as a denial of provider attack.

Table 1. Password cracking, dictionary attack and brute force via cyber hackers

Pattern	Calculation	Result	Time to Guess (2.6×10^{18} tries/month)
Personal Info: interests, relatives		20	Manual 5 minutes
Social Engineering		1	Manual 2 minutes
American Dictionary		80,000	< 1 second
4 chars: lower case alpha	26^4	5×10^5	
8 chars: lower case alpha	26^8	2×10^{11}	
8 chars: alpha	52^8	5×10^{13}	
8 chars: alphanumeric	62^8	2×10^{14}	3.4 min.
8 chars alphanumeric +10	72^8	7×10^{14}	12 min.
8 chars: all keyboard	95^8	7×10^{15}	2 hours
12 chars: alphanumeric	62^{12}	3×10^{21}	96 years
12 chars: alphanumeric + 10	72^{12}	2×10^{22}	500 years
12 chars: all keyboard	95^{12}	5×10^{23}	
16 chars: alphanumeric	62^{16}	5×10^{28}	

The Compromised Computers are known as Zombies

Figure 5. University systems of Georgia, information, technology and services
Source: URL Link https://www.slideshare.net/BilmyRikas/usgsecurityawarenessprimerpptx

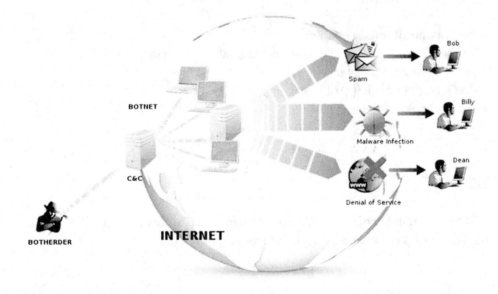

MAN IN THE MIDDLE ATTACK

An attacker pretends to be your final destination on the community. Whilst someone attempts to hook up with a particular destination, an attacker can mislead him to a different carrier and fake to be that network gets right of entry to factor or server.

Figure 6. University of Georgia, cyber security, information, technology and service 2010

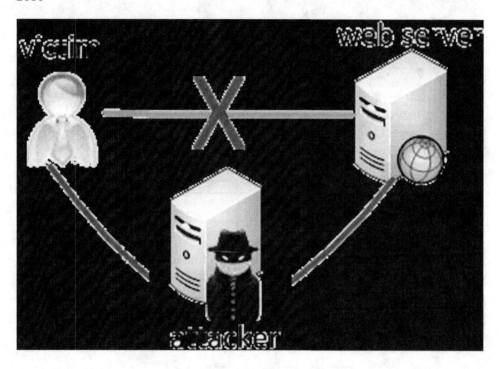

BEST PRACTICES TO AVOID THESE THREATS

To keep away from the cyber safety attack there is a defense mechanism that's used extensive a couple of layers of protection to cope with technical, personnel and operational troubles and its challenges. (See the discern –7 and 8)

Figure 7. Refers about the defense in depth layers

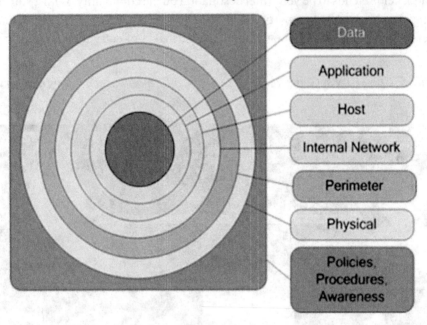

Figure 8. Refers about the of cyber security attack mechanism
Source: URL Link https://www.slideshare.net/BilmyRikas/usgsecurityawarenessprimerpptx

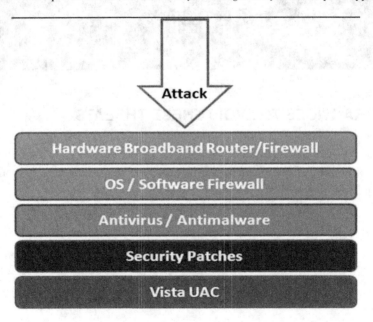

ANTI-VIRUS AND ANTI-SPYWARE SOFTWARE

For shield cyber -assault, we have to have taken the prior precaution or use of anti-virus software program because of;

a. Anti-virus software detects positive kinds of malwares and might destroy it earlier than any damage is performed.
b. Installation and preserve anti-virus and anti-adware software.
c. Make certain to keep anti-virus software up to date.
d. Many unfastened and industrial options exist.
e. Touch your technology guide expert for help.

METHOD OF STUDY

On this phase, we the researcher have taken both the strategies of statistics collection, but maximum of records amassed from posted assets and additionally accrued information of three hundred respondents from 10 agencies and places of work for the duration of India by a Google shape survey on on-line for entire the aforesaid research paintings.

HYPOTHESIS

For justification of assigned research paintings, the subsequent speculation has been taken unanimously by means of the researcher up to date:

Null Hypothesis: (Ho)

This speculation refers that application of digital generation and artificial Intelligence (AI) and preventive software program aren't control the cyber security within the gift context due to updated fast cyber issues improved by means of every day.

Alternative Hypothesis: (He)

This hypothesis refers that use of preventive antivirus and anti-cyber protection software up to date mass consciousness is the nice remedy for sup updated cybercrime and control.

DETECTING NEW THREATS

AI can be used updated stumble on cyber dangers and doubtlessly harmful behavior. Traditional software program systems without a doubt can't hold up with the massive volume of new viruses developed every week, thus that is an area wherein AI can be really useful. AI systems are being trained up to date identify malware, run sample reputation, and detect even the smallest behaviors of malware or ransom ware assaults earlier than they attain the gadget using superior algorithms. AI allows better predictive intelligence thru herbal language processing, which curates cloth on its own with the aid of scraping articles, news, and cyber hazard studies.

This may provide records on new abnormalities, cyber-attacks, and preventative strategies. In the end, hackers, like everybody else, follow tendencies, so what's famous with them changes all the time. AI-up to detailed and updated cyber-security structures can offer the most idea about understanding of world and enterprise-particular threats, allowing you up to date make greater knowledgeable prioritization selections up to detailed and updated no longer just on what might be used updated attack your structures, but also on what's most possibly up-to-date assault your systems .For justification of assigned research work, the following hypothesis has been taken unanimously by the researcher.

BATTLING BOTS

Bots account for a large part of net traffic in recent times, and they may be deadly. Bots may be an actual danger, from account takeovers the use of stolen passwords to fraudulent account introduction and statistics theft. Manual replies will now not suffice to combat computerized threats. AI and system gaining knowledge of help in growing a complete know-how of internet site traffic and distinguishing between proper bots (consisting of search engine crawlers), malicious bots, and human beings. AI enables us to evaluate huge amounts of records and permits cyber-protection groups to regulate their approach to an ever-converting terrain

BREACH RISK PREDICTION

AI systems assist in figuring out the IT asset stock, which is a specific and thorough document of all devices, customers, and apps with varying stages of access to numerous structures. contemplating the asset stock and hazard publicity (described above), AI-primarily based systems can now forecast how and where you're most probable to be hacked, permitting you to devise and allocate assets to areas with the finest risks.

BETTER ENDPOINT PROTECTION

The wide variety of devices applied for far flung work is rapidly expanding, and AI will play a crucial role in safeguarding all of those endpoints. Positive, antivirus software and VPNs may also help protect towards remote malware and ransom ware assaults, but they regularly rely on signatures. This implies that so one can be covered against the most current assaults, signature definitions must be stored updated. This may be a hassle if virus definitions are out of present day, both due to a failure to update the antivirus solution or a lack of understanding on the part of the software program manufacturer. As a result, if a brand new form of malware attack emerges, signature safety can be rendered ineffective.

"AI-pushed endpoint security makes use of an exceptional method, setting up a baseline of endpoint behavior thru a repetitive schooling system." If something out of the usual happens, AI can stumble on it and take suitable motion, including notifying a technician or restoring to a secure nation after a ransom ware attack. "Instead of watching for signature updates, this enables proactive protection towards attacks," explains Tim Brown, VP of safety and security structure at Solar-winds.

WHAT CYBER-SECURITY EXECUTIVES THINK ABOUT AI

The Capgemini research Institute tested the importance of AI in cyber-safety, and their paper titled Reinventing Cyber-security with synthetic Intelligence strongly advises that modern-day corporations ought to improve cyber-protection defences the usage of AI. Respondents to the ballot (850 executives from cyber-safety, IT records protection, and IT operations from ten international locations) felt that AI-enabled reaction is required considering cyberpunks are already using AI generation to perform cyber-attacks.

SOME OF THE REPORT'S KEY TAKEAWAYS INCLUDE:

According to 3 out of every 4 Executives polled, AI permits their company to reply to breaches greater quick and the intention to respond to cyber-attacks, sixty nine percentage of corporations accept as true with AI is needed.in accordance to a few out of every five businesses, utilizing AI enhances the accuracy and efficiency of cyber analysts.

AI gives higher solutions to an agency's cyber-security concerns as networks get larger and records grows greater complicated. Simply stated, human beings are incapable of coping with the growing complexities on their very own, and the employment of AI will become unavoidable ultimately.

DOWNSIDES OF AI IN CYBER-SECURITY

The blessings indexed above constitute most effective a small part of AI's capacity for enhancing cyber-protection.

However, like with the whole thing, there are widespread drawbacks to using AI on this industry. Groups might require a ways more assets and economic commitments to establish and operate an AI system.

Moreover, because AI structures are educated the use of records units, you'll want to accumulate a huge number of diverse units of malware codes, non-malicious codes, and abnormalities. Acquiring all of those facts units takes time and entails expenses that most groups can't find the money for AI structures can provide faulty conclusions and/or fake positives inside the absence of massive quantities of statistics and events. Acquiring misguided information from untrustworthy assets may potentially backfire.

Another principal drawback is that cybercriminals also can use AI to research their malware and launch greater superior assaults, which brings us to the following point…want extra tech information? Join Computing aspect newsletter nowadays!

USE OF AI BY ADVERSARIES

In preference to continuously monitoring for suspicious sports, cyber-safety employees may additionally utilize AI to reinforce best practices and decrease the assault floor. Alternatively, cybercriminals may also use the identical AI structures for malevolent objectives. in step with Accenture, adverse AI "causes device gaining knowledge of models to misconceive inputs into the machine and act in a manner this is useful to the attacker."

For Example

For an iPhone's "Face identity" access characteristic recognizes faces the usage of neural networks, rendering it susceptible to hostile AI assaults. Hackers would possibly create opposed snap shots to circumvent Face identification safety features and effortlessly maintain their attack without attracting interest to them.

Table 2. Respondents model for preventing cyber attack (ID Security)

Users	Anti-SOFT ware for Control of cyber attack	Respondent's With equal gender equality and equity	% of Positive Response			Negative	Mean value
			M	F	TG		
Central /State Govt. offices	MacAfee	30	12	11	03	04	**86.67**
Tata	Kaspersky	30	14	12	02	02	**93.33**
Reliance	AVIRA	30	13	11	02	04	**86.67**
Hinduja	NOD-32	30	10	13	02	05	**83.33**
Maruti-	Norton	30	11	14	01	04	**86.67**
Mahindra	TREND	30	13	12	01	04	**80.00**
Hindustan Leaver limited	AVG Antivirus	30	12	12	03	03	**90.00**
Indigo	Bit defender	30	11	12	02	05	**83.33**
NALCO	F-Secure	30	13	11	04	02	**93.33**
Jindal and Ispat	Avasti	30	12	13	02	03	**90.00**
Total		300	**121**	**121**	**22**	**36**	**88.00**

Source: Data collected from the own sources of questionnaire by authors

Semiotic Models in Pie Chart of respondent's

Figure 9. Semiotic models of respondents in bar graph

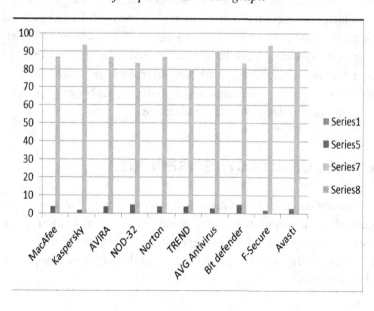

Figure 10. Semiotic models of respondents in pie chart

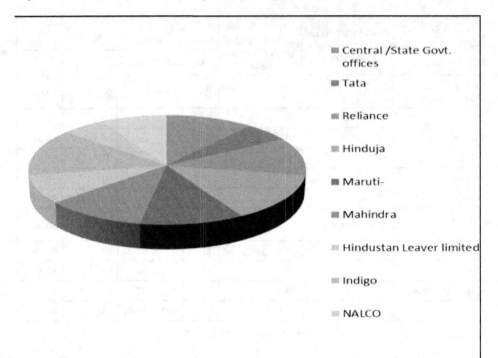

HYPOTHESIS TESTING:

In this phase, from the above statistics evaluation, we may take a look at that each male and female personnel/employees/group of workers of the afore stated offices/ organizations are used antivirus software program for shielding cyber-attack and the proportion of shielding may be very excessive, the null hypothesis (Ho) is completely false (incorrect) and it is not sizable in each the level of alpha o,01 and zero,05 degree consequently, the alternative hypothesis has been widely wide-spread because of its quite positive cost and significance.

ADVANTAGES OF AI IN CYBER-SECURITY

AI has several blessings and uses in various fields, one among that's cyber-protection. With modern-day unexpectedly growing cyber-assaults and fast tool proliferation, AI and system learning can help in preserving up with cybercriminals, automating risk identification, and responding greater correctly than traditional software-pushed or manual approaches

CONCLUSION

In conclusion, we draw the outcome that cyber security is a broad term and it is an area which relates with various organizations and governments, each at different level, usually from solitary to country wise. So, Artificial Intelligence (AI) along with Machine Learning (ML) techniques is being used over the spectrum of security. Most of these technologies have their own future prospects and provide security to the community by reducing fraud in digital transactions, etc. Thus, the previous talks show that synthetic intelligence (AI) is rapidly emerging as a need to have technology for improving the effectiveness of IT security teams. Humans cannot scale to thoroughly relax an agency stage assault surface, and AI gives the lot wanted analysis and hazard identification that can be used by security professionals to minimize breach hazard and decorate safety posture via prioritizing the use of antivirus and cyber assault preventive software, in addition to more non-public attention about cyber hackers not to contact them on social media. In conclusion, we draw the outcome that cyber security is a broad term and it is an area which relates with various organizations and governments, each at different level, usually from solitary to country wise. So, Artificial Intelligence (AI) along with Machine Learning (ML) techniques are being used over the spectrum of security. Most of these technologies have their own future prospects and provide security to the community by reducing fraud in digital transactions, etc. Thus, the previous talks show that synthetic intelligence (AI) is rapidly emerging as a need to have technology for improving the effectiveness of IT security teams. Humans cannot scale to thoroughly relax an agency stage assault surface, and AI gives the lot wanted analysis and hazard identification that can be used by security professionals to minimize breach hazard and decorate safety posture via prioritizing the use of antivirus and cyber assault preventive software, in addition to more non -public attention about cyber hackers not to contact them on social media. In addition, AI helps identify and prioritize risks, respond to incidents, and identify malware attacks. Therefore, despite the shortcomings of functionality, AI enhances cyber protection and helps organizations improve their security regimes.

REFERENCES

Bandyopadhyay, S., Sengupta, M., Maiti, S., & Dutta, S. (2011). Role of middleware for internet of things: A study. *International Journal of Computer Science & Engineering Survey*, 2(3), 94–105. doi:10.5121/ijcses.2011.2307

Cybenko, G., & Hallman, R. (2021). Resilient distributed adaptive cyber-defense using block-chain. *Game Theory and Machine Learning for Cyber Security*, *22*, 485–498. doi:10.1002/9781119723950.ch23

Dinh, H. T., Lee, C., Niyato, D., & Wang, P. (2013). A survey of mobile cloud computing: Architecture, applications, and approaches. *Wireless Communications and Mobile Computing*, *13*(18), 1611. doi:10.1002/wcm.1203

Gubbi, J., Buyya, R., Marusic, S., & Palaniswami, M. (2013). Internet of things (IoT): A vision, architectural elements, and future directions. *Future Generation Computer Systems*, *29*(7), 1645–1660. doi:10.1016/j.future.2013.01.010

Juneja, A., Juneja, S. V., Bali, V., Jain, & Upadhyay, H. (2021). Artificial intelligence and cyber security: Current trends and future prospects. *The Smart Cyber Ecosystem for Sustainable Development*, *27*, 431–441. doi:10.1002/9781119761655.ch22

Mathew, A. (2021). Artificial intelligence for offence and defense-the future of cyber security. *Educational Research*, *3*(3), 159–163.

Misra, G., Kumar, V., Agarwal, A., & Agarwal, K. (2016). Internet of things (IOT)–a technological analysis and survey on vision, concepts, challenges, innovation directions, technologies, and applications (an upcoming or future generation computer communication system technology). *American Journal of Electrical and Electronic Engineering*, *4*(1), 23–32.

Patel, K. K., & Patel, S. M. (2016). Internet of things-IOT: definition, characteristics, architecture, enabling technologies, application & future challenges. *International Journal of Engineering Science and Computing, 6*(5).

Sahay, S. K., Goel, N., Jadliwala, M., & Upadhyaya, S. (2021). Advances in secure knowledge management in the artificial intelligence era. *Information Systems Frontiers*, *23*(4), 807–810. doi:10.100710796-021-10179-9

Salman, O., Elhajj, I., Kayssi, A., & Chehab, A. (2015). Edge computing enabling the internet of things. *2015 IEEE 2nd World Forum on Internet of Things (WF-IoT)*, 603–608. 10.1109/WF-IoT.2015.7389122

Sarma, M., Matheus, T., & Senaratne, C. (2021). Artificial intelligence and cyber security: a new pathway for growth in emerging economies via the knowledge economy. In *Business Practices* (pp. 51–67). Growth and Economic Policy in Emerging Markets.

Sethi, P., & Sarangi, S. R. (2017). Internet of things: Architectures, protocols, and applications. *Journal of Electrical and Computer Engineering, 2017*, 9324035. doi:10.1155/2017/9324035

Smys, S. (2020). A survey on internet of things (IoT) based smart systems. *Journal of ISMAC, 2*(4), 181–189. doi:10.36548/jismac.2020.4.001

Taylor, M., Reillya, D., & Wren, C. (2020). Internet of things support for marketing activities. *Journal of Strategic Marketing, 28*(2), 149–160. doi:10.1080/096525 4X.2018.1493523

The use of Artificial Intelligence and Cyber security. (n.d.). www.computer.org/publications/tech-news/trends/the-use-of-artificial-intelligence-in-cybersecurity

Vermesan, O., Friess, P., & Guillemin, P. (2011). Internet of things strategic research roadmap. *Global Technological and Societal Trends, 1*, 9–52.

Yan, Z., Zhang, P., & Vasilakos, A. V. (2014). A survey on trust management for internet of things. *Journal of Network and Computer Applications, 42*, 120–134. doi:10.1016/j.jnca.2014.01.014

Zeng, D., Guo, S., & Cheng, Z. (2011). The web of things: A survey. *Journal of Communication, 6*(6), 424–438.

Chapter 3
Analysis and Mitigation Strategies of Security Issues of Software–Defined Networks

Aswani Kumar Aswani Cherukuri

https://orcid.org/0000-0001-8455-9108
Vellore Institute of Technology, India

Sushant Sinha
Vellore Institute of Technology, India

ABSTRACT

The rapid development in telecommunication technologies in the last decade gave rise to a new set of sophisticated security threats. Software-defined networking (SDN) is a new network paradigm that isolates the network control plane from the data plane. This provides network programmability, which reduces operating costs and enables business growth. However, this new technology has several security threats, which is a major concern in its adaptation. This chapter presents a comprehensive review of the security issues of SDN and mitigation strategies.

INTRODUCTION

SDN concept is not entirely new; it existed even decades ago. Particular infrastructures were used to decouple the data plane from the control plane. This decoupling was needed for computing systems requiring high speeds and large scale roles. Traditionally, computer networks have been segregated into three planes, data plane, control plane and management plane.

DOI: 10.4018/978-1-6684-3448-2.ch003

Figure 1. SDN architecture

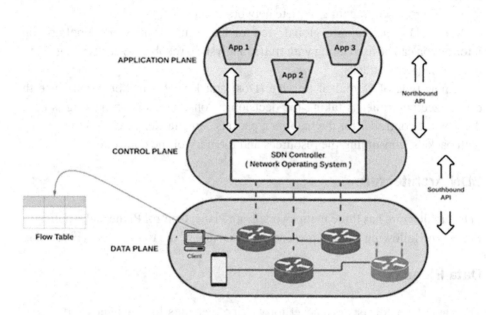

Data Plane, which handles the traffic, consists of devices that forward the packets. Control Plane consists of forwarding tables and enables the data plane functions. Management Plane consists of software services used to configure the control functionality. In this way, the network infrastructure can be virtualized. Thus simplifying it to configure and manage the network centrally.

SDN uses a centralized control application running on a server or virtual machine to allow control over network flows. The control plane decides where the packet is needed to be sent, and the data plane forwards the packet to the destination. The controller defines rules defining how the packets are handled and routed. Routers and switches become slave of application driven controller when these rules are installed.

From the cost perspective, SDN is considerably cheap. It's due to the universal nature of the data forwarding switching devices that follow specific standards and provide more control over network traffic flow than the conventional network devices.

SDN's layered architecture follows the 'separation of concern' principle. This means, in theory, it should have improved security of networks.

SDN increases the attack surface and misses out on appropriate security mechanisms like authorization. Using a centralized approach has positive effects on many policy types, including centralized routing algorithms, firewalls, and network-monitoring techniques. The negative implications include the situation when a central unit fails. This downgrades the resilience of a distributed system. As SDN is centralized, an external adversary might need less vulnerable SDN components to be compromised to gain complete network control.

Since SDN maintains a global view of the complete network topology, this information can be used along with traffic analysis to reliably detect existing Denial of Service (DoS) attacks.

A new type of Denial of Service (Dos) attack vector has emerged since the centralized controller is taking the decisions. Constant decision making is being done by the controller for the incoming packets. An attacker can flood the network with packets, consuming the resources and memory of the controller.

SDN Architecture

SDN architecture has three main layers: Data Plane, Control Plane and Application Plane. The following section presents an overview of the three layers (Figure 1).

Data Plane

The data plane consists of packet forwarding elements like switches and routers. However, unlike forwarding elements of traditional networks, these have no embedded intelligence to take autonomous decisions. Here the OpenFlow interface comes into play. Different devices communicate through OpenFlow interfaces with the controller. This ensures configuration and communication compatibility between different devices.

An OpenFlow enabled forwarding device maintains a forwarding table with three sections: Rule Matching, Actions to be executed for matching packets, and Counters for matching packet statistics. Rule Matching fields include Switch Port, Source MAC, Destination MAC, Ethernet Type, VLAN ID, Source IP, Destination IP, TCP Source Port, TCP Destination Port.

Southbound API

This is the bridge between forwarding devices and the control plane. It provides a standard interface for the upper layers enabling the controller to use different southbound APIs like OpenFlow and OpenState, and protocol plug-ins like SNMP and BGP to manage new or existing physical or virtual devices. OpenFlow provides three main types of information to the Network Operating Systems: Packet_in message, Event based messages, and Flow statistics generated by the forwarding devices. Packet_in message is sent whenever a forwarding device doesn't have a matching flow in the flow table for a packet or an explicit rule for a packet. Event_based message is sent each time a link or port change is triggered.

SDN Controller

The controller performs the task of abstracting the lower-level details and makes them available to the application plane through essential services like network topology and standard APIs to developers.

SDN controller provides the following functionalities: shortest path for forwarding, topology manager, stat manager, device manager, notification manager, and security mechanisms provide services like isolation between services and application.

There are three possibilities for the controller's architecture: centralized, decentralized or distributed.

In the centralized controller, only one entity is responsible for managing all forwarding devices. This architecture has two main limitations: Scaling limitations, and Single point failure threat.

Distributed controllers have better scaling support and are highly resilient to failures as the independent controllers are spread across different network segments. Controllers also have Westbound APIs and Eastbound APIs. These APIs allows the controller to exchange data, monitoring information and algorithms for consistency.

Northbound API

The Northbound API provides a standard interface for developing applications. The low-level instruction sets used by southbound interfaces to program the forwarding devices are abstracted by the northbound API. It provides security, routing, data path computation functions and includes global automation and data management applications.

There is no standardization of this API yet, and the existing controllers implement their own northbound API with different programming languages and specifications. Maybe the different types of applications that can be installed at the Application Plane can cause the lack of standardization of this API.

Application Plane

Applications define the behaviour of the forwarding devices. These applications submit high-level policies to the control plane, which in turn enforces them as flow rules on network forwarding devices. This plane might consist more than one network application like security and visualization.

Most applications of SDN fall in the following: mobility, wireless and measurement and monitoring, security and dependability, data centre networking and traffic engineering. Policy Enforcement as a Service (PEPS) has interlayer and interdomain access control, enabling a 'defence in depth' protection model. Here unsuccessful

Figure 2. Security related characteristics having security issues

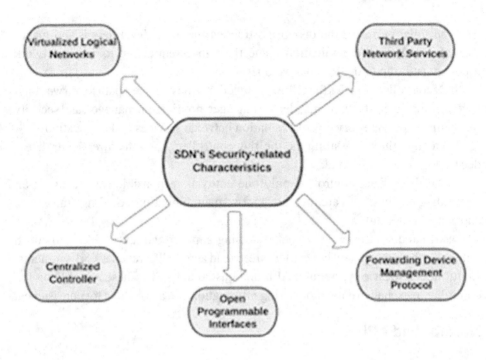

access requests are dropped before they even engage with the data provider server. This can mark the development of next-generation firewalls to improve perimeter security against Denial of Service (DoS) attacks.

SDN VULNERABILITIES

The following properties of SDN increase the number of vulnerabilities in the network: virtualized logical networks, third party network services, centralized controller, open programmable interfaces and forwarding device management. The following sections analyze the above five properties (Figure 2).

Virtualized Logical Networks

SDN and Network Function Virtualization (NFV) are highly dependent on each other, i.e. highly interconnected. NFV is used for virtualizing the services which were previously based on hardware components. Network functions like DNS are decoupled for optimizing the network services. SDN can be linked to serve virtualization. This is done by using multiple forwarding devices which are being shared over a physical device.

Third Party Network Services

SDN controllers are capable of installing various third-party network services and can also execute them.

Applications can be either instantiated during runtime like OpenDayLight (ODL). ODL is the modular open platform used for customizing networks. Other alternatives of ODL includes UniFi, which is absolutely free; Beehive SDN Controller and Wi-5 are some more free and Open Source alternatives.

Applications can also be compiled as a part of controller module like NOX and POX. NOX is the first OpenFlow controller and is written in C++, Python API is also available. POX is called the younger sibling of NOX and is the Python only version of NOX.

Centralized Controller

The controller maintains a global view of the entire network topology. Controllers were initially designed to be the sole devices, i.e. to be used individually. But due to Scalability and Reliability issues, recently distributed controllers are being used.

In distributed controllers, one controller is assigned a certain set of forwarding devices. Master/Slave deployment model is being followed between the controllers and forwarding devices.

Open Programmable Interfaces

SDN is made programmable due to the presence of the following three programmable interfaces:

1) Northbound API, which resides between Application Plane and Control Plane. REST API is an example. It enables SDN applications to submit policies to the control plane of the network.
2) This allows communication between different inter-connected controllers which may or may not be using the same domain.
3) Southbound API is a highly discussed interface out of all the interfaces of SDN. A controller is allowed to program a forwarding device irrespective of the hardware and software used in the controller or the forwarding device. OpenFlow is the standard used for the controller to data plane communications.

Figure 3. Relation between SDN's five main components and the attack scopes
(Gupta, B. B., Perez, G. M., Agrawal, D. P., & Gupta, D. (2021) pp. 341-387)

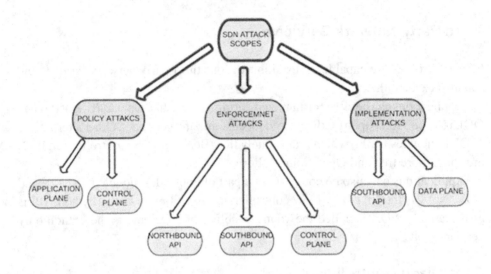

Forwarding Device Management Protocol

Forwarding devices are configured and managed using the OpenFlow configuration and the forwarding device management protocol.

OF-Config (OpenFlow Configuration and Management Protocol) is a special set of rules that defines a mechanism for OpenFlow controllers. These are used to access and modify configuration data on an OpenFlow Switch.

Attack Vectors and Impacts

Definition and storage of network policies are separated from their implementations in SDN architecture. Thus the attacks on SDN are categorized into five main sections (Figure 2 and Figure 3) based on their impacts on the policy, enforcement and implementation.

Implementation Attacks

These attacks target the Data Plane and the Southbound API.

Data Plane

The data plane can be compromised by using either: Device Attack, Side Channel Attack or Protocol Attack.

1) Device Attack involves exploiting SDN-capable switch's vulnerabilities. These vulnerabilities can be software or hardware. Software bugs are targeted in firmware attacks, thus this attack falls in the software vulnerability category. For hardware, TCAM memory of the forwarding device can be exploited.
2) Side Channel Attack involves the deduction of the forwarding policy of the network by the attacker. This is done by observing the performance of the forwarding device. For example, if input buffer is being used to identify rules, the analysis of the packet processing times can be used by the attacker to deduce the forwarding policy.
3) Protocol Attack targets the data plane. This attack involves targeting the network protocol vulnerabilities of the forwarding devices. The OpenFlow-enabled switch implements independent and custom switch firmware with varying potential. An example of this attack is mentioned in (Gupta, B. B., Perez, G. M., Agrawal, D. P., & Gupta, D. (2021) pp. 341–387), which involves HP 3500yl and 3800 switch models that do not support all the OpenFlow specified 12-tuple match fields in the TCAM flow table. This is a vulnerability which can be used to install crafted rules by malicious applications, which can override existing flow rules (IP matching) with hardware-unsupported match fields (MAC matching) specified.

Southbound API

Primary attacks (Gupta, B. B., Perez, G. M., Agrawal, D. P., & Gupta, D. (2021) pp. 341–387) on Southbound API are Eavesdrop Attack, Availability Attack, TCP Attack and Interception Attack.

1) Eavesdrop attack involves the adversary learning about the information exchanged between the control and the data plane as a part of a larger attack plot.
2) Availability attack implies Denial of Service (DoS) attack. The Southbound API is flooded with requests causing the network to be unable to address the genuine requests. Flow rules can be discovered by examining and analysing the packets and evaluating the delay time from probing packets and classifying them into classes. Now, plentiful rule-matched packets are sent which results

in the packet-in packets being triggered. These packet-in packets then overload the SDN controller.

3) Interception attack involves corrupting the network behaviour by modifying the messages being exchanged. An example of a man-in-the-middle attack is presented by Brooks, M., & Yang, B. (2015, September). Here, ARP poisoning is used for intercepting the traffic between the SDN controller and a Client. These attacks can be further extended to corrupt the network behaviour.

Enforcement Attacks

The ambition of this attack is to prevent SDN from properly instructing how, when and where the policies are to be enforced. Thus, the attacks that target the Southbound API, Northbound API and the Control Plane may be associated with attacks targeting policy enforcement.

1) Attacks against Southbound API may also have an adverse impact on policy enforcement. For example, in the man-in-the-middle attack, an attacker may modify the message exchanges like the packet-in message or flow-mod. This modification can tamper with the controller's understanding of the requirements of the data plane. The insufficiency of well-defined standards and constant amendments in the Southbound API can lead to malicious involvement in the policy enforcement process. This can be signified in a scenario where improperly configured message exchange end up having an invalid or conflicting instruction being set or distributed in the Data Plane.

2) The nature of attacks on Northbound API are almost identical to that on the Southbound API. But the attacker needs higher level of access to the system and is potentially sitting in the application plane. Northbound API lacks any standardization, unlike the Southbound API, where OpenFlow is assumed as the standard. Insecure developments are the result of each controller having its own specification for the Northbound API. Malicious applications can exploit the faults in the Northbound API to manipulate the behaviour of other applications by the eviction of active sessions, tampering with control messages exchanges, etc. the consequences of a compromised Northbound API is much more adverse given that information exchanged between the control unit and Application Plane affect network-wide policies.

3) Attacks against Control Plane are the most acute threats against the SDNs. These can be classified into three categories: Availability Attack, Manipulation Attack and Software Hack.

    a) In availability attacks, the aim is to make the controller inaccessible for a certain duration of time for all parts of the network. This can be achieved by flooding the controller with packet-in messages – given that these are not authenticated.

b) Manipulation attacks involve subverting the controllers understanding of the data plane, which ultimately sways to improper decision making.

c) Software hacks involve altering a system variable to turn the controller offline effectively.

Policy Attacks

Policy Attacks involves threats to the SDN's ability to define and store proper network policies. An adversary aiming to target the network's policy level aims for compromising SDN's application and control plane. Compromising the controller gives the attacker the ability to modify the information shared with applications and compromise their decision making.

1) In Control Message Attack, a malicious application may take down the entire network by transmitting control messages that modify or clear the flow table entries of the switches. Thus, a stray message circulated by an application can be disastrous. An example of this attack was stated by Shin, S., & Gu, G. (2013). The condition is, there are no restrictions for the control messages generated by the application. Therefore an SDN application can generate any control message at any time. A vicious application continuously generates flow rules to fill the flow tables of switches repeatedly, and the switches cannot handle any more issued flow rules.

2) Resource Attack involves the exhaustion of system resources like memory and CPU by malicious applications and thereby seriously hampering the performance of the controller. In extreme cases, controller instances can be dismissed by the malicious SDN application.

3) Storage Attack involves the manipulation of internal databases to exploit the network behaviour. This is possible because SDN applications are approved for access privilege to shared storage.

4) Access Control Attack is the term used for all the attacks that violate the required access authorization. Current controllers have only a certain degree of control over the authentication, accountability and authorization. All the above 3 Policy Attacks, i.e. Control Message, Resource and Storage Attack, involve access violation.

SDN SECURITY THREATS

SDN suffers from the following security threats: I. Link Flooding Attack (LFA), II. Distributed Denial of Service (DDoS), III. Packet Injection, IV. Worm-Hole Attack and V. Topology Poisoning Attack.

Link Flooding Attack (LFA) (Scaranti, G. F., Carvalho, L. F., Barbon, S., & Proenca, M.L. (2020)) (Rasool, R. U., et al. (2019))

Figure 4 shows SDN under no attack, whereas Figure 6 shows Link Flooding Attack (LFA) model. Here a link connecting to a target server is attacked by flooding, making the link highly congested. This congestion makes it difficult for legitimate traffic to reach the target server.

Traceroute commands are used to create a link map around the target server. Then, certain hosts called decoy servers are placed around the path of the target link. Now, a set of bots are used to produce enough traffic to flood the link. In the end, the decoy servers are manipulated by the bots to send low rate traffic to each other so as to create enough congestion that disrupts the target server from the rest of the network.

Rasool, R. U., et al. (2019) proposed CyberPulse as a solution. It detects and mitigates LFA on the SDN controller. Deep learning is used in CyberPulse for flood traffic classification.

SDN uses OpenFlow (OF) protocol for communication between the controller and the data plane. OF contains flow tables known as flow rules to send the traffic to its destination. All incoming packets are compared with the entries in the flow table. If there is no matching flow entry, a control packet is sent to the controller for further proceedings. This packet is called PACKET_IN; it contains the header information of the packet and is forwarded to the controller for further instructions as to how to handle it. The controller then sends the PACKET_OUT that contains the flow rule to OF switch, which then forwards the packet to the destination and updates the flow table.

Adversaries send low rate legitimate flow to the selected servers around the target link, which are the decoys. Initially the network slows down and as time passes the network becomes irresponsive. LFA mimics the same kind of activity that is generated by a normal traffic and uses its low rate nature to avoid detection and hence successfully flood the complete network. Low rate traffic is hard to detect and are sent to the decoy servers until the complete link is congested.

In CyberPulse, ANN technique is selected for classification of LFA (Figure 5), as it was able to accurately classify the malicious traffic, thus making it easy to mitigate the attack.

Figure 4. Normal traffic scenario in SDN
(Rasool, R. U., et al. (2019))

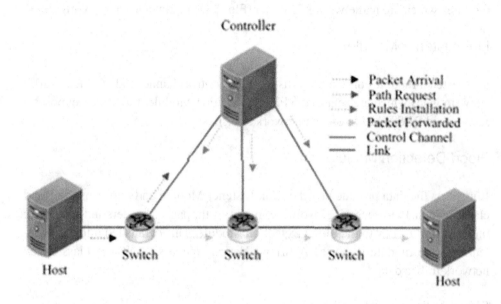

Figure 5. LFA Classification using MLP
(Rasool, R. U., et al. (2019))

Algorithm 1 LFA Classification Using MLP

Require: Traffic Flow F, packet statistics, dataset T
Ensure: Flow Class: *Flooding, Legitimate*
1: Get traffic flows
2: **for** Flow $f \in F$ **do**
3:     Get Flow Statistics
4:     Extract Features
5: **end for**
6: Pre-process T
7: Train ANN-MLP model using T
8: Classify flows using ANN-MLP
9: Export classification
10: **return** Flow Class: *Flooding, Legitimate*

CyberPulse uses the Northbound REST API of SDN to communicate with the controller. It works concurrently with all the other modules of SDN. It has three modules which are namely, Link Listener, Flood Detection and Flood Mitigation.

Link Listener Module

Link listener module continuously inspects the control channel and produces traffic flow statistics which are sent to the Flood Detection Module. Floodlight exposes a Java-Based REST API to extract network statistics.

Flood Detection Module

It inspects the data provided by the Link Listener Module and performs the flood classification. Pre-processing involves eliminating the packet-headers and presenting only the traffic flow to the Flood Detection Module. This data is fed into the deep-learning sub-module that uses Artificial Neural Network (ANN) to classify the network traffic data.

Flood Mitigation Module

Processed data from the previous module is sent to this module which mitigates the attack using the null routing technique.

Packets matching the null route will be dropped. The null route creates a block-hole, which is a kernel routing table entry that leads to nowhere.

MLP is characterized by an input, an output, and one or more hidden layers that are interlinked with each other. On the contrary, there is no connection between the nodes in the same layer, and there are no bridging connections either.

Output Layer

Output layer is the number of possible classes in the dataset that is desired to predict and is denoted by 'y'. Here it is equal to two, Legitimate and Flooding.

Hidden Layer

Hidden layers correspond to the number of intermediate connections that are used in the experiment, and by default, this number is selected as 1. The number of hidden layers depends on the mean value of the input and output layers. When data is linearly separable, the number of hidden layers to use is 0. These layers actually

Figure 6. LFA Model
(Rasool, R. U., et al. (2019))

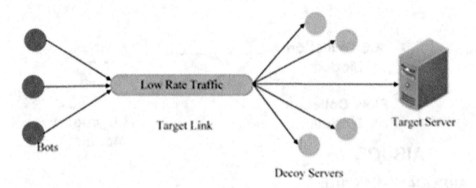

transform the single layer perception into multilayer, which is denoted by h: (h1, h2, . . ., hn). Where hidden layer can comprise 1 to a maximum number of n layers.

Backward Propagation

It is used to continuously update the weights of the layers so as to minimize the difference between the generated output and the expected output. Using this, the gradient descent can be calculated, which is further used to calculate the weights and to train the MLP model.

In Scaranti, G. F., Carvalho, L. F., Barbon, S., & Proenca, M.L. (2020), Artificial Immune System and Fuzzy Logic to Detect Flooding Attacks is proposed (Figure 7).

AIS-IDS is a biological inspired IDS. It uses fuzzy logic to automate the detection and mitigation of network anomalies. The proposal is placed on the control plane and has three modules with specific functions. The three modules are responsible for collecting flows, detection and mitigation.

Using the normal traffic behaviour, the anomaly traffic flow can be recognized. Fuzzy Interference System is used to solve the uncertainty in detecting the anomaly.

The mitigation module will recognize the suspicious IP addresses and ports to determine the mitigation strategies to mitigate/block the attack.

For evaluating the efficiency of AIS-DIS, this model is compared with KNN, LOF (Local Outlier Factor) and Naive Bayes for the simulated DDoS.

AIS-DIS has three modules in the SDN controller, Flow Collector, AIS Detection and Mitigation. The first module periodically gets the IP flows from the data plane using the OpenFlow (OF) protocol. This data is further processed and sent to the subsequent module, i.e. AIS Detection. This module categorizes the network

Figure 7. AIS-DIS
(Scaranti, G. F., Carvalho, L. F., Barbon, S., & Proenca, M. L. (2020))

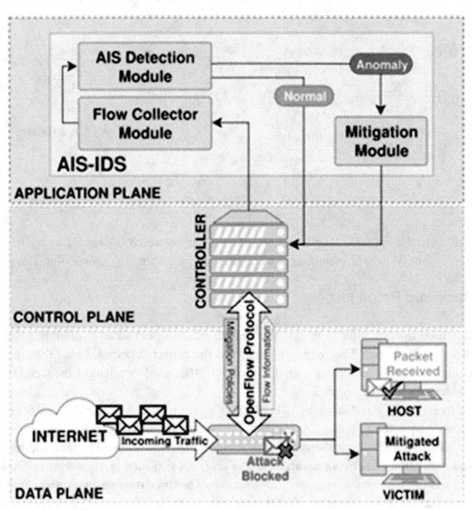

behaviour into normal or abnormal. If the behaviour is found to be abnormal, the Mitigation module blocks the traffic by creating forwarding rules.

The three modules are described below:

A.   Flow Collector Module (Figure 8) collects the data which is needed by the AIS Detection module (Figure 9). OpenFlow protocol is used. Every instant, many flows are created and expired in SDN. If the collection of flows information is more frequent, anomaly detection becomes more accurate and makes it possible to take faster action to mitigate the attack. But there is a disadvantage

Figure 8. Flow collector module
(Scaranti, G. F., Carvalho, L. F., Barbon, S., & Proenca, M. L. (2020))

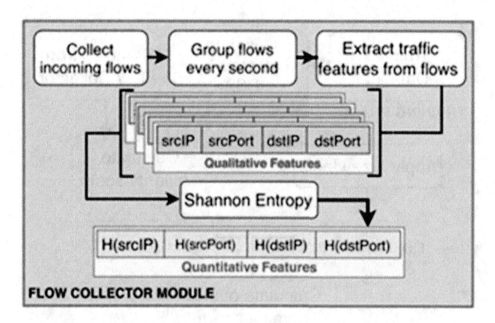

in the periodic data collection, which is the volume of the flow which is being analyzed. Here creating an IDS that reacts accurately in real-time when detecting threats is a challenging issue.

B.   AIS is inspired by biological immune systems. One of the best know algorithms for AIS is the Negative Selection Algorithm (NSA). It simulates the recognition of biological antibody to the job of self and non-self-classification. NSA is a computational model to generate immune detectors (Figure 10). This approach gives the advantage to detect threats without training the model with abnormal examples in the datasets. Each detector is complete only when its features have similarity values greater than the minimum similarity with the training dataset. This new detector is added to the detectors' collection, and the generation process terminates when this collection reaches n detectors. This is followed by classification.

C.   Mitigation Module (Figure 11) gets all the flow of anomalous traffic which was routed by the AIS Detection module (Figure 9). Then the mitigation module applies packet dropping policies to mitigate the detected attack. Depending on the types of anomalies: DDoS or PortScan attack, there are two types of mitigation strategies.

Figure 9. AIS detection module
(Scaranti, G. F., Carvalho, L. F., Barbon, S., & Proenca, M. L. (2020))

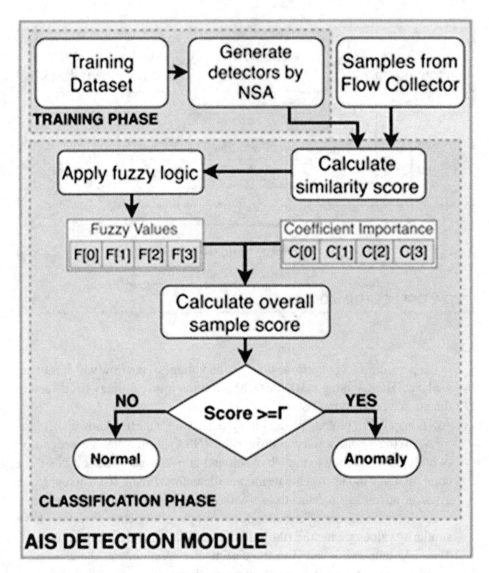

The results of the experiments concluded AIS-IDS to have F-measure over 99.9%, showing that the IDS proposed by the authors is reliable for protecting networks. On testing with public dataset, f-measure was found to be over 92%. The mitigation module was also able to drop the anomalous packets and block the attacks. Hence AIS-IDS has proved to be effective for detecting and mitigating Flooding Attacks in SDN.

Figure 10. Pseudocode for detectors generation
(Scaranti, G. F., Carvalho, L. F., Barbon, S., & Proenca, M. L. (2020))

Input : Training Data (tData), number of detectors (n)
and minimum similarity (k)

Output: Detectors Collection (Ω_l)

1 $\Omega_l \leftarrow \emptyset$
2 $numDetectors \leftarrow 0$
3 **while** $numDetectors \leq n$ **do**
4   **foreach** *feature* $\in$ *tData* **do**
5   *featColumn* $\leftarrow$ *tData[feature]*
6   *detFeatColumn* $\leftarrow$ Ω_l*[feature]*
7   *isused* $\leftarrow$ *no*
8   **while** *isused* $=$ *no* **do**
9   *rFeature* $\leftarrow$ *genRandomFeature()*
10   **if** *getSimilarity(rFeature, featColumn)* $\geq k$
and
getSimilarity(rFeature, detFeatColumn) $\geq k$
then
11   *newDetector[feature]* $\leftarrow$ *rFeature*
12   *isused* $\leftarrow$ *yes*
13   **end**
14   **end**
15   **end**
16     $\Omega_l \leftarrow \Omega_l \cup$ *newDetector*
17   *numDetectors* $\leftarrow$ *numDetectors* $+ 1$
18 **end**
19 **return** Ω_l

DDoS Attack

DDoS attack involves a huge number of packets being sent to the target. If the

Figure 11. Pseudocode for mitigation module
(Scaranti, G. F., Carvalho, L. F., Barbon, S., & Proenca, M. L. (2020))

Input : Data to be classified (newData), detectors collection (Ω_t), importance values (impValues) and minimum similarity (k)

Output: Classification Result

1 *score* $\leftarrow$ 0
2 **foreach** *attribute* $\in$ *newData* **do**
3   *attrColumn* $\leftarrow$ Ω_t[*attribute*]
4   *simScore* $\leftarrow$ *getSimilarity(attribute, attrColumn, k)*
5   *fuzzyValue* $\leftarrow$
   calcGaussianFuzzy(simScore, k, sigma)
   score $\leftarrow$ *score* + (*fuzzyValue* $\times$ *impValues*[*attribute*])

6 **end**
7 **if** *score* > Γ **then**
8   **return** *anomalous*
9 **end**
10 **else**
11   **return** *normal*
12 **end**

---

attack is successful, the controller will be disconnected from the rest of the network. Separation of controller results in losing its centralized control. This single point of failure can be dealt with architecture proposed by Tan, L., et al. (2020).

The architecture proposed by Tan, L., et al. (2020) consists of detection and defence mechanism. It comprises four divisions: A) DDoS Detection Trigger Mechanism on Programmable Data Plane, B) Flow feature Extraction, C) DDoS Detection Algorithm, and D) DDoS Defence Mechanism. These four divisions are described below:

A)   DDoS Detection Trigger Mechanism on Programmable Plane: The method used for DDoS attack detection uses fixed time intervals to detect network traffic. The efficiency of DDoS attack detection and performance of the controller is largely affected by the detection cycle periods. If the time interval is set to be too large, then the response time will be too high. This also increases the workload on the controller and the switches. And if the time interval is too small, then the attack detection will be started by the controller frequently, which increases the workload on the controller.

To solution to the above problem of periodic triggering of DDoS attack detection in SDN environment is to introduce a detection trigger mechanism which determines the start time of the DDoS attack detection through the trigger mechanism. This method is successful in breaking the problem of regular trigger detection method.

The detection trigger mechanism is deployed on the data plane and is implemented by counting packet_in messages on the switch. When the DDoS attack is initiated, there will be a huge spike in the number of packet_in messages, this abnormal increase in packet_in is used as a sign of a DDoS attack being initiated (Tan, L., et al. (2020)).

B)   Flow Feature Extraction: The accuracy of the algorithm is greatly affected by the feature section as the flow feature determines the basis of classification of the attack flow and normal flow. Firstly, since the attack aims to exhaust the resources of the network or occupy the bandwidth of the links, the attacker sends a large amount of traffic to the network in a short span of time. Secondly, in communication between hosts, the network is mostly bidirectional. Thus the percentage of traffic is highly symmetrical. But, when there is a DDoS attack, the symmetry decreases as the one directional flow (from the attacker) increases drastically. Thirdly, in order to ensure the normal service to the legitimate users, it is necessary to be able to distinguish between legitimate network flow and DDoS attack traffic. To address the above problem, Tan, L., et al. (2020) introduced the rate of change of asymmetric traffic. If the burst in traffic is legitimate, then the symmetry in network traffic will increase accordingly. While in a DDoS attack, the request waits for no response from the server. Due to this, the traffic will be highly asymmetric. An attacker needs to send a large number of packets in a short time span to crash the network quickly. There is a high chance that there is a DDoS attack, if the number of flows with small number of packets is too large. Whereas in legitimate traffic, a large of packets are needed for sending valid information. Thus the ratio of flows with small number of packets can be used to reflect the strength of the DDoS attack.

After the detection of abnormal traffic by the switches, the controller detects the abnormal traffic through the switches. The controller then sends OFPT_FLOW_MOD messages to the switches, which asks the switch to buffer packet from the abnormal traffic and send those packets to the controller for analysis. This is followed by the extraction of basic information of the flow, then the controller calculates the five feature values (Figure 12) of the flow using the following formula. These values are stored in the database.

Figure 12. Calculation of 5 features
(Tan, L., et al. (2020))

1) Average bytes per unit time at time Tn: the average number of bytes of flows per unit time.

$$br = \frac{b_{Tn} - b_{T_{n-1}}}{T_n - T_{n-1}} \tag{1}$$

2) Average durations per flow: the average duration of each flow.

$$adf = \frac{\sum_{i=0}^{flow\_nums_T} dur_i}{flow\_nums_T} \tag{2}$$

3) Percentage of pair-flows: The percentage of the symmetric flow to the total flows per unit time.

$$ppf = \frac{\sum_{i=0}^{flow\_nums_T} N_{pair\_flows}}{\sum_{i=0}^{flow\_nums_T} N_{pair\_flows} + \sum_{i=0}^{flow\_nums_T} N_{single\_flows}} \tag{3}$$

4) Variation rate of single flows: Change of the rate of asymmetric flow per unit time.

$$vrsf = \frac{flow\_nums_T - \sum_{i=0}^{flow\_nums_T} N_{single\_flows}}{T_n - T_{n-1}} \tag{4}$$

5) Percentage of flows with a few packets: The percentage of flows with a small number of packets in all flows.

$$pfsp = \frac{\sum F_i (N_p < V)}{flow\_nums_T} \tag{5}$$

C) DDoS Detection Algorithm (Figure 13): K-Means-based training data processing module and K-nearest neighbour-based traffic detection module are used in DDoS Detection Algorithm. K-means is used to cluster the data to compare the distance between the detection point and various clustering centres when using the KNN algorithm for detection. To determine whether the flow is normal flow or attack flow, k-nearest points are classified to normal group or attack

Figure 13. Pseudocode for K-means algorithm
(Tan, L., et al. (2020))

1: for $i = 1 : N + M$ do
2:    for j=1:5 do

3:      Normalized $x'_{ij} = \dfrac{x_{ij} - \min\{x_j\}}{\max\{x_j\} - \min\{x_j\}}$

4:    end for
5: end for
6: Randomly select k initial centers $X_{c1}^{label}, X_{c2}^{label}, \ldots, X_{ck}^{label}$

7: repeat
8:    for $i = 1 : N + M - k$ do
9:      for s=1: k do

10: Calculate the distance between the sample X_i^{label} and the center of each cluster

$$D_{is}\left(X_i^{label}, X_{cs}^{label}\right) = \sqrt{\left(X_i^{label} - X_{cs}^{label}\right)^2} = \sqrt{\sum_{j=1}^{5}\left(x_{ij} - x_{cj}\right)^2}$$

11: According to the distance D_{is}, the sample X_i^{label} is classified into the nearest cluster
12:    end for
13: end for
14: for s=1: k do

15:    Calculate new cluster center vector $\left(X_{cs}^{label}\right)'$

16:    if $\left(X_{cs}^{label}\right)' = X_{cs}^{label}$ then

17:      keep the current mean vector unchanged
18:    else

19: update the current cluster center vector X_{cs}^{label} to $\left(X_{cs}^{label}\right)'$

20:    end if
21: end for
22: until the current cluster center vector is not updated
23: for s=1: k do

24: calculate the radius of each cluster $r_s = \dfrac{\sum_{i=1}^{N_s} D_{is}}{N_s}$

25: end for

group. Traditionally, in KNN algorithm, it is necessary to calculate the distance between the point to be measured and all the other training data. And then, select the k nearest points to determine the type of the point to be measured. The algorithm proposed by Tan, L., et al. (2020) has reduced the calculation cost of detection and thus reduced the impact of special data on detection algorithm results. The detection algorithm is used only in the training phase and does not affect detection time. The purpose of using K-means algorithm is to segregate the traffic data with similar features into multiple categories. This makes it very convenient for the KNN algorithm to achieve rapid matching of the traffic features and can reduce the workload of the detection module and the impact of special data on detection results.

D)   DDoS Defence Mechanism (Figure 14): The commonly used techniques for mitigating DDoS attacks are to forward, modify or block the attack traffic. Even after successful mitigation of attack, a large number of malicious flow entries generated by the attack flow will remain in the switches. These entries will affect the flow of legitimate traffic because the flow entries keep occupying the storage resources of switches. Thus, the malicious flow entries should be deleted after blocking the traffic generated by the attack. Figure 15 presents a comparison between different methods on the basis of precision, recall and false alarm. The performance metrics were evaluated using NSL-KDD Dataset. This dataset contains 41 features like duration, src_bytes, dst_bytes, protocol_type, etc.

Wang, Y., Hu, T., Tang, G., Xie, J., & Lu, J. (2019) proposed Safe-Guard Scheme (SGS), which combines anomaly traffic detection in data plane and controller dynamic defence in control plane. Here a flow monitoring approach was used in anomaly traffic detection module. To distinguish attack flows from legitimate traffic, anomaly detection module extracts four tuple vector from the flows of switches based on rate feature and asymmetry feature. Back Propagation Neural Network (BPNN) method has been improved here.

Figure 16 is the Finite State Machine which manages the entire SGS System.

A)   Initial State: Here the network is running. SGS receives the packets from the host and transmits those to the switches.

B)   Detection State: Here, the identification of potential DDoS attack is executed. If anomalous traffic was detected, the system goes to Defence State. Else, the system returns to Safe State.

C)   Defence State: This state mainly runs in Control Plane. In this state, the system has confirmed that there is a DDoS attack on the controller and enables the controller dynamic defence module. Controller sends access control messages

Figure 14. DDoS defence mechanism
(Tan, L., et al. (2020))

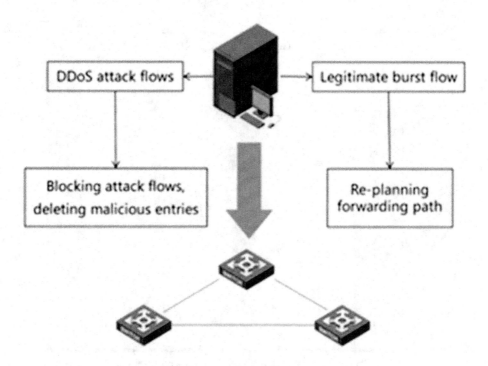

to switches to block anomalous flow from the source and clean malicious flow entry of the affected switches.

D) Safe State: The system forwards packets and returns to the Initial State.

The Anomaly Traffic Detection (Figure 17) module runs on the data plane of the switches. This module has three functionalities: Feature Extraction, Detection Reacting and Results Executing.

Figure 18 shows the validation results of the four-tuple vector for DDoS Attack Detection. The four tuples are (a) Byte rate, (b) Symmetric flows percentage, (c) Variation rate of asymmetric flow and (d) Flow percentage with small amount packets.

On evaluation of the performance of SGS with baseline schemes, the results showed that SGS can quickly detect and react to DDoS attacks. Controller response time of SGS was reduced by 42.1% at least, and flow setup time was reduced by 30.4% on average.

Figure 15. Comparison of different methods
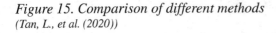
(Tan, L., et al. (2020))

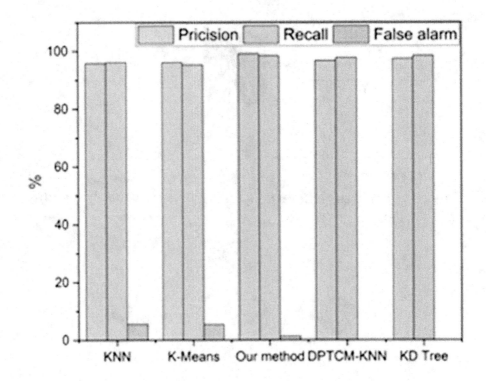

Packet Injection

Packet Injection attack involves the adversary taking control of more than one host to inject manipulated packets. Also, no additional privileges than the regular user are needed by the adversary to compromise the controller's system.

By monitoring packet-in messages, the topology management service learns the host information and updates the topology information along with the host profiles. The legitimacy of the packet-in messages caused by unmatched packets cannot be ensured because of the absence of such mechanism in the controller. This means any unmatched packet can trigger the packet-in messages. The above fact can be exploited by the attackers who control the end hosts to mount Packet Injection attacks by sending large amounts of fake packets. When these packets reach the OpenFlow switch and are tried to match with the entries, no matching flow entry is found in the table. This results in packet-in messages being sent from the switch to the SDN controller through the OpenFlow channel. The fake packets have no destination. Thus, the controller instructs the switch to flood these packets to other ports except the one it came from in the form of packet-in messages. The explosion of the topology information leads to huge performance degradation of the applications that are built on top of the Rest API.

Figure 16. Finite state machine managing SGS system
(Wang, Y., Hu, T., Tang, G., Xie, J., & Lu, J. (2019))

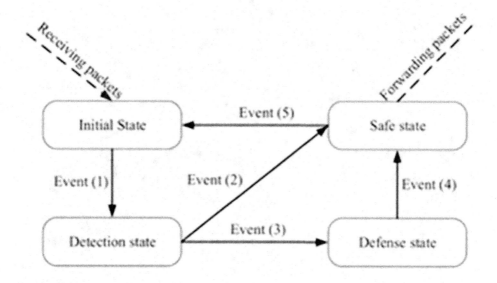

Figure 17. Anomaly detection module
(Wang, Y., Hu, T., Tang, G., Xie, J., & Lu, J. (2019))

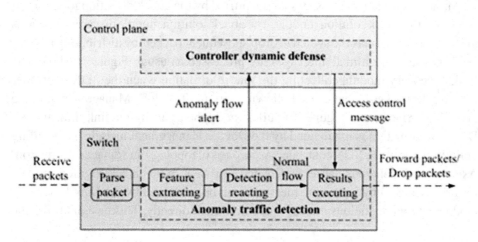

Figure 18. Validation results
(Wang, Y., Hu, T., Tang, G., Xie, J., & Lu, J. (2019))

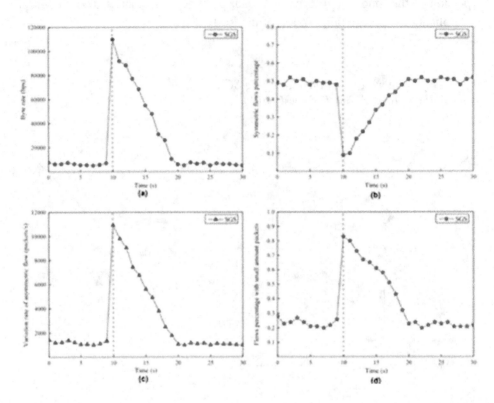

PacketChecker is proposed by Deng, S., Gao, X., Lu, Z., & Gao, X. (2018) in the form of an extension to assist SDN controller in handling fake packets. PacketChecker is an extension to the existing SDN controller.

Malicious packet-in messages are identified by the attack detection module and are sent to the attack solution module. The attack solution module discards malicious messages and instructs the switch to drop subsequent packets by distributing a Flow-Mod message. Legitimate messages are processed as usual. Figure 19 shows the Link Discovery module collecting the link information when the SDN controller receives the packet-in messages. Following this, the Topology Management module (Topology Manager in Figure 19) builds the topology using the link information. Device information is maintained by the Device Management module. Forwarding policy is made by the SDN controller on the basis of topology and device information. As soon as a malicious packet is detected, it is sent to the attack solution module for processing. Only legitimate messages can be processed by the Link Discovery module and the malicious messages are discarded directly. This design allows the

Figure 19. Flow diagram for packet-in messages
(Deng, S., Gao, X., Lu, Z., & Gao, X. (2018))

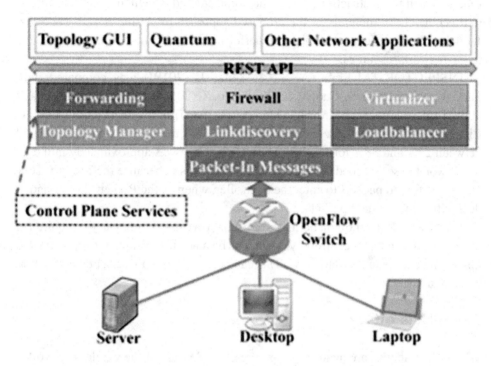

PacketChecker to work as an extension to the existing controller without revamping the SDN hardware.

Alshra'a, A. S., & Seitz, J. (2019) proposed INSPECTOR as a solution. It adds an isolated component (INSPECTOR) to the network architecture to check all the new packets before they reach the controller.

All the complex network logic exists only at the extreme/edge switches. These switches are the ingress and egress switches, and the rest of the core switches are kept as simple as possible. The core switches perform the task of packet forwarding, whereas the edge switches are required to end-host addresses like IPv4 or IPv6 for forwarding.

INSPECTOR maintains a database for all the authenticated hosts like IP address, In-port number, Data Path Identifier (DPID) of the connected edge switch. A packet_in message is sent to the INSPECTOR by the edge switch whenever a host requests a service for the first time. INSPECTOR then looks into the header packet field information to ensure that the host's request has authentication to use the network resources. Especially during Packet Injection attack, the packet load is distributed between the controller and the INSPECTOR.

Each new source address passes through the INSPECTOR either for the first time or when the instructions inside the connected edge switch were deleted due to timeout. The complexity of the proposed approach by Alshra'a, A. S., & Seitz, J. (2019), has no effect on the network performance while the host is authenticated to the network resources.

INSPECTOR (Alshra'a, A. S., & Seitz, J. (2019)) was compared with PacketChecker (Deng, S., Gao, X., Lu, Z., & Gao, X. (2018)), and presented 200% and 400% Ternary Content-Addressable Memory (TCAM) improvement rate. OpenFlow Channel workload was decreased by 85%, and the memory usage was reduced between 22% and 38% for INSPECTOR. CPU usage was approximately null and, in the worst case, reached 2% for INSPECTOR. This is because the INSPECTOR denies the forged packets to enter the controller, whereas the PacketChecker had to deal with all the forged packets.

INSPECTOR itself might be compromised. So a trusted third party is required to ensure this doesn't happen. Improvements can be made if searching for authenticated hosts can be done in constant time. This can be achieved if a smarter data structure is being used.

Worm-Hole Attack

Worm-Hole attacks are against the routing control plane of the wireless networks. It involves packets at one node of the Worm-Hole link being replayed at the other node of the link. This creates an illusion of the presence of a shorter path for further forwarding. The influenced nodes will then forward the traffic through malicious nodes. This forwarded traffic can be recorded, or altered or even dropped.

One of the most widely used controllers in SDN for discovering the network topology is Link Layer Discovery Protocol (LLDP). However, it has been proven that LLDP does not guarantee the integrity of its messages.

There are two major vulnerabilities in LLDP (Hua, J., Zhou, Z., & Zhong, S. (2021)):

1) Absence of authentication for ensuring LLDP packets' integrity.
2) Simple semantics of LLDP makes it easy to falsify the LLDP packets.

These vulnerabilities can be exploited for fabricating LLDP packets to declare a fake link connecting two switches that are not linked in reality. Consequently, the SDN controller would acquire the wrong network topology and forward the data to the fake link. Extremely serious attacks like DoS, eavesdropping and even hijacking attacks can be caused.

The fact that the fake link is not connected in reality leads to 100% packet loss because there is no transmission. This information can be used by the controller to detect the attack. Hua, J., Zhou, Z., & Zhong, S. (2021) presents a "true" worm-hole attack by building an in-band covert channel between the two compromised switches. This channel is built by introducing a relay host between the two cheating switches. On the basis of experimental analysis, it's been concluded that, as the position of the relay hosts is changed, the degree of effect on the network also changes.

To detect whether the link is fake or not, a detection measure is proposed in Hua, J., Zhou, Z., & Zhong, S. (2021) based on latencies. This detection measure provides efficient protection against worm-hole attacks and is scalable too. When the SDN is not under attack, the traffic is forwarded via the shortest path. But, under Worm-Hole attack, the flow is forwarded to the relay host. This relay host then forwards the data to the destination.

Most of the time, the path which includes the relay host is longer than that of the original path. Thus the delay time can be used to detect the presence of a Worm-Hole attack. There are two cases of Worm-Hole attacks:

1) When the link is running for a period of time and all the data of the network is collected by the controller. The detection algorithm has three steps:
   a) The controller saves the mean delay time between two switches, for all the switch pairs.
   b) When a new link is added to the existing network, the controller finds all the flows which flow through the newly added link. The new latencies of the new flows are compared with those of the previous latencies.
   c) The new link is considered to be a fake link if the percentage of the timeout flows surpasses the pre-defined threshold. If the link is identified to be a fake link, the controller notifies the neighbours of the terminals of the fake link to isolate this link from the network.
2) In this case, the link is being configured for the first time. The controller has got no data regarding the latencies. The new detection algorithm is;
   a) The shortest latency between two switches is stored in the controller for every pair of switches.
   b) When one switch can forward packets to tother switch via a direct link, this link is expected to be a normal link. If no direct link exists, then the controller picks up the second shortest latency link and compares it with the original latency. If the original latency is longer than the latter, this link between the two switches must be marked vicious. A threshold is used to reduce number of misjudgements.

On the basis of testing, the threshold is set to be 20%. This is because, for 95% of the delays out of 1000 times, the delays did not increase more than 20% of the normal delay. Also, as the data traffic increases, there might be more congestion in the network. This congestion is the cause for the latency to vary in a wider range, and hence, the detection might neglect some attacks. When the hop from the relay host to the compromised switches are increased, the defense success rate increases. This is because, as the hop increases, the influenced flows will have greater latency. Thus making it easier to detect the attacks. Success rate reaches 100% when the hop is 11 from the relay host to the compromised switch.

Topology Poisoning Attack

A Topology Poisoning attack can be performed after compromising one of the hosts in the network. One such attack can be LLDP spoofing attack which can mislead the topology view of the controller.

As discussed in the worm-hole attack section, LLDP lacks an authentication mechanism for testing the integrity of the received packets. This leads to the reception of random packets, which also includes the forged ones. With the aid of network monitor tools, adversaries can obtain and analyze the LLDP packets to implement tempering. On the basis of fabricated LLDP packets, the controller updates the network topology. This may influence future management leading to serious network collapse.

Two attack strategies are discussed by Wang, J., Tan, Y., Liu, J., & Zhang, Y. (2020) regarding topology poisoning attacks in vehicular edge networks. The two strategies are, fake LLDP packet injection and LLDP packet relay.

In fake LLDP packet injection, as the name suggests, fake LLDP packets are fabricated and injected into the network to poison the network topology. Attackers can obtain the LLDP packets and the frame structure by monitoring the traffic. A packet analysis tool can be used to know the meaning of each field in the packet. In the next stage, the attackers can modify the contents of the LLDP packets to achieve their intentions.

In LLDP packet relay, based on the threat model, the attacker can control at least two hosts that connect the target. The compromised host can communicate with each other through wired or wireless medium. A fake link is established by encapsulating the illusive LLDP packet into a packet-in message and sending it to the controller.

There are two differentiating factors between the fake LLDP packet injection and LLDP packet relay, these are:

1) Fake LLDP packet injection method needs two compromised hosts, whereas the LLDP packet relay method needs only one.

2) Fake LLDP packet injection method needs modification and analysis of the LLDP packets. Whereas the LLDP packet relay method simply uses the packet intercepted from the compromised host.

Wang, J., Tan, Y., Liu, J., & Zhang, Y. (2020) also proposed a novel attack-tolerance scheme based on deep enforcement learning (DRL), which complements the existing ones. The future scope of this scheme targets to perfect the tolerance scheme.

SUMMARY AND CONCLUSION

This chapter presented Software Defined Network's architecture and its vulnerabilities. Factors responsible for increasing the vulnerabilities in SDN along with their targets was discussed. SDN's security threat was classified into five major categories: Link Flooding Attack (LFA), Distributed Denial of Service (DDoS), Packet Injection, Worm-Hole Attack and Topology Poisoning Attack. Detection and mitigation strategies proposed by various researchers were presented for corresponding attack types along with their strengths and weaknesses. SDN has many advantages for securing networks. Meanwhile it gave birth to many new vulnerabilities as it has an increased attack surface. Keeping SDN simple aids its security. But keeping SDN simple is complex. Maintaining a clear security road map is important, else its security issues might overshadow its benefits.

REFERENCES

Abdullaziz, O. I., Wang, L. C., & Chen, Y. J. (2019). HiAuth: Hidden Authentication for Protecting Software Defined Networks. *IEEE eTransactions on Network and Service Management*, *16*(2), 618–631. doi:10.1109/TNSM.2019.2909116

Aladaileh, M. A., Anbar, M., Hasbullah, I. H., Chong, Y. W., & Sanjalawe, Y. K. (2020). Detection Techniques of Distributed Denial of Service Attacks on Software-Defined Networking Controller–A Review. *IEEE Access: Practical Innovations, Open Solutions*, *8*, 143985–143995. doi:10.1109/ACCESS.2020.3013998

Alshra'a, A. S., & Seitz, J. (2019). Using INSPECTOR Device to Stop Packet Injection Attack in SDN. *IEEE Communications Letters*, *23*(7), 1174–1177. doi:10.1109/LCOMM.2019.2896928

Brooks, M., & Yang, B. (2015, September). A Man-in-the-Middle attack against OpenDayLight SDN controller. *Proceedings of the 4th Annual ACM Conference on Research in Information Technology*. 10.1145/2808062.2808073

Comer, D., & Rastegarnia, A. (2019). Externalization of Packet Processing in Software Defined Networking. *IEEE Networking Letters*, *1*(3), 124–127. doi:10.1109/LNET.2019.2918155

Deng, S., Gao, X., Lu, Z., & Gao, X. (2018). Packet Injection Attack and Its Defense in Software-Defined Networks. *IEEE Transactions on Information Forensics and Security*, *13*(3), 695–705. doi:10.1109/TIFS.2017.2765506

Dong, S., & Sarem, M. (2020). DDoS Attack Detection Method Based on Improved KNN With the Degree of DDoS Attack in Software-Defined Networks. *IEEE Access: Practical Innovations, Open Solutions*, *8*, 5039–5048. doi:10.1109/ACCESS.2019.2963077

Eom, T., Hong, J. B., An, S., Park, J. S., & Kim, D. S. (2019). A Systematic Approach to Threat Modeling and Security Analysis for Software Defined Networking. *IEEE Access: Practical Innovations, Open Solutions*, *7*, 137432–137445. doi:10.1109/ACCESS.2019.2940039

Gao, S., Peng, Z., Xiao, B., Hu, A., Song, Y., & Ren, K. (2020). Detection and Mitigation of DoS Attacks in Software Defined Networks. *IEEE/ACM Transactions on Networking*, *28*(3), 1419–1433. doi:10.1109/TNET.2020.2983976

Gupta, B. B., Perez, G. M., Agrawal, D. P., & Gupta, D. (2021). Handbook of Computer Networks and Cyber Security: Principles and Paradigms. In Software-Defined Network (SDN) Data Plane Security: Issues, Solutions, and Future Directions (pp. 341–387). Springer.

Haider, S., Akhunzada, A., Mustafa, I., Patel, T. B., Fernandez, A., Choo, K. K. R., & Iqbal, J. (2020). A Deep CNN Ensemble Framework for Efficient DDoS Attack Detection in Software Defined Networks. *IEEE Access: Practical Innovations, Open Solutions*, *8*, 53972–53983. doi:10.1109/ACCESS.2020.2976908

Hua, J., Zhou, Z., & Zhong, S. (2021). Flow Misleading: Worm-Hole Attack in Software-Defined Networking via Building In-Band Covert Channel. *IEEE Transactions on Information Forensics and Security*, *16*, 1029–1043. doi:10.1109/TIFS.2020.3013093

Imran, M., Durad, M. H., Khan, F. A., & Abbas, H. (2020). DAISY: A Detection and Mitigation System Against Denial-of-Service Attacks in Software-Defined Networks. *IEEE Systems Journal*, *14*(2), 1933–1944. doi:10.1109/JSYST.2019.2927223

Kim, S., Yoon, S., Narantuya, J., & Lim, H. (2020). Secure Collecting, Optimizing, and Deploying of Firewall Rules in Software-Defined Networks. *IEEE Access: Practical Innovations, Open Solutions, 8*, 15166–15177. doi:10.1109/ACCESS.2020.2967503

Phan, T. V., Nguyen, T. G., Dao, N. N., Huong, T. T., Thanh, N. H., & Bauschert, T. (2020). DeepGuard: Efficient Anomaly Detection in SDN With Fine-Grained Traffic Flow Monitoring. *IEEE eTransactions on Network and Service Management, 17*(3), 1349–1362. doi:10.1109/TNSM.2020.3004415

Qureshi, K. I., Wang, L., Sun, L., Zhu, C., & Shu, L. (2020). A Review on Design and Implementation of Software-Defined WLANs. *IEEE Systems Journal, 14*(2), 2601–2614. doi:10.1109/JSYST.2019.2960400

Rasool, R. U., Ashraf, U., Ahmed, K., Wang, H., Rafique, W., & Anwar, Z. (2019). Cyberpulse: A Machine Learning Based Link Flooding Attack Mitigation System for Software Defined Networks. *IEEE Access: Practical Innovations, Open Solutions, 7*, 34885–34899. doi:10.1109/ACCESS.2019.2904236

Sallam, A., Refaey, A., & Shami, A. (2019). On the Security of SDN: A Completed Secure and Scalable Framework Using the Software-Defined Perimeter. *IEEE Access: Practical Innovations, Open Solutions, 7*, 146577–146587. doi:10.1109/ACCESS.2019.2939780

Scaranti, G. F., Carvalho, L. F., Barbon, S., & Proenca, M. L. (2020). Artificial Immune Systems and Fuzzy Logic to Detect Flooding Attacks in Software-Defined Networks. *IEEE Access: Practical Innovations, Open Solutions, 8*, 100172–100184. doi:10.1109/ACCESS.2020.2997939

Shin, S., & Gu, G. (2013). Attacking software-defined networks. *Proceedings of the Second ACM SIGCOMM Workshop on Hot Topics in Software Defined Networking - HotSDN '13*. 10.1145/2491185.2491220

Tan, L., Pan, Y., Wu, J., Zhou, J., Jiang, H., & Deng, Y. (2020). A New Framework for DDoS Attack Detection and Defense in SDN Environment. *IEEE Access: Practical Innovations, Open Solutions, 8*, 161908–161919. doi:10.1109/ACCESS.2020.3021435

Varadharajan, V., & Tupakula, U. (2020). Counteracting Attacks From Malicious End Hosts in Software Defined Networks. *IEEE eTransactions on Network and Service Management, 17*(1), 160–174. doi:10.1109/TNSM.2019.2931294

Wang, J., Tan, Y., Liu, J., & Zhang, Y. (2020). Topology Poisoning Attack in SDN-Enabled Vehicular Edge Network. *IEEE Internet of Things Journal, 7*(10), 9563–9574. doi:10.1109/JIOT.2020.2984088

Wang, Y., Hu, T., Tang, G., Xie, J., & Lu, J. (2019). SGS: Safe-Guard Scheme for Protecting Control Plane Against DDoS Attacks in Software-Defined Networking. *IEEE Access: Practical Innovations, Open Solutions, 7*, 34699–34710. doi:10.1109/ ACCESS.2019.2895092

Xu, Y., Sun, H., Xiang, F., & Sun, Z. (2019). Efficient DDoS Detection Based on K-FKNN in Software Defined Networks. *IEEE Access: Practical Innovations, Open Solutions, 7*, 160536–160545. doi:10.1109/ACCESS.2019.2950945

Yoon, S., Cho, J. H., Kim, D. S., Moore, T. J., Free-Nelson, F., & Lim, H. (2020). Attack Graph-Based Moving Target Defense in Software-Defined Networks. *IEEE eTransactions on Network and Service Management, 17*(3), 1653–1668. doi:10.1109/ TNSM.2020.2987085

Zhang, P., Zhang, F., Xu, S., Yang, Z., Li, H., Li, Q., Wang, H., Shen, C., & Hu, C. (2021). Network-Wide Forwarding Anomaly Detection and Localization in Software Defined Networks. *IEEE/ACM Transactions on Networking, 29*(1), 332–345. doi:10.1109/TNET.2020.3033588

Zhijun, W., Qing, X., Jingjie, W., Meng, Y., & Liang, L. (2020). Low-Rate DDoS Attack Detection Based on Factorization Machine in Software Defined Network. *IEEE Access: Practical Innovations, Open Solutions, 8*, 17404–17418. doi:10.1109/ ACCESS.2020.2967478

Chapter 4
Role of Bangladesh Bank on Cybersecurity in FinTech

Saila Sarmin Rapti
Bangladesh Bank, Bangladesh

Nabila Fahria
Bangladesh Bank, Bangladesh

Sunita Rani Das
Bangladesh Bank, Bangladesh

ABSTRACT

Following the COVID-19 outbreak, the world has seen another rising challenge of accessing financial services. By limiting the transmission of COVID-19, fintech accelerated access to financial services for all aspects of society, allowing individuals to become more flexible and comfortable with fintech. However, cyber-attacks can hinder the progress of this evolution by attacking any type of banking channel, including traditional banking, internet banking, credit cards, ATMs, agent banking, and mobile banking. From the standpoint of central bank risk management, this chapter investigates fintech and the associated field of cybersecurity.

INTRODUCTION

The COVID-19 pandemic has created numerous chances for FinTech firms. In order to ride the digital transformation wave that everyone wants to be a part of, customer penetration has reached new highs. It's crucial to remember, though, that every advantage comes with some risk. Security Dangers, Breach of Privacy, Service Disparity, Cybercrime, Systemic Risks, and other risks are all related with the

DOI: 10.4018/978-1-6684-3448-2.ch004

widespread use of digital banking. When it comes to providing financial services, financial technology, or FinTech, is a sort of technology and innovation that tries to compete with traditional banking methods. Technology is used to advance financial transactions in this relatively new industry. This technology includes the use of smartphones in banking services, sometimes known as cellular banks, as well as investment services via mobile phone and Cryptocurrencies, which aims to make financial services accessible to the general public.

Financial technology companies are made up of new projects, financial institutions, and well-established technology enterprises that strive to improve or replace the use of financial services provided by existing financial firms. Many existing financial institutions are utilizing financial technology solutions and technologies to improve and streamline their operations in order to increase their services and strengthen their market position (Peters et al., 2015). As a result, we learn that improvements in financial technology work hard to increase the efficiency of the financial system for all public and private sectors, firms, and consumers, exposing financial technology to financial risks and losses. Policymakers, titles, and regulations attempt to protect all parties involved in financial innovation and support the expansion of these services in order to foster financial innovation and encourage the growth of these services (Philippon, 2016; Shah et al., 2018).

As a result of technological improvements, the field of finance has evolved over time. As a result of technology-based innovations in finance, consumer access to numerous services in the sectors of payments, loans, insurance, savings, and investment has improved considerably over the last decade; this is now within their reach at an unparalleled pace and scope (Kim et al., 2015). However, it raises privacy concerns, such as if dealing in technology exposes and compromises client data, and whether related technologies such as machine learning and artificial intelligence will be used in banking risk management (Kareem et al., 2020). As a result of these improvements, cyber-attacks are changing and becoming more common. Attack operations professionals strive to enhance their methods in order to advance. It's vital to define the sort of threat and comprehend the risks associated with cybersecurity and their implications for financial services faster than security teams can accomplish so that their techniques become more sophisticated. Stronger cybersecurity solutions are essential as the relevance of financial technology develops. As a result, the benefits of financial technology are preserved. This will demand some preparedness in a number of areas, including cyber governance, which will necessitate a greater awareness and study of Internet technology and security facts, as well as security partnerships. The main issue is that, because financial and banking services have recently developed and high capabilities, great risks have arisen, and these services are accompanied by fierce attacks that institutions must prepare for, because financial and banking services have recently developed and high capabilities. Banking operations supervision and regulatory organizations should monitor oversight systems that are in line with the rise of electronic banking operations and the hazards they involve, because financial companies are the most vulnerable to these threats.

The paper is organized in the following manner: Section 2 included Literature review, Section 3 provided the definition of Fintech, Section 4 highlighted The evolution and growth of FinTech and Digital Payment Systems within the Bangladesh's Monetary system, Section 5 described the performance of Bangladesh in FinTech and Cyber Security and Section 6 depicts the cyber security problems in FinTech in Bangladesh. Section 7 highlighted Antifraud measures and cybersecurity for Fintech By Bangladesh Bank and Section 8 concluded.

LITERATURE REVIEW

Al Duhaidahawi et al. (2020) measured the relationship between Fintech variables and cybersecurity, where Fintech variables were explanatory variables and cybersecurity was dependent and the observations of the study were revealed significant relationship between the dependent and independent variables at 5.00% level of significance with 90.80 percent of complementary among the Fintech variables.

A study of Ng, Artie W. et al. (2017) aiming at emergence of formulation of policies for technologies financial services and cybersecurity of Hong Kong revealed that both technical and moral fitness are crucial for minimizing the risks arisen from Fintech on cybersecurity and with the efficiency of both policies, territories of fraud exposures may be explored which is helpful to Fintech developments.

Vucinic M. (2020) linked between financial technology and market structure through financial stability, risks and benefits, according to the study Fintech brings opportunities and risks simultaneously for market players which may threat financial stability in prospect of micro and macroeconomic risks along with these cyber risks will be increased because of technological solutions of access point that hackers could target.

Another study of Rahman Benazir et al. (2021) displayed the ecosystem, opportunities and challenges in prospects of Fintech in Bangladesh, with the help of primary survey the study found the growth of Fintech in Bangladeshi financial sector, Fintech has significant effect on financial sector, there are various improved activities for fintech and there exist different obstacles on the way of the growth of Fintech in Bangladesh through four Chi-square (χ^2) test hypotheses testing.

Jayalath J A R C & Premaratne S. C. (2021) portrayed in their study of "Analysis of Key Digital Technology Infrastructure and Cyber Security Consideration Factors for Fintech Companies," that cyber threat is increasing rapidly as financial platforms are disclosed to the public through internet, that is why, a well-structured digital technological infrastructure is needed for the Fintech companies, banks and finance companies so that they can provide digital solutions to reduce the cyber threat.

A study of Khan Mr. Ashraf & Malaika Majid (2021) mentioned central bank as the key decision maker but the decision-making body are not fully up to date to cybersecurity and fintech improvement issues while fintech has made central bank operations: financial supervision, reserve management and currency management risky. International Monetary Fund (IMF) has suggested the central banks to have "appropriate hierarchical levels", a "committee structure", and a clear independence of the investment side from the risk management side to reduce cybersecurity risk.

WHAT IS FINTECH

FinTech is an acronym for financial technology that associates technology with financial services (Schueffel, 2016). It shows how modern internet-related technologies like cloud computing, mobile internet, and big data analytics are linked to commercial activities including payments, lending, mortgages, loans, and the stock market. FinTech is an abbreviation for financial technology, and it refers to businesses that use technology to conduct financial transactions.

Financial Technology (FinTech) has emerged as a distinct technical word that primarily represents the financial technology sectors in a wide range of activities for firms or organizations, with a focus on improving service quality through the use of Information Technology (IT) applications. (Schueffel, P., 2016)

Mr. Abraham Leon Bettinger, Vice President of the bank Manufacturers Hanover Trust, provided the following definition in a scholarly article detailing models on how he had analyzed and solved daily banking problems encountered at the bank (Prabook, 2016): "FINTECH is an acronym that stands for financial technology, combining bank expertise with modern management science techniques and the computer." (Bettinger, p.62, 1972)

THE EVOLUTION AND GROWTH OF FINTECH AND DIGITAL PAYMENT SYSTEMS WITHIN THE BANGLADESH'S MONETARY SYSTEM

Payment and settlement systems are seen as important to a country's financial system's efficient operation. These systems allow the transferring the funds among financial institutions, businesses, and individuals. As a regulatory body, Bangladesh Bank (BB) has encouraged scheduled banks to keep up smooth and robust e-banking operations. BB has taken necessary initiatives to start e-commerce, e-banking, Automated Clearing House System (ACHS), mobile phone banking, etc. Now, in these days, Banks are able to perform online money transactions, payment of utility bills, transfer of funds, payments for exports-imports or trade through e-channels like Internet, ATM, Mobile phone or other electronic devices. Other major successful projects of BB are NPSB,BACPS, BEFTN, CIB, Data warehouse, etc.

Figure 1. Evolution of FinTech and digital payment

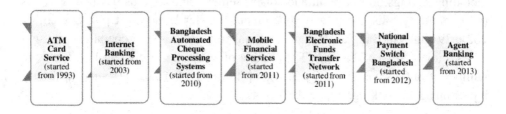

The chart below is showing the evolution of FinTech and digital payment systems within the monetary system of Bangladesh:

Bangladesh Bank authority and Government have taken collaborative efforts so that the scheduled banks of Bangladesh can conduct inter-bank online transactions and can operate unceasing full-fledged online banking in Bangladesh. Bangladesh Bank conducts several operations in this sector:

Internet Banking

The Dutch-Bangla Bank is Bangladesh's first fully automated bank to offer electronic banking. The automation was completed in 2003, but new features and additions are being added and modified on a regular basis. Banks provide any branch banking services via their respective bank online network, which includes services such as transaction through any branch under the respective bank online network; payment against pay order or pay order encashment, demand draft encashment, opening or redemption of FDR from any branch of the same bank; remote fund transfer, cash withdrawal, cash deposit, account statement, clearing and balance enquiry within branches of the same bank; and L/C opening. (source: Bangladesh bank)

Agent Banking

Bangladesh Bank has introduced agent banking in the country through issuing a guideline in 2013. Agent banking is defined as banking services delivered by engaged agents under a legitimate agency agreement outside of traditional bank branches. An Agent must provide, as a minimum, cash deposit and cash withdrawal services. The major goal is to provide a secure alternative delivery route for banking services to the underprivileged and underserved people, who are typically located in geographically isolated areas outside the reach of standard banking networks. (source: guidelines of agent banking, Bangladesh Bank)

Through an agent, banks can provide a number of financial services to customers, including savings, loans, remittance disbursement, and various payment services (such as utility bills, taxes, and government transfer benefits). Up to September 2021, 29 banks in Bangladesh have undertaken agent banking operations through 18,077outlets of 13,470 agents. The number of agents has grown by 4.32% and the number of outlets has grown by 5.44% up to September 2021. (source: quarterly report on agent banking, Bangladesh Bank)

ATM Card Service

It was Standard Chartered Bank (SCB) which introduced ATMs in Bangladesh. The first booth was set up at Dhaka's Banani in 1993. An Automated Teller Machine (ATM) is a device that allows users of a financial institution to conduct automated financial transactions. Customers can use an ATM to access their bank accounts and make cash withdrawals, cash advances, fund transfers across accounts, and check account balances. The Bangladesh Bank has issued guidelines for white label ATMs and white label merchant acquiring services to help spread banking services across the country at an affordable cost.

Mobile Financial Services (MFS)

Bangladesh Bank has introduced efficient off-branch Mobile Financial Services (MFS) during 2011 in Bangladesh as the country acquired an omnipresent mobile phone network experienced, large number of mobile phone users and improved IT infrastructure. Within ten years, this exponentially growing Bank-Led model of MFS has become the largest MFS market in the world. Bangladesh Bank permits Cash in, Cash out, Person to Person (P2P), Person to Business (P2B), Business to Person (B2P), Person to Government (P2G) and Government to Person (G2P) payment services through MFS domestically. No cross border money transfer is allowed under this service. However, local disbursement of inward foreign remittance through banking channels is permitted. Any adult can open an MFS account with any provider at an agent point or bank branch with a photo and legal identification. In this case, having more than one MFS account by one person with the same provider is not permitted.

Bangladesh Automated Cheque Processing Systems (BACPS)

Since inception in October, 2010 BACPS is the only state-of-the art cheque clearing facility. It uses the Cheque Imaging and Truncation (CIT) technology for electronic presentation and payment of paper-based instruments (i.e. cheque, pay order, dividend & refund warrants, etc). BACPS operates in a batch processing mode.

Bangladesh Electronic Funds Transfer Network (BEFTN)

BEFTN was the first paperless electronic inter-bank funds transfer system in the country when it launched in February 2011. As a lead over cheque clearing system, it allows for both credit and debit transactions. Payroll, international and domestic remittances, social security payments, company dividends, bill payments, corporate payments, government tax payments, social security payments, and person-to-person payments are all possible through this network. Debit transactions, such as utility bill payments, insurance premium payments, Club/Association payments, EMI payments, and so on, are also accommodated. BEFTN processes the majority of government salaries, social benefits, and other government payments.

National Payment Switch Bangladesh (NPSB)

Operational since 2012, NPSB is meant for establishing interoperability among participating banks for their account and card based transactions. Currently, it caters interbank Automated Teller Machines (ATM), Point of Sales (POS) and Internet Banking Fund Transfer (IBFT) transactions while the Mobile Financial Services interoperability is under active consideration. 53 Banks are now interconnected through NPSB for their ATM transactions. Currently, four types of interbank ATM transactions (i.e. cash withdrawal, balance enquiry, fund transfer and mini statement) could be done through NPSB. As of October 2021, 53 banks are interoperable for POS transactions and 30 banks are interconnected for their IBFT transactions. There are different limits for individual and institutional IBFT transactions. For individuals, the maximum value of each transaction is 3,00,000 taka and the frequency are maximum 10 times a day and not more than 10,00,000 taka per day. For corporations, a limit has been set on each transaction as 5,00,000 taka and maximum frequency as 20 times a day and 25,00,000 taka per day. It is mandatory for the participating banks to ensure Two Factor Authentications (2FA) for any online/e-commerce/interbanking/ card not present transactions.

PERFORMANCE OF BANGLADESH I/N FINTECH AND CYBER SECURITY

Figure 2 depicts the use of financial technology (fintech) throughout a three-year period, beginning in December 2018 and ending in December 2021. The trend in the fintech industry is depicted in this graph, which demonstrates how the use of fintech has increased over time. For example, the total number of card transactions was roughly 18 million in December 2018, and it nearly doubled to 31 million in December 2021. This shift is primarily due to consumers preferring plastic money to paper money. The same can be true for internet banking, where total transactions climbed from.8 million to 4.2 million in three years.

Figure 2. Uses of Fintech over time in Bangladesh

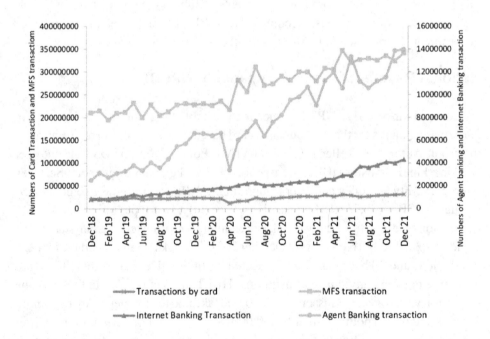

In terms of mobile financial services (MFS) and agent banking, the most significant changes may be seen. From 2018 to 2021, MFS transactions surged from 210 million to 341 million, while agent banking transactions increased from 2.4 million to a stunning 13 million. Another thing to note from the graph is that in most cases, the increases in transactions were not uniform, i.e., the rise/increase was not always steady, and there were also troughs in the trend. The fact that the world has been under the authority of COVID-19 since 2020, and the epidemic has put us all on lockdown, explains this transaction trend. Because people were staying at home during that time, physical transactions were essentially non-existent, as shown in the graph. As people became more familiar with technology and quit dealing in person, the upward trend began in February 2020 and continued for all types of transactions indicated. FinTech is becoming more popular and has begun to replace traditional financial transactions.

In the National Cyber Security Index published by the Estonia-based e-Governance Academy Foundation, Bangladesh has advanced 27 steps. Bangladesh has moved up to 33rd place in the survey, which examines the level of cyber security and digital growth in 180 countries worldwide. The National Cyber Security Index assesses the central government's cyber security capabilities in the country. Greece is ranked first with a score of 96.10 on the NCSI website, while Bangladesh is ranked second with a score of 67.53. Bangladesh is the top-ranked country in South Asia, while India is ranked 46th.

The Figure:3 tells us about the number of cyber-attacks that were registered over the period of 6 years. The trend we can see here is an increasing trend, with the least number of registered attacks in 2016 and the highest in 2020. As the pandemic hit us in 2020, people became more inclined towards online and paperless transactions to avoid physical altercations. This is when and where the hackers get the opportunity to commit credit card fraud, ghost transactions, identity theft and many other kinds of cybercrime. Also, during these times, the government/ the central bank became

Table 1. Overall review of Bangladesh according to e-Governance Academy Foundation

Index score	Cyber Security Indicators
33rd National Cyber Security Index	Protection of digital services (scored 1 in scale of 5)
53rd Global Cybersecurity Index	Protection of essential services (scored 5 in scale of 6)
147th ICT Development Index	E-identification and trust services (scored 7 in scale of 9)
95th Networked Readiness Index	Cyber incidents response (scored 5 in scale of 6)

Source: NCSI is held and developed by e-Governance Academy Foundation, Estonia

Figure 3. Per year registered incidents of cyber attacks in Bangladesh

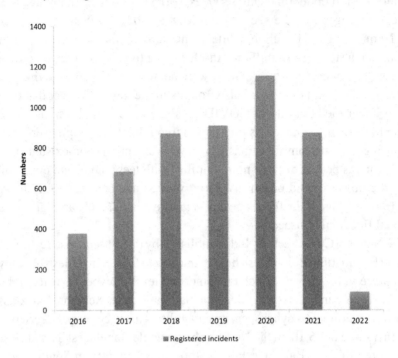

more aware of the cyber security threat and were more active in diminishing such threats. Thus, people also registered more cases with the law enforcers in order to catch the culprits. We can see that the number of registered cases fell in 2021 due to the government's crackdown on the perpetrators and also because the law enforcers were more active in stopping cybercrimes in all their forms.

CYBER SECURITY PROBLEMS IN FINTECH IN BANGLADESH

The pandemic has increased cyber risk because more staff are working remotely, banks restricted gathering in branches, fear of virus spreading etc. The main targets will be anybody who regularly accesses sensitive data such as staff holding information about customers and customers who have less knowledge in technology. Banks have had to deal with a variety of threats, including employee errors, state-sponsored attacks, errors involving third-party vendors, and the use of complicated technologies for well over a decade. The following are some of the most typical ways that cyber-security is jeopardized: Viruses, Trojan horses, spyware, ransomware, and adware are examples of malware. Botnets, SQL injection, Phishing, Vishing, Smishing, DNS Phishing, Farming, Man-in-the-Middle attack, Denial-of-Service assault, and other cyber attacks are also included. Dridex malware (December 2019), romance scams (February 2020), and Emotet malware (late 2019) are only a few of the world's most recent cyber threats. The definitions of this threats are included in Appendix (Annex-I). There are different kind of cyber security threats in Fintech, it could be human made or machine-made threats. Now we will see several types of cyber security risk in FinTech sector of Bangladesh:

I. Technological vulnerabilities: Technological vulnerabilities includes the risk originates due to the fault in technological systems. The following are some of the most prevalent technology-related vulnerabilities that financial organizations experience.

    ◦   Lack of Updates in antivirus and other protection systems: Antivirus version that is out of date, Unpatched operating systems and apps, Installing programs and software from an untrustworthy source, Inadequate endpoint security are the most common mistakes made by financial institutions. Most of these vulnerabilities occur due to the lack of financial provisions for the cyber-security systems.

    ◦   Insecure connection to server and website: URL redirection to malicious web page and websites are common user end problems in the financial institutions. The employees who have confidential data may use malicious websites unknowingly and may harm the security. Malware, unlike other sorts of attacks, can enter through a variety of channels, including emails, pop-ups, malicious websites, third-party software, and so on. These assaults are particularly dangerous because they have a high data transfer rate and can bring entire networks down.

II. Human made vulnerabilities: Even if all these technological precautions are made but they all can fail due to the human vulnerabilities. Human weaknesses are far more destructive than technological flaws. Consider the case of a customer who wants to use an mobile financial services to send money. Even if the mobile banking software is secure and funds are delivered safely, a human error in typing the recipient's number or leaking the password can result in an inaccurate fund transfer or loss of money. It also indulges the cybercriminals. Individuals or groups who attack systems for monetary gain or to cause disruption are referred to as cybercriminals. There are several types of Human vulnerabilities. In cases of ATM card counterfeit, fraud involve skimming, a process where genuine data on a card's magnetic stripe is electronically copied onto another. In mobile financial services, fraud stole the PIN. Internet banking users who are victims, they are directed by the criminal to fake websites usually by emails which appear to originate from legitimate sources. The victims are then tricked into revealing personal information, including bank details.

- ○ Password related risks: Some may save their login credentials rather than remembering them. Stealing them cybercriminals easily can hack the system and steal away the funds from the owners.

- ○ Lack of technological education: Some people may think; bankers or financial institutions do not necessarily need to be expert in IT related things. However, IT related knowledge and being aware of using network is essential for every one especially the bankers and users.

- ○ Unawareness of cyber security: Many users habituating in clicking suspicious emails and filling up personal identifiable information in open websites. Many people shares their password with friends, colleagues and family which left them vulnerable to the cyber criminals. Users are targeted by adware that offers them free gifts, certificates, and vacation deals. These false offers are designed to get people to click on phony adverts that lead to harmful websites.

- ○ Unlocking Computers: When employees leave their offices for a short time, they leave their computers unlocked which give the opportunity to hackers.

- ○ Transaction related problems: Most of the financial transactions are completed through cloud-based servers nowadays. If the users do not keep enough knowledge in transaction vulnerabilities, hackers can easily steal the information and take away the money.

III. Institutional Vulnerabilities: A cybersecurity governance and risk management program that is appropriate for the size of the organization should be designed. Proper IT governance procedures within an organization are also essential.

- ○ Cloud based Risk: Digital banking, payment gateways, internet banking services, and other financial services are increasingly reliant on cloud-based infrastructure. Cloud computing's advantages are undeniable: speed, accessibility, and scalability, to mention a few. It does, however, have a lot of data moving through it, which makes it an ideal smoke screen for attackers. This is why it's critical to find a reputable cloud provider with a proactive and up-to-date security approach. If the security is compromised, every piece of data sent or received through the cloud server can be breached. The act of disclosing sensitive or confidential data to any untrusted person, whether purposefully or unintentionally, is known as a data breach.

- ○ Complying with standard: Depending on the type of financial institution (Specialized Bank, Electronic Money Institution, Payment Institution), owners are required to adhere to different security and data protection standards, among other things. Failure to comply with the regulations can result in expensive fines, but more critically, major security problems.

Hackers have launched an attack. The more devices used to access a single account, the more likely that account will be compromised. This risk is amplified by the use of mobile banking, ATM cards, and internet banking. While speed is important in FinTech, it's also a good idea to only add new supported platforms after thorough security testing. Customers want quick access to banking services. FinTech companies are well aware that they must frequently pick between ease and security. However, as the number of regulatory agencies and compliance requirements in FinTech grows, the business will be forced to strike a balance between convenience and security before introducing a new product.

ANTIFRAUD MEASURES AND CYBERSECURITY FOR FINTECH BY BANGLADESH BANK

Cyber security is a technique for securing computers, servers, mobile devices, electronic systems, networks, and data from malicious attacks. It's also known as information technology security or electronic information security. The term is used in a variety of applications, from business to mobile computing, and it may be divided into several groups.

Application security aims to protect software and devices from malicious assaults. Network security is the process of protecting a computer network from intruders, whether they be targeted attackers or opportunistic malware. Information security safeguards data integrity and privacy during storage and transfer. Operational security includes the processes and decisions for handling and securing data assets. This umbrella encompasses the protocols that regulate how and where data may be stored or shared, as well as the rights that users have when accessing a network. With an increasing number of data breaches each year, the global cyber threat is continually evolving. In the first nine months of 2019, data breaches exposed 7.9 billion records, according to a survey published by Risk Based Security. This is more than 112 percent more than the number of records disclosed in the same time period the previous year. As the extent of the cyber threat grows, the International Data Corporation predicts that global spending on cyber-security solutions would reach a whopping $133.7 billion by 2022. In response to the growing cyber danger, governments around the world have produced suggestions to assist firms in developing robust cyber-security strategies. The United States' National Institute of Standards and Technology (NIST) has created a cyber-security architecture. To combat the propagation of hazardous viruses and aid in early detection, the framework encourages continuous, real-time monitoring of all electronic resources.

Endpoint security, often known as end-user protection, is an important part of cyber security. After all, it's common for an individual (the end-user) to unintentionally download malware or another type of cyber danger to their computer, laptop, or mobile device. End-users and systems are protected in the following ways by cyber-security measures: To begin, cryptographic protocols are used to encrypt emails, files, and other sensitive data. This safeguards information not just while it is in transit, but also against loss or theft. Here are some helpful hints for staying safe online: Updating software and operating system, use anti-virus software, use strong passwords that aren't easy to guess, don't open email attachments from unknown senders (they could include malware), don't click on links in emails from unknown senders, and so on.

Roles of Bangladesh Bank on cyber security for Fintech sector are as follows:

1. Guideline on ICT Security For Banks and Non-Bank Financial Institutions, May 2015.: The ICT landscape is vulnerable to various forms of attacks. The frequency and malignancy of such attacks are increasing. It is imperative that Bank or NBFI implements security solutions at the data, application, database, operating systems and networks to adequately address related threats. Appropriate measures shall be implemented to protect sensitive or confidential information such as customer personal information, account and transaction data which are stored and processed in systems. Customers shall be properly authenticated before access to online transactions, sensitive personal or account information.Bank or NBFI must have an approved Disaster Recovery Plan.

2. The ATMs and Point-of-Sale (POS) devices have facilitated cardholders with the convenience of withdrawing cash as well as making payments to merchants and billing organizations. However, these systems are targets where card skimming attacks are perpetrated. To secure consumer confidence in using these systems, the Bank or NBFI shall consider putting in place several measures to counteract fraudsters' attacks on ATMs and POS devices. Such as, The Bank or NBFI shall install anti-skimming solutions on ATM devices to detect the presence of unknown devices placed over or near a card entry slot,

3. Regulations on Electronic Fund Transfer-2014: a personal identification number (PIN), password/one time password(OTP), biometric recognition, code or any other device providing a means of certified access to a customer's account for the purposes of, among other things,initiating a electronic fund transfer.

4. Bangladesh Automated Cheque Processing System (BACPS) V 2.0, Operating Rules & Procedures: "Public Key Infrastructure" is the framework of encryption and cyber security that protects communications among the parties of a system. PKI ensures data authenticity, integrity and nonrepudiation. It works by using

two different cryptographic keys, a public key and a private key and are based on digital certificates.

5. NPSB Switch Operating Rules & User Manual: Dispute Management Rules:fraud activity report to NPSB. If a fraudulent transaction takes place or reported by issuer banks BB takes responsibility to solve the complaints.

6. Bangladesh Real time Gross settlement system Rule-2015: is responsible for, (once RTGS has technically accepted the Payment Instruction for processing), integrity, security and confidentiality of a Payment Instruction until it is dispatched to the Receiver.As System Operator of BD-RTGS, BB administers the operation of the daily business cycle, manages the creation of reports and charts and is responsible for the security of RTGS data, central software/ services, including managing backups and fallback situations of the central system.

7. Besides, Bangladesh Bank has published EOI for PCI DSS certification and evaluation is going on. Moreover, ISO 27001 certification is under process. Both IT departments and PSD are working on this issue. As per the instructions of the Ministry of ICT and Ministry of Finance Bangladesh Bank asked all banks and NBFIs to get PCI DSS and ISO 27001 certification with the mentioned deadlines.Bangladesh Bank is going to implement a Security Operation Center (SOC) soon. Security Information and Event Management (SIEM), Anti Advanced Persistent Threat (Anti-APT), Privileged Access Management (PAM) solutions are going to be implemented soon.

8. The Bangladesh Bank is going to launch a computer emergency response team for the financial sector (Fin-Cert) to avert cyber attacks like the one in which hackers managed to steal $81 million from its accounts with the Federal Reserve Bank of New York five years ago – in the biggest digital heist in the country's banking history.

9. Cyber Security Unit (CSU) was formed in Bangladesh Bank in July 2019.The activities of the said unit started from May 2020 with the joining of Md. Mehedi Hasan was designated by the Chief Information Security Officer (CISO) as the head of CSU, Bangladesh Bank.

Cyber security unit will cover the specific areas of the security concerns as below (source: Annual Report 2019-20, Bangladesh Bank):

i. Design and implement BB's information security infrastructure to monitor IT installations and systems for detection and prevention of unauthorized access and use; steering to completion of BB's ongoing cyber security strengthening program and conduct annual reviews thereof to identify, access and coordinate remediation of weaknesses in BB's IT security systems.

ii.   Take necessary steps in areas of Security Engineering (SE), Security Threat and Vulnerability Management (STVM), Information Security Operations Center (ISOC), Security Information and Event Management (SIEM), Financial Sector wide Critical Incident Response Team (CIRT) and Cyber Security Intelligence (CSI), putting in place adequate documented processes, procedures and internal technical controls in all these areas.

iii.   Assess knowledge/skill enhancement needs for staff in the new CSU, set up appropriate training routines of cyber security capacity building with up-to-date understanding of emerging trends in information security technology.

iv.   Ensure BB's response-preparedness to IT security incidents through development and regular exercise of incidence response and procedures, forecast leadership skills in getting things done in inter-departmental/inter-agency team environments.

v.   Foster and facilitate a cyber security risk aware culture among all staffers in BB offices and departments and ensure effective, efficient and balanced protection of all BB information assets.

vi.   Develop security standards for IT platform in conformance with BB's IT architecture, risk profile and policy requirements.

vii.   Interface with business units and IT stakeholders in identifying requirements and assess their applicability to BB's IT infrastructure.

viii. Identify efficiencies to improve the performance and responsiveness of BB's security work programs.

ix.   Review and offer suggestions on setting the technical requirements in procurements of IT equipment/consumables in conformance with BB's information security architecture and risk profile.

x.   Design short-term and long-term security policy and implementation plan for BB.

xi.   Take necessary measures to upgrade and maintain the security infrastructure of BB according to the implementation plan.

xii.   Assist in arrangement of regular security testing on the ICT infrastructure of BB, audit existing systems and provide comprehensive risk assessments.

xiii. Ensure regular review of logs of user activities in order to recognize suspicious behavior.

xiv.   To design automatic (machine learning based) monitoring and financial fraud detection policy.

xv.   Design monitoring plan of the implementation process of security policy by Banks and NBFI's of Bangladesh.

xvi.   Guide Banks and NBFI's of Bangladesh to take appropriate preventive measures in case of any security threat/incident at any of the financial institutes in Bangladesh or relevant organizations abroad.

xvii. Facilitate security awareness program for all employees of the bank at regular intervals.

xviii. Prepare a team for digital forensic investigation to investigate any incident.

xix. Assist to integrate IT systems for development with security policies and information protection strategies.

xx. Collaborate with key stakeholders to establish an IT security risk management program.

xxi. Anticipate new security threats and stay-up-to-date with evolving infrastructures.

CONCLUSION

New technologies like Artificial intelligence and cybersecurity helped to bloom FinTech innovation significantly. FinTech has provided the financial sector with new opportunities. Because more businesses are done online, its value has grown throughout the COVID-19 epidemic. People use technology to conduct online business and keep track of social distances. Digital banking is quickly replacing the traditional banking and becoming an integral part of our modern lives. In today's world, contactless payments are widely accepted as a global payment method. In every area, including transportation, health care, grocery, banking, commerce, and education, FinTech has reached out to the general public. The environment of FinTech is rapidly changing, and we will see even more changes in the next years, posing several hazards, challenges, and security issues. In light of this research, it can be realized that any clarity about all the security attributes that can be compromised or have been compromised will issue a great threat for the banking sector. Bangladesh Bank has established a variety of cyber security measures. IT departments of Bangladesh bank are now organizing various training and awareness programs on a regular basis. The bank has already established a separate Cyber Security Unit (CSU) to lead the cyber security of banking. In addition, Bangladesh Bank has issued an EOI for PCI DSS certification and requested all banks and NBFIs to obtain PCI DSS and ISO 27001 certification in accordance with the international standard. Other measures such as installing a Security Operation Center, solutions such as Security Information and Event Management, Anti-Advanced Persistent Threat, and Privileged Access Management will be introduced soon. To protect valuable data and systems from hostile assaults, Vulnerability Assessment and Penetration Testing will also be implemented. Additionally, BB will introduce Fin-Cert which will highly focus on the financial institutions for emergency security and will respond quickly to stave off any imminent cyber attack.

ACKNOWLEDGEMENT

*The views and opinions expressed in the paper are solely author's responsibility, do not necessarily reflect that of Bangladesh Bank.

REFERENCES

Al Duhaidahawi. (2020). Analysing the effects of FinTech variables on cybersecurity: Evidence form Iraqi Banks. *International Journal of Research in Business and Social Science, 9*(6), 123–133.

Ashraf & Majid. (2021). Central Bank Risk Management, Fintech and Cybersecurity. *International Monetary Fund Working Papers, 2021*(105), 6-55.

Benazir, R., Oeshwik, A., & Shireen, S. (2021). Fintech in Bangladesh: Ecosystem, Opportunities and Challenges. *International Journal of Business and Technopreneurship, 11*, 73–90.

Callen-Naviglia, J., & James, J. (2018). *Fintech, regtech and the IMP.* Academic Press.

Gai, K., Qiu, M., & Sun, X. (2018). A survey on FinTech. *Journal of Network and Computer Applications, 103*, 262–273.

Jayalath & Premaratne. (2021). Analysis of Key Digital Technology Infrastructure and Cyber Security Consideration Factors for Fintech Companies. *International Journal of Research Publications (IJRP), 84*(1), 128-135. doi:. doi:10.47119/IJRP1008419202212246

Kareem, H. M., Duhaidahawi, A., Zhang, J., Abdulreza, M. S., & Sebai, M. (2020). An efficient model for financial risks assessment based on artificial neural networks; Evidence from Iraqi Banks (2004-2017). *Journal of Southwest Jiaotong University, 55*(3). Advance online publication. doi:10.35741/issn.0258-2724.55.3.8

Khan, M. A., & Malaika, M. (2021). *Central Bank Risk Management, Fintech, and Cybersecurity.* International Monetary Fund.

Kim, Y., Park, Y.-J., Choi, J., & Yeon, J. (2015). An Empirical Study on the Adoption of "Fintech" Service: Focused on Mobile Payment Services. December. *Advanced Science and Technology Letters, 114*(26), 136–140. doi:10.14257/astl.2015.114.26

Milena, V. (2020). Fintech and Financial Stability Potential Influence of FinTech on Financial Stability, Risks and Benefits. *Journal of Central Banking Theory and Practice, 9*(2), 43–66.

Najaf, K., Mostafiz, M. I., & Najaf, R. (2021). Fintech firms and banks sustainability: Why cybersecurity risk matters? *International Journal of Financial Engineering, 8*(02), 2150019. doi:10.1142/S2424786321500195

Ng & Kwok. (2017). Emergence of Fintech and cybersecurity in a global financial centre: Strategic approach by a regulator. *Journal of Financial Regulation and Compliance.*

Ng, A. W., & Kwok, B. K. (2017). Emergence of Fintech and cybersecurity in a global financial centre: Strategic approach by a regulator. *Journal of Financial Regulation and Compliance.*

Peters, G. W., Panayi, E., & Chapelle, A. (2015). Trends in Crypto-Currencies and Blockchain Technologies: A Monetary Theory and Regulation Perspective. SSRN *Electronic Journal, 3*(3). doi:10.2139/ssrn.2646618

Philippon, T. (2016). The Fintech Opportunity. *National Bureau Of Economic Research, 8*(3), 6–10. https://www.nber.org/papers/w22476

Schueffel, P. (2016). Taming the beast: A scientific definition of fintech. *Journal of Innovation Management, 4*(4), 32–54.

Shah, S. S. H., Xinping, X., Khan, M. A., & Harjan, S. A. (2018). Investor and manager overconfidence bias and firm value: Micro-level evidence from the Pakistan equity market. *International Journal of Economics and Financial Issues, 8*(5), 190.

APPENDIX

Threat Categories

FinTech institutions face the most prevalent cyber threats. This section defines significant cyber threats to FinTech startups.

- **Malware:** Malware is malicious software specially designed to disrupt, damage, or gain unauthorized access to a computer system to steal sensitive information. Malware can be classified as: Adware, Ransomware, Riskware, Scareware, Spyware, Trojan horse, Virus, Worm, and Zero-day.
- **Adware:** Adware represents advertisement malware. It is a malicious application that throws unwanted advertisements on the user screen. Adware lures the user towards flashing advertisements that offer lucrative products and attract them to click on the advertisement.
- **Ransomware:** Ransomware is malware that encrypts files and directories on the machine to make them inaccessible to users. It asks for a handsome amount of ransom to provide the decryption key that is used to unlock the data.
- **Riskware:** Riskware is a legitimate program that poses potential risks to the security vulnerabilities on the device. Although it is a genuine program, it is used to steal information from the device and redirect users to malicious websites.
- **Scareware:** Scareware is a fear coaxer that raises fear in users' minds to encourage them to download or buy malicious apps.
- **Spyware:** Spyware is malicious software that can steal sensitive information once installed on the device. The data collected by spyware is passed to advertisers, external agencies, or firms.
- **Trojan:** Trojans are sneaky impersonators that behave like legitimate programs. They can hide in the background and steal information from the device.
- **Virus:** Virus is a computer program that replicates itself by changing other programs and inserting its own code.
- **Worm:** Worm is a computer program that does not require a host program. It replicates itself to spread to other computer systems. A worm uses the target machine to infect other machines on the network.

Chapter 5

Cyber Security Legal Framework in India:
An Appraisal

Diptirekha Mohapatra
Sambalpur University, India

ABSTRACT

Cybercrimes have become a global phenomenon due to the digital world. Cybercrimes in India are no exception. Because of this, it becomes very difficult to ensure cyber security. This adversely affects not only individuals but also companies, government, and society at large. As huge data is lost as a result of such crime, a law in India was enacted called the Information Technology Act, 2000 with an objective to prevent all types of crime relating to cyber security. Accordingly, other laws were amended like Indian Penal Code, 1860; The Negotiable Instrument Act, 1881; and the Indian Evidence Act, 1882. But, in spite of these stringent laws, the data of National Crimes Bureau shows an upward trend in every head relating to cybercrimes, thereby ensuring cyber security.

INTRODUCTION

In this information age, cyber crimes have attracted the attention of the world quite recently. Cyber crimes evolved with the introduction and growth of information technology in everyday life As a category of white collar crime, it emerged with digital world. Cyber crime is a comprehensive concept coined by Sussman and Heuston in the year 1995. It ranges from online fraud, computer hacking, forgery, credit card fraud to child pornography, cyber stalking, cyber terrorism, etc. Cyber

DOI: 10.4018/978-1-6684-3448-2.ch005

crime is an illegal activity where computer is used as primary means for commission of such crime and for storage of evidence. (U.S. Department of Justice).

With a view to control and prevent such crime in the society many countries have come up with stringent laws. India is no exception to it. The Information Technology Act, 2000 was enacted with such objectives. Accordingly many laws more particularly penal laws are also amended in consonance with the information Technology Act,2000. Even then many countries like India fail to combat such crime.

Security may be defined "as a process to protect an object against physical damage, unauthorised access, theft or loss by maintaining high confidentiality and integrity of information about the object and making information available whenever required." (Kizza, (2013)

Cyber security plays a critical role in the field of data technology. Protection and preservation of data in cyber space has become a challenge now-a-days. As a result of this, cyber crimes are increasing tremendously. (Samuel & Osman,2014)

Ensuring the security asserts protection to both IoT devices and services from unauthorised access from within devices as well as externally. Security should protect the services, hardware resources, information and data both in transition and storage. (Mohamaad and Gair,2015)

Cyber attackers mostly attack Government websites, financial systems, news and media websites, military networks as well as public infrastructure systems. Attack motives of these attackers ranges from identity theft, intellectual property theft and financial fraud to critical infrastructure attacks. (Mohammad and Gair,2015)

In a computing context, cyber security comprises cyber security and physical security both are used by the enterprises to remain safe against unauthorised access to data control and other computerised systems. The security, which is designed to maintain the confidentiality, integrity and availability of data is a subset of cyber security. (Seema et.al.,2018)

Security is the main problem of cyber security and must be based on proper policies and strictly enforced. It is a major challenge with cloud computing, as to the question of jurisdiction of criminal proceedings which in contrary puts lots of challenges to governance and territoriality. The effective level of quality security will ensure the acceptance of these new services. (Joshi and Singh,2013)

PURPOSE

The main purposes of this chapter are:

i.   To discuss the legal framework developed both nationally and internationally to deal with cyber crimes as cyber crimes has become global issue.

ii.   To appreciate the various motivating factors for commission of cyber crimes.

iii. To analyse the selected data recorded and reported by the National Crime Records Bureau.

iv.   To examine the efficacy of selected laws in India to address the issues of cyber crimes

INTERNATINAL INSTRUMENTS WITH REGARD TO CYBER SECURITY

The Convention on Cyber Crime,2001 known Budapest Convention is the first ever convention on cyber crime seeks to address the issues related to cyber crime.. It addresses the issues relating to improve investigating procedures, harmonisation of national laws and and fostering international cooperation with this regard. Till 2020,there are 67 signatories to such treaty. But India has not yet signed or ratified this treaty although it aspires for digital India. The Council of Europe (COE) in 2001 with 47 countries came forward with first International Convention on cyber crime,where USA,Japan and Canada signed with 46 member states. But however, only 25 countries ratified this convention. (Ahmed et.al.,2008)

The TEL(Telecommunication and Working Group) of Asia Pacific Economic Cooperation (APEC) issued the cyber security strategy to deal with cyber security in August 2002 which later on included in Lima Declaration in 2005. The declaration raised the issues relating to network security and reiterated the establishment of Computer Emergency Response Teams (Ajayi,2016)

The Organisation of Economic Cooperation and Development (OECD) comprising of 34 countries published a guidelines for the security of Information Systems and Networks: Towards a culture of security to ensure cyber security to the society.

The Commonwealth of Nations in 2002 presented a modal law drafted in accordance with Convention on Cyber Crime,2001. (International Telecommunication Union,2009) which provides a legal framework that harmonises legislation within the Commonwealth nations and secure international cooperation.

The Economic Community of West African States (ECOWAS) comprising 15 member States adopted in 2009, the Directive on fighting cyber crime in ECOWAS that provides a legal framework for the member states, which includes substantive criminal law as well as procedural law. (Nicholas,2008)

The United Nations (UN) General Assembly in 1990 adopted a resolution dealing with computer crime legislation. In 2000, it adopted a resolution on combating the criminal misuse of information technology, while in 2002, it adopted a second resolution on the criminal misuse of information technology.(Nicholas,2008)

The G8 made public in 1997, a ministerial communiqué with action plan and principles to combat cyber crime and protect data and systems from unauthorised impairment It further mandated all law enforcement personnel must be trained and equipped to address cyber crime and designates all member countries to take a point of contact on 24 hours a day and 7 days week basis.(Chang et.al.)

The International Telecommunication Union (ITU) intermingled with telecommunication and cyber security issues, the United Nations in 2003 came up with Geneva Declaration of Principles and Geneva Plan of Action and where it highlighted the importance of measures in the fight against cyber crimes.

LEGAL FRAMEWORK TO PREVENT CYBER CRIMES AND PRESERVE CYBER SECURITY IN INDIA:

The Provisions under the Information Technology Act, 2000 (Herein after the I.T.Act, 2000)

The main provisions to deal with cyber crimes under the Information Technology Act,2000 are:

Sec.65: Tampering with computer source documents.–."Whoever knowingly or intentionally conceals, destroys or alters or intentionally or knowingly causes another to conceal, destroy, or alter any computer source code used for a computer, computer programme, computer system or computer network, when the computer source code is required to be kept or maintained by law for the time being in force, shall be punishable with imprisonment up to three years, or with fine which may extend up to two lakh rupees, or with both."[1]

Sec.66: Computer related offences.–"If any person, dishonestly or fraudulently, does any act referred to in section 43he shall be punishable with imprisonment for a term which may extend to three years or with fine which may extend to five lakh rupees or with both."[2]

Section 43: Penalty and compensation for damage to computer, computer system, etc.–"If any person without permission of the owner or any other person who is in charge of a computer, computer system or computer network,– (a) accesses or secures access to such computer, computer system or computer network 7 [or computer resource]; (b) downloads, copies or extracts any data, computer data base or information from such computer, computer system or computer network including information or data held or stored in any removable storage medium; (c) introduces or causes to be introduced any computer contaminant or computer virus into any computer, computer system or computer network; (d) damages or causes to be damaged any computer, computer system or computer network, data, computer data base or any other programmes residing in such computer, computer system or computer network; (e) disrupts or causes disruption of any computer, computer system or computer network; (f) denies or causes the denial of access to any person authorised to access any computer, computer system or computer network by any means; (g) provides any assistance to any person to facilitate access to a computer, computer system or computer network in contravention of the provisions of this Act, rules or regulations made there under; (h) charges the services availed of by a person to the account of another person by tampering with or manipulating any computer, computer system, or computer network;(i) destroys, deletes or alters any information residing in a computer resource or diminishes its value or utility or affects it injuriously by any means; (j) steal, conceal, destroys or alters or causes any person to steal, conceal, destroy or alter any computer source code used for a computer resource with an intention to cause damage; he shall be liable to pay damages by way of compensation to the person so affected."[3]

Section 66A. Punishment for sending offensive messages through communication service, etc.–"Any person who sends, by means of a computer resource or a communication device,– (a) any information that is grossly offensive or has menacing character; or (b) any information which he knows to be false, but for the purpose of causing annoyance, inconvenience, danger, obstruction, insult, injury, criminal intimidation, enmity, hatred or ill will, persistently by making use of such computer resource or a communication device; (c) any electronic mail or electronic mail message for the purpose of causing annoyance or inconvenience or to deceive or to mislead the addressee or recipient about the origin of such messages, shall be punishable with imprisonment for a term which may extend to three years and with fine"[4]

Section 66A has been struck down by Supreme Court's Order dated 24th March, 2015 in the Shreya Singhal vs. Union of India.[5]

Section 66B. Punishment for dishonestly receiving stolen computer resource or communication device.–"Whoever dishonestly receive or retains any stolen computer resource or communication device knowing or having reason to believe the same to be stolen computer resource or communication device, shall be punished with imprisonment of either description for a term which may extend to three years or with fine which may extend to rupees one lakh or with both." [6]

Section 66C. Punishment for identity theft.–"Whoever, fraudulently or dishonestly make use of the electronic signature, password or any other unique identification feature of any other person, shall be punished with imprisonment of either description for a term which may extend to three years and shall also be liable to fine which may extend to rupees one lakh."[7]

Section 66D. Punishment for cheating by personation by using computer resource.–"Whoever, by means of any communication device or computer resource cheats by personation, shall be punished with imprisonment of either description for a term which may extend to three years and shall also be liable to fine which may extend to one lakh rupees." [8]

Section 66E. Punishment for violation of privacy.–"Whoever, intentionally or knowingly captures, publishes or transmits the image of a private area of any person without his or her consent, under circumstances violating the privacy of that person, shall be punished with imprisonment which may extend to three years or with fine not exceeding two lakh rupees, or with both."[9]

Section 66F. Punishment for cyber terrorism.–"(1) Whoever,– (A) with intent to threaten the unity, integrity, security or sovereignty of India or to strike terror in the people or any section of the people by– (i) denying or cause the denial of access to any person authorised to access computer resource; or (ii) attempting to penetrate or access a computer resource without authorisation or exceeding authorised access; or (iii) introducing or causing to introduce any computer contaminant, and by means of such conduct causes or is likely to cause death or injuries to persons or damage to or destruction of property or disrupts or knowing that it is likely to cause damage or disruption of supplies or services essential to the life of the community or adversely affect the critical information infrastructure specified under section 70; or (B) knowingly or intentionally penetrates or accesses a computer resource without authorisation or exceeding authorised access, and by means of such conduct obtains access to information, data or computer data base that is restricted for reasons of the security of the State or foreign relations; or any restricted information, data or computer data base, with reasons to believe that such information, data or computer data base so obtained may be used to cause or likely to cause injury to the interests of the sovereignty and integrity of India, the security of the State, friendly relations with foreign States, public order, decency or morality, or in relation to contempt of court, defamation or incitement to an offence, or to the advantage of any foreign nation, group of individuals or otherwise, commits the offence of cyber terrorism. (2) Whoever commits or conspires to commit cyber terrorism shall be punishable with imprisonment which may extend to imprisonment for life." [10]

Section 67. Punishment for publishing or transmitting obscene material in electronic form.–"Whoever publishes or transmits or causes to be published or transmitted in the electronic form, any material which is lascivious or appeals to the prurient interest or if its effect is such as to tend to deprave and corrupt persons who are likely, having regard to all relevant circumstances, to read, see or hear the matter contained or embodied in it, shall be punished on first conviction with imprisonment of either description for a term which may extend to three years and with fine which may extend to five lakh rupees and in the event of second or subsequent conviction with imprisonment of either description for a term which may extend to five years and also with fine which may extend to ten lakh rupees."[11]

Section 67A. Punishment for publishing or transmitting of material containing sexually explicit act, etc., in electronic form.–"Whoever publishes or transmits or causes to be published or transmitted in the electronic form any material which contains sexually explicit act or conduct shall be punished on first conviction with imprisonment of either description for a term which may extend to five years and with fine which may extend to ten lakh rupees and in the event of second or subsequent conviction with imprisonment of either description for a term which may extend to seven years and also with fine which may extend to ten lakh rupees."[12]

Section 67B. Punishment for publishing or transmitting of material depicting children in sexually explicit act, etc., in electronic form.–"Whoever,–(a) publishes or transmits or causes to be published or transmitted material in any electronic form which depicts children engaged in sexually explicit act or conduct; or (b) creates text or digital images, collects, seeks, browses, downloads, advertises, promotes, exchanges or distributes material in any electronic form depicting children in obscene or indecent or sexually explicit manner; or (c) cultivates, entices or induces children to online relationship with one or more children for and on sexually explicit act or in a manner that may offend a reasonable adult on the computer resource; or (d) facilitates abusing children online, or (e) records in any electronic form own abuse or that of others pertaining to sexually explicit act with children, shall be punished on first conviction with imprisonment of either description for a term which may extend to five years and with fine which may extend to ten lakh rupees and in the event of second or subsequent conviction with imprisonment of either description for a term which may extend to seven years and also with fine which may extend to ten lakh rupees."[13]

Section 67C. Preservation and retention of information by intermediaries.–"(1) Intermediary shall preserve and retain such information as may be specified for such duration and in such manner and format as the Central Government may prescribe. (2) any intermediary who intentionally or knowingly contravenes the provisions of sub-section (1) shall be punished with an imprisonment for a term which may extend to three years and also be liable to fine."[14]

The Provisions of Information Technology Act primarily deal with extraction of data,etc. Hence, companies cannot get total protection of their data. For this, they have to enter into separate agreements.(Sharma, 2016)

After the enactment of the Information Technology Act,2000 necessary amendments are made in Indian Penal Code, 1860;Indian Evidence Act,1872; and the Negotiable Instruments Act,1881.

The Provisions under the Indian Penal Code, 1860 (Herein after the IPC, 1860)

The Indian Penal Code, 1860 also contains provisions dealing with the menace of cyber crimes.

Section 469. Forgery for purpose of harming reputation: "Whoever commits forgery, intending that the document or electronic document forged shall harm the reputation of any party, or knowing that it is likely to be used for that purpose, shall be punished with imprisonment of either description for a term which may extend to three years, and shall also be liable to fine."[15]

Section 470. Forged document or electronic record: "A false document or electronic record made wholly or in part by forgery is designated a forged document or electronic record."[16]

Section 499. Defamation: "Whoever, by words either spoken or intended to be read, or by signs or by visible representations, makes or publishes any imputation concerning any person intending to harm, or knowing or having reason to believe that such imputation will harm, the reputation of such person, is said to defame that person"[17]

Section 503 of IPC. Criminal intimidation: "Whoever, threatens another with any injury to his person, reputation or property, or to the person or reputation of any one in whom that person is interested, with intent to cause alarm to that person, or to cause that person to do any act which he is not legally bound to do, or to omit to do any act which that person is legally entitled to do, as the means of avoiding the execution of such threats, commits criminal intimidation. Section 503 of IPC covers the offence of criminal intimidation by use of e-mails and other electronic means of communication for threatening or intimidating any person or his property or reputation. It is punishable with imprisonment for a term which may extend to 2 years, or fine, or both under section 504. The offence is non-cognizable, bailable and compundable."[18]

The Negotiable Instruments Act, 1881 (Herein after the NI Act, 1881)

The Negotiable Instruments Act,1881 was also amended accordingly with regard to cyber crimes..

Section 64: Presentment for Payment

"(1)..........

Sub-Section(2) "Notwithstanding anything contained in section 6, where an electronic image of a truncated cheque is presented for payment, the drawee bank is entitled to demand any further information regarding the truncated cheque from the bank holding the truncated cheque in case of any reasonable suspicion about the genuineness of the apparent tenor of instrument, and if the suspicion is that of any fraud, forgery, tampering or destruction of the instrument, it is entitled to further demand the presentment of the truncated cheque itself for verification: Provided that the truncated cheque so demanded by the drawee bank shall be retained by it, if the payment is made accordingly."[19]

Section 81. Delivery of instrument on payment, or indemnity in case of loss:

"(1)............

(2) Where the cheque is an electronic image of a truncated cheque, even after the payment the banker. who received the payment shall be entitled to retain the truncated cheque. (3) A certificate issued on the foot of the printout of the electronic image of a truncated cheque by the banker who paid the instrument, shall be prima facie proof of such payment."[20]

Section 89. Payment of instrument on which alteration is not apparent:

"(1) ....

(2) Where the cheque is an electronic image of a truncated cheque, any difference in apparent tenor of such electronic image and the truncated cheque shall be a material alteration and it shall be the duty of the bank or the clearing house, as the case may be, to ensure the exactness of the apparent tenor of electronic image of the truncated cheque while truncating and transmitting the image. (3) Any bank or a clearing house which receives a transmitted electronic image of a truncated cheque, shall verify from the party who transmitted the image to it, that the image so transmitted to it and received by it, is exactly the same."[21]

Indian Evidence Act, 1872 and Cyber Crimes

The Indian Evidence act also amended to incorporate the necessary changes to appreciate evidentiary value of electronic nature.

Section 45A. Opinion of Examiner of Electronic Evidence.:

"When in a proceeding, the court has to form an opinion on any matter relating to any information transmitted or stored in any computer resource or any other electronic or digital form, the opinion of the Examiner of Electronic Evidence referred to in section 79A of the Information Technology Act, 2000 (21 of 2000), is a relevant fact."[22]

Section 47A. Opinion as to digital signature, when relevant:

"When the Court has to form an opinion as to the 2 [electronic signature of any person, the opinion of the Certifying Authority which has issued the 3 [electronic Signature Certificate] is a relevant fact."[23]

Section 65A. Special provisions as to evidence relating to electronic record.:

"The contents of electronic records may be proved in accordance with the provisions of section 65B."[24]

Section 65B. Admissibility of electronic records.:

"(1) Notwithstanding anything contained in this Act, any information contained in an electronic record which is printed on a paper, stored, recorded or copied in optical or magnetic media produced by a computer (hereinafter referred to as the computer output) shall be deemed to be also a document, if the conditions mentioned in this section are satisfied in relation to the information and computer in question and shall be admissible in any proceedings, without further proof or production of the original, as evidence or any contents of the original or of any fact stated therein of which direct evidence would be admissible. (2) The conditions referred to in sub-section (1) in respect of a computer output shall be the following, namely: — (a) the computer output containing the information was produced by the computer during the period over which the computer was used regularly to store or process information for the purposes of any activities regularly carried on over that period by the person having lawful control over the use of the computer; (b) during the said period, information of the kind contained in the electronic record or of the kind from which the information so contained is derived was regularly fed into the computer in the ordinary course of the said activities; (c) throughout the material part of the said period, the computer was operating properly or, if not, then in respect of any period in which it was not operating properly or was out of operation during that part of the period, was not such as to affect the electronic record or the accuracy of its contents; and (d) the information contained in the electronic record reproduces or is derived from such information fed into the computer in the ordinary course of the said activities. (3) Where over any period, the function of storing or processing information for the purposes of any activities regularly carried on over that period as mentioned in clause (a) of sub-section (2) was regularly performed by computers, whether— (a) by a combination of computers operating over that period; or (b) by different computers operating in succession over that period; or (c) by different combinations of computers operating in succession over that period; or (d) in any other manner involving the successive operation over that period, in whatever order, of one or more computers and one or more combinations of computers, all the computers used for that purpose during that period shall be treated for the purposes of this section as constituting a single computer; and references in this section to a computer shall be construed accordingly. (4) In any proceedings where it is desired to give a statement in evidence by virtue of this section, a certificate doing any of the following things, that is to say, — (a) identifying the electronic record containing the statement and describing the manner in which it was produced; (b) giving such particulars of any device involved in the production of that electronic record as may be appropriate for the purpose of showing that the electronic record was produced by a computer; (c) dealing with any of the matters to which the conditions mentioned in sub-section (2) relate, and purporting to be signed by a person occupying a responsible official position in relation to the operation of the relevant device or the management of the relevant activities (whichever is appropriate) shall be evidence of any matter stated in the certificate; and for the purposes of this subsection it shall be sufficient for a matter to be stated to the best of the knowledge and belief of the person stating it. (5) For the purposes of this section, — (a) information shall be taken to be supplied to a computer if it is supplied thereto in any appropriate form and whether it is so supplied directly or (with or without human intervention) by means of any appropriate equipment; (b) whether in the course of activities carried on by any official, information is supplied with a view to its being stored or processed for the purposes of those activities by a computer operated otherwise than in the course of those activities, that information, if duly supplied to that computer, shall be taken to be supplied to it in the course of those activities; (c) a computer output shall be taken to have been produced by a computer whether it was produced by it directly or (with or without human intervention) by means of any appropriate equipment."[25]

Section 67A. Proof as to electronic signature.:

"Except in the case of a secure [electronic signature], if the [electronic signature] of any subscriber is alleged to have been affixed to an electronic record the fact that such [electronic signature] is the [electronic signature] of the subscriber must be proved."[26]

Section 81A. Presumption as to Gazettes in electronic forms:

"The Court shall presume the genuineness of every electronic record purporting to be the Official Gazette, or purporting to be electronic record directed by any law to be kept by any person, if such electronic record is kept substantially in the form required by law and is produced from proper custody."[27]

Section 85A. Presumption as to electronic agreements.:

"The Court shall presume that every electronic record purporting to be an agreement containing the electronic signature of the parties was so concluded by affixing the electronic signature of the parties."[28]

Section 85B. Presumption as to electronic records and electronic signatures.:

"(1) In any proceedings involving a secure electronic record, the Court shall presume unless contrary is proved, that the secure electronic record has not been altered since the specific point of time to which the secure status relates.

(2) In any proceedings, involving secure digital signature, the Court shall presume unless the contrary is proved that— (a) the secure electronic signature is affixed by subscriber with the intention of signing or approving the electronic record; (b) except in the case of a secure electronic record or a secure 5 [electronic signature], nothing in this section shall cerate any presumption, relating to authenticity and integrity of the electronic record or any electronic signature."[29]

Section 85C. Presumption as to Electronic Signature Certificates:

"The Court shall presume, unless contrary is proved, that the information listed in a Electronic Signature Certificate is correct, except for information specified as subscriber information which has not been verified, if the certificate was accepted by the subscriber."[30]

Section 88A. Presumption as to electronic messages.: "The Court may presume that an electronic message, forwarded by the originator through an electronic mail server to the addressee to whom the message purports to be addressed corresponds with the message as fed into his computer for transmission; but the Court shall not make any presumption as to the person by whom such message was sent."[31]

Section 90A. Presumption as to electronic records five years old.:

"Where any electronic record, purporting or proved to be five years old, is produced from any custody which the Court in the particular case considers proper, the Court may presume that the electronic signature] which purports to be the electronic signature of any particular person was so affixed by him or any person authorised by him in this behalf."[32]

MOTIVATIONAL FACTORS FOR CYBER CRMINALS

Cyber criminals are greatly motivated in various ways, including financial gains, emotional stability,social norms and lack of legislation and punishment.(Alansari et.al.,2019)

According to Seema et.al.,2018 Cyber criminals can be categorise into three groups that reflect their motivation to commit cyber crimes.

Type 1: Cyber Criminal hungry for recognition. They are: Hobby hackers, IT professionals, politically motivated hackers and terrorist organisations.

Type 2: Cyber criminals not interested for recognition. These include: psychologically unsound persons, financially motivated hackers, State-sponsored hackers for espionage or sabotage and organised criminals.

Type 3: Cyber criminals –insiders. These are: former employees seeking revenge and competing companies for economic gain through damage

The major causes or motivating factors for increasing cyber crime are profit motive and the pecuniary advantage the criminals receive on committing offence outweighs the punishment they are inflicted with. Many researchers are trying to explore the possible causes of rising trend of such crimes not only in India but also worldwide in spite of stringent laws. It is one of the challenge as well as legislative strategy to create cyber security and on the contrary cyber crime needs more extensive and secure practice.

According to the study of Ajayi (2016), the major motivating factor for cyber crimes is profit motive and pecuniary advantage. In addition to that difficulty in identification of the further encourages the cyber criminals. In some cases they are not solely motivated by the pecuniary advantage rather they derive satisfaction in having unauthorised access to computer and its network. Lastly, the challenge they take to intrude into the privacy of another.

INCIDENCE OF CYBER CRIMES

E-crimes are increasing by number of incidents thereby causing huge damage to governments, companies, individual and society as well. (Broadthrust and Grabasky,2005).

In several occasions India has encountered cyber threats like Indira Gandhi International Airport cyber attack in 2013; 26/11 Mumbai attack; Varanasi bomb blast in 2010; CBI website hacking by Pakistani cyber army in 2010. Furthermore, every day Pakistani cyber criminals deface and hack nearly 60 Indian websites. (Raman and Sharma,2019)

Keeping pace with cyber security, strategy and operations can be a challenge, particularly in a government and enterprise networks where in their most innovative form, cyber threats often take aiming at secret political and military assets of a nation or its people. Some of the common threats are cyber terrorism, cyber warfare and cyber espionage.(Seema et.al.)

From strategic point of view, cyber crime is seen as an offence to cyber-security namely, attacks to digital networks for the purpose of seizing control, paralysing them or even destroying infrastructures that are vital to governments and sectors of strategic importance.(Joshi and Singh,2013)

Table 1. Shows incidence of cyber crimes in India

Year/ Number of total cyber crimes	2010	2011	2012	2013	2014	2015	2016	2017	2018	2019	2020
India	966	1791	2876	5693	9622	11592	12317	21796	27248	44735	50035

Source: National Crime Records Bureau (NCRB)

NATIONAL CRIME RECORDS BUREAU DATA ANALYSIS

The author has collected data from National Crime Records bureau from 2013-2020. By analysing those data not only incidence of reported cases will be revealed but also the rate of conviction and rate pendency of cases under different heads of cyber crimes will attract attention of the target group.

The ten years data reported by National Crimes Records Bureau (NCRB) from 2010-2020 is given in the above table. It is quite evident that the cyber crime in India is steadily increasing every year. In 2010, it was 966 and increased to 1791 in 2011,again it rose to 2876 in 2012 . Further it increased to 5693 in 2013,9622 in 2014,11592 in 2015, 12317 in 2016, 21796 in 2017,27248 in 2018, 44735 in 2019 and finally 50035 in 2020. Even in most of the years it increased more than 100% than previous year like in 2011,2012,2013 and 2019. No particular reason can be ascribed to such increase. There is not only rise in total number of incidences of cyber crimes but also rise in major heads of cyber crime as is evident from the table given below.

From the above table it is revealed that the data for the year 2013, according to crime heads is not available even with NCRB which is a dedicated organisation of the government of India to maintain and report all kinds of data relating to crimes in India. But, the total cyber crimes in the year2013 is reported by the NCRB. Further, if we will examine particular head of cyber crime we will not find a regular trend from 2014 to 2020. For example, tampering computer source documents under section 65 of the Information Technology Act (ITA),2000 cases reported in the year 2014 was 89 and it decreased to 88 in 2015 and further to 78 in 2016. But in the year 2017, it remarkably increased to 233 and 257 in 2018. Again, it reduced to 173 in 2019 and further swiftly increased to 338 in 2020. However, it is revealed in the data that the crime of tampering computer source documents has made a spectacular increase from 2014 to 2020 i.e.in only six years gap it increased from 89 to 338 i.e. nearly four times increase in crime rate.

Cases in which Charge sheet submitted+ Cases in which Charge sheet not laid but as true as submitted

Table 2. Indicates incidence of cases under major heads

Particulars	2013	2014	2015	2016	2017	2018	2019	2020
Tampering Computer Source Documents (Sec-65)	-	89	88	78	233	257	173	338
Computer Related Ofeences (Sec-66)	-	5548	6567	6818	10108	14141	23612	21926
Cyber Terrorism (Sec-66F)	-	5	13	12	13	21	12	26
Unauthorised Access/ Attempt To Access Protected Computer System (Sec-70)	-	0	8	-	2	0	2	2

Source: National Crime Records Bureau (NCRB)

The table given above shows the rate of charge sheeting under section 65 of the IT Act,2000 as to tampering computer source document from 2014-2020, as data for the year 2013 is not available.

The percentage of charge sheeting in the year 2014 was 54.5%; 50% in 2015;39.6% in 2016;35.5% in 2017;45.4% in 2018; 29.8% in 2019;43.7% in 2020. The data in the above table reveals the fact that in most of the years the rate of charge sheeting even less than 50% except in 2014 and 2015.

Cases in which Charge sheet submitted+ Cases in which charge sheet not laid but as true as submitted

The data in the table given above mentions the rate of charge sheeting under section 66 of the I.T. act,2000 with regard to computer related offences where 2013 data is unavailable. In 2014 the charge sheeting rate was 51.9%;2015 records 43.9%; in 2016 it is 37.1%; 2017 charge sheeting rate was 29.2%; it was 35.1% in 2018;36% in 2019 and 46.6% in 2020. It is also revealed from the table that except in 2014 in all other years the percentage of charge sheeting was as low as les than 50%.

Table 3. Shows police disposal of cyber crimes under Sec-65 tampering computer source document

Particulars	2013	2014	2015	2016	2017	2018	2019	2020
Cases Reported	-	89	88	78	233	257	173	338
Chargesheeted	-	18	36	32	54	122	42	76
Rate of Chargesheeting	-	54.5%	50%	39.6%	35.5%	45.4%	29.8%	43.7%

Source: National Crime Records Bureau (NCRB)

Note:: Rate of charge sheet= <u>Cases in which charge sheet were submitted</u> * 100

Table 4. Shows police disposal of cyber crimes under Sec-66 computer related offences

Particulars	2013	2014	2015	2016	2017	2018	2019	2020
Cases Reported	-	5548	6567	6818	10108	14141	23612	21926
Chargesheeted	-	1094	1841	2018	2091	2730	3702	6435
Rate of Chargesheeting	-	51.9%	43.9%	37.1%	29.2%	35.1%	36%	46.6%

Source: National Crime Records Bureau (NCRB)

Note:: Rate of charge sheet= <u>Cases in which charge sheet were submitted</u> * 100

Table 5. Indicates police disposal of cyber crimes under Sec-66F cyber terrorism

Particulars	2013	2014	2015	2016	2017	2018	2019	2020
Cases Reported	-	5	13	12	27	10	12	26
Chargesheeted	-	0	1	6	0	5	3	4
Rate of Chargesheeting	-	0	25%	15%	12.5%	33%	33.3%	33.3%

Source: National Crime Records Bureau (NCRB)

Note:: Rate of charge sheet= <u>Cases in which charge sheet were submitted</u> * 100

Cases in which Charge sheet submitted+ Cases in which

Charge sheet not laid but as true as submitted

The data shown in the above table clearly shows the grim picture with regard to the percentage of charge sheeting of offences under section 66-F of the I.T.Act,2000 with regard to cyber terrorism. Data is not available for the years 2013 and the rate of charge sheeting is 0 in 2014. The performance in other years is also quite dissatisfactory. In 2015, the rate of charge sheeting was 25%,15% in 2016;12.5% in 2017; 33% in 2018,33.3% in 2019 and 2020.

Table 6. Indicates police disposal of cyber crimes under Sec-70 unauthorized access /attempt to access to protected computer system

Particulars	2013	2014	2015	2016	2017	2018	2019	2020
Cases Reported	-	0	8	7	0	0	2	2
Chargesheeted	-	0	3	0	0	0	2	0
Rate of Chargesheeting	-	0	60%	100%	100%	-	100%	-

Source: National Crime Records Bureau (NCRB)

Note:: Rate of charge sheet= <u>Cases in which charge sheet were submitted</u> * 100

Cases in which Charge sheet submitted+ Cases in which

Table 7. Shows court disposal of cyber crimes under Sec-65 tampering computer source documents

Particulars	2013	2014	2015	2016	2017	2018	2019	2020
Rate of Conviction	-	NA	50%	63%	22.2%	33.33%	100%	90.9%
Rate of Pendenecy	-	67%	94.6%	84.3%	92.9%	95.3%	99.2%	95%

Source: National Crime Records Bureau (NCRB)

Charge sheet not laid but as true as submitted

With regard to the offences relating to unauthorised access/attempted access to protected computer system the data given in the above table clearly shows that for most of the years records are not available like in 2013,2014,2018 and 2020. But in other years the performance as to charge sheeting not only more than 50% but also in some years it is 100%.

The table shows the rate of conviction and rate of pendency of cases in courts as to the offences under section 65 of the I.T.Act,2000. As far as rate of conviction is concerned data is not available for 2013 and 2014. It is 50% in 2015;63% in 2016;22.2% in 2017;33.33% in 2018; 100% in 2019; and 90.9% in 2020. But conversely, the rate of pendency of cases in courts records a high rate. In 2014 it is 67%,;in 2015 it is 94%; 84.3% in 2016; 92.9% in 2017; 95.3% in 2018;99.2% in 2019 and even it is still more in 2020 i.e.95%.;

Table 8. Shows court disposal of cyber crimes under Sec-66 computer related offences

Particulars	2013	2014	2015	2016	2017	2018	2019	2020
Rate of Conviction	-	NA	41.2%	30.5%	17.6%	61%	39.0%	68.5%
Rate of Pendency	-	67%	88.1%	90.8%	94.8%	90%	94.2%	79.6%

Source: National Crime Records Bureau (NCRB)

The table given above reveals the data relating to rate of conviction and rate of pendency of cases under section 66 of the IT Act,2000 i.e. computer related offences. Inevery year the pendency cases are more than 60% whereas conviction rate is less than 50%.

The data with regard to court disposal of cyber crimes under Section 66F i.e. cyber terrorism as depicted in the above table is quite dissatisfactory. In all years from 2013 to 2020 conviction rate is nil and pendency of cases is 100% except in 2014.

The above table clearly shows that the crimes under section 70 of the I.T.Act,2000 are mostly unavailable with regard to rate of conviction except in 2020 where the

Table 9. Indicates court disposal of cyber crimes under Sec-66F cyber terrorism

Particulars	2013	2014	2015	2016	2017	2018	2019	2020
Rate of Conviction	-	-	-	-	-	-	-	00
Rate of Pendency	100%	33.3%	100%	100%	100%	100%	100%	100%

conviction rate is 100%. At the same time rate of pendency is 100% in 2015,2018,2019 and 2020 and it is 90% in 2017. For all other years the data is unavailable.

After analysing various international and national legal instruments for prevention of cyber crimes, reported data of National Crime. Records Bureau, the author arrives at certain concluding remarks.

CONCLUSION

Although there are plethora of legislations and conventions to prevent cyber crimes not only in India but also worldwide but there are high repored cases. In spite of stringent measures the incidence of cyber crimes is increasing at a spectacular rate. In some cases the data is not available and in other cases the rate of conviction is very low and rate of pendency of cases is very high showing that even after lapse of more than five years the cases are under trial. In many cases the charge sheeting rate is very depressing indicating there by that in most of cases even the charge sheet is not framed. Even in high profile cases like cyber terrorism the percentage of charge sheeting is as low as 33% and even less than that. And the rate of conviction is either unavailable and nil and rate of pendency of cases is 100% in most of the years. From this it is inferred that the law enforcement authorities are quite apathetic to the issues of cyber crimes. After thorough analysis the author arrives at following observations.

i.   There is no dearth of stringent measures to deal with the issues of cyber crimes. Rather the enforcement mechanism need to be strengthened.

Table 10. Shows court disposal of cyber crimes under Sec-70 unauthorised access/ attempt to access to protected computer system

Particulars	2013	2014	2015	2016	2017	2018	2019	2020
Rate of Conviction	-	-	-	-	-	0	-	100%
Rate of Pendenecy	-	0	100%	-	90.0%	100%	100%	100%

Source: National Crime Records Bureau (NCRB)

ii. The NCRB must create facilities to make available and maintain proper data and records of cyber crimes.

iii. The time frame for investigation into and trial of cases to be framed for timely disposal of cases as justice delayed is justice denied.

REFERENCES

Ahmed, M., Amster, D., Barette, M., Cross, T., & Heron, G. (2008). Emerging Cyber Threats Report for 2009. Georgia Tech Information Security Centre.

Ajayi, E. F. G. (2016). Challenges to Enforcement of Cyber Crime Laws and Policy. *Journal of Internet and Information Systems.*, 6(1), 1–12. doi:10.5897/JIIS2015.0089

Alansari, M. M., Aljazzaf, Z. M., & Safraz, M. (2019). On Cyber Crimes and Cyber Security. In M. Sarfraz (Ed.), *Developments in Information Security and Cybernetic Wars* (pp. 1–41). IGI Global. doi:10.4018/978-1-5225-8304-2.ch001

Ambohara, M., & Koien, G. M. (2015). Cyber Security and the Internet of Things: Vulnerabilities, Threats, Intruders and Attacks. *Journal of Cyber Security.*, 4, 65–88. doi:10.13052/jcsm2245-1439.414

Camqc, N. (2008). *Emerging Trends in Cyber Crime. In 13th Annual Conference. New Technologies in Crime and Prosecution Challenge and Opportunities. International Association of Prosecutors.* http://www.odpp.nsw.gov.ahe/default-source/speeches. by.nicholas.cowdery/emerging-transformation-cyber-crime.pdf

CCDCOE. (n.d.). *The NATO Cooperative Cyber Defence Centre of Excellence is a multinational and Interdisciplinary Cyber Defence Hub.* Retrieved from https:// ccdcoe.org/ https://ccdcoe.org › organisations › apec

Chang, W., Chung, W., Chen, H., & Chou, S. (2003). An International Perspective on Fighting Cyber Crime. *ISI Proceedings of the 1st NSF/NIJ Conference on Intelligence and Security Informatics*, 379-384.

Joshi, Y., & Singh, A. (2013). A Study on Cyber Crime and Security Scenario in India. *International Journal of Engineering and Management Research.*, 3(3), 13–18.

Kizza, J. M. (2013). *Guide to Computer Network Security.* Springer. doi:10.1007/978-1-4471-4543-1

National Crime Records Bureau. (n.d.a). Retrieved from https://ncrb.gov.in/en/Crime-in-India-2020

National Crime Records Bureau. (n.d.b). Retrieved from https://ncrb.gov.in/en/ Crime-in-India-2019

National Crime Records Bureau. (n.d.c). Retrieved from https://ncrb.gov.in/en/ Crime-in-India-2018

National Crime Records Bureau. (n.d.d). Retrieved from https://ncrb.gov.in/en/ Crime-in-India-2017

National Crime Records Bureau. (n.d.e). Retrieved from https://ncrb.gov.in/en/ Crime-in-India-2016

Samuel, K. O., & Osman, W. R. (2014). Cyber Technology Attack of the Contemporary Information Technology Age: Issues, Consequences and Panacea. *International Journal of Computer Science and Mobile Computing., 3*(5), 1082–1090.

Seema, P. S., Nandini, S., & And Sowmiya, M. (2018). Overview of Cyber Security. *International Journal of Advanced Research in Computer and Communication Engineering, 7*(11), 125–128. doi:10.17148/IJARCCE.2018.71127

Sharma, M. (2016). Issue and Legal Consequences. *International Journal of Scientific and Engineering Research, 7*(12), 168–172.

The Indian Evidence Act,1872(Act I of 1872)

The Indian Penal Code,1860 (Act 45 of 1860)

The Information Technology Act,2000(Act 45 of 1860)

The Negotiable Instruments Act,1881(Act 16 0f 1881)

ENDNOTES

[1] Section 65, The Information Technology Act,2000(Act 21 of 2000)
[2] Section 66, The Information Technology Act,2000(Act 21 of 2000)
[3] Section 43, The Information Technology Act,2000(Act 21 of 2000)
[4] Section 66A, The Information Technology Act,2000(Act 21 of 2000)
[5] Shreya Singhal vs. Union of India,AIR 2015 SC1523
[6] Section 66B, The Information Technology Act,2000(Act 21 of 2000)
[7] Section 66C, The Information Technology Act,2000(Act 21 of 2000)
[8] Section 66D, The Information Technology Act,2000(Act 21 of 2000)
[9] Section 66E, The Information Technology Act,2000(Act 21 of 2000)
[10] Section 66F, The Information Technology Act,2000(Act 21 of 2000)

[11]   Section 66A, The Information Technology Act,2000(Act 21 of 2000)
[12]   Section 67A, The Information Technology Act,2000(Act 21 of 2000)
[13]   Section 67B, The Information Technology Act,2000 (Act 21 of 2000)
[14]   Section 67C, The Information Technology Act,2000(Act 21 of 2000)
[15]   Section 469,The Indian Penal Code, (Act 45 of 1860)
[16]   Section 470,The Indian Penal Code, (Act 45 of 1860)
[17]   Section 499,The Indian Penal Code, (Act 45 of 1860)
[18]   Section 503,The Indian Penal Code, (Act 45 of 1860)
[19]   Section 64, The Negotiable Instruments Act,1881(Act 16 of 1881)
[20]   Section 81, The Negotiable Instruments Act,1881(Act 16 of 1881)
[21]   Section 89, The Negotiable Instruments Act,1881(Act 16 of 1881)
[22]   Section 45A, The Indian Evidence Act,1872 (Act I of 1872)
[23]   Section 47A, The Indian Evidence Act,1872 (Act I of 1872)
[24]   Section 65A, The Indian Evidence Act,1872 (Act I of 1872)
[25]   Section 65B, The Indian Evidence Act,1872 (Act I of 1872)
[26]   Section 67A, The Indian Evidence Act,1872 (Act I of 1872)
[27]   Section 81A, The Indian Evidence Act,1872 (Act I of 1872)
[28]   Section 85A, The Indian Evidence Act,1872 (Act I of 1872)
[29]   Section 85B, The Indian Evidence Act,1872 (Act I of 1872)
[30]   Section 85C, The Indian Evidence Act,1872 (Act I of 1872)
[31]   Section 88A, The Indian Evidence Act,1872 (Act I of 1872)
[32]   Section 90A, The Indian Evidence Act,1872 (Act I of 1872)

Chapter 6
A Study on Big Data Privacy in Cross-Industrial Challenges and Legal Implications

Tilottama Singh
iD https://orcid.org/0000-0001-6152-4658
Amity University, India

Richa Goel
Amity University, India

Sukanta Kumar Baral
iD https://orcid.org/0000-0003-2061-714X
Indira Gandhi National Tribal University, India

ABSTRACT

Data privacy (also known as information privacy or data protection) refers to the legal right of the data subject to access, use, and collection of data. For the development of a digital economy, privacy protection and identity management are critical. The current regulatory framework's efficiency has been called into consideration from a legal standpoint. In both industry and academia, big data has become a hot issue for research. This chapter presents a succinct but comprehensive examination of data security and privacy issues at all phases of the data life cycle. The chapter then goes over some of the current solutions. Finally, this chapter discusses future research projects related to data security and privacy protection. It further explores other facets of the privacy problem that turn out to be critical for the broad adoption of privacy-enhancing technology, giving a more holistic picture of the situation.

DOI: 10.4018/978-1-6684-3448-2.ch006

INTRODUCTION

Viewing privacy through the lens of ethics can assist businesses in developing and improving their code of conduct. By considering privacy from an ethical standpoint and developing a code of conduct, all employees in an organization, not just security personnel, are held accountable for safeguarding sensitive information. Technology has drastically expanded not only the amount of personal data collected, but also the ability to store, process, and distribute that data. Cloud computing and social networks have accelerated the capture, sharing, and processing of personal data, resulting in a number of privacy breaches. As a result, privacy, broadly defined as the right to be left alone, is becoming an increasingly common worry. Due to socio-techno risk, a new security problem, data privacy protection is complicated. This danger arises from the misuse of data storage and processing technology. Using technology in a way that violates ethical values causes ethical risk, which is a new category of risk. When contemplating the potential breach of business and personal confidentiality, the ethical risk (in addition to the technological and financial risks) arises. This danger is tied to both technology and people, making it a technological-cum-social risk, or a socio-techno risk. People are the benefactors of Internet technology in the era of big data. For Internet service providers, data has a high financial value, but its analysis and use will be more sophisticated and difficult to govern, putting personal privacy at risk. People leave a lot of data footprints on the Internet every day, thanks to the rapid expansion of the Internet. This allows criminals to acquire information on the Internet and then use it for illicit purposes such as reselling, fraud, and so on, not only for people. Life has brought difficulties and financial losses, wreaking havoc on social stability and harmony. How to deal with security and privacy issues in the context of big data is an essential necessity for people to have a decent answer in the era of big data.

The goal of this contribution is to illustrate the most pressing legal concerns in the domain of privacy and identity management, expanding on prior research and taking socioeconomic and technical advancements into account.

Two avenues for legal action in this area are proposed in the following sections. A primary field concerns the legal and other sorts of regulatory options, namely, how to identify the correct blend of different types of regulatory instruments and processes to assure genuine impact on practises.

The second area of possible legal action is the relationship between regulation and technological advancements. We propose four possible streams:

1) how to avoid and monitor the development of privacy-degrading technologies and application fields,
2) regulatory concerns relating to the use of privacy-enhancing technology, and

3)   legislation relating to the administration and use of (many) identities.

It is important to note that one of the key 'transversal' tasks of legal professionals in all future advancements is to ensure that privacy and identity management technologies are properly regulated. Many research and papers have concluded that technology and regulation have no or little mutual impact on their respective developments, and that solutions to bridge the gap between technology and regulation should be devised. To avoid a situation where technology rules de facto the processing of personal data, initiatives from both the legal and technological sides should be implemented, with reciprocal participation. Information is transmitted at a breakneck speed in the age of big data. The usage of data information is not of high value and data is reduced at the same time as information is transmitted owing to insufficient supervision of data information, lack of technological support, an inefficient supervisory system, and the vulnerability of information loss. Individuals, businesses, and even society will suffer several unfavourable and negative consequences because of the value of itself, resulting in higher economic losses.

LITERATURE REVIEW

The issue of data privacy isn't unsolvable. Technical and social strategies can be used to attain data privacy. Protecting data from unauthorized or unintentional access or loss is one of the technical solutions. Customers must be able to accept and understand whether and how their data is being used, and this must be done in an open and confidential manner. Raghunathan (2022), highlighted the aspects of Digital India, the pillars, cyber governance, cyber policing in the States, and cyber diplomacy. He examined a case study of Kerala's cyber policing based on institutional visits and interviews with various organizations, institutions, and other agencies. The article discusses establishing organizational and governance structures, developing cyber risks across the country, and international cyber governance collaboration with various countries and international agencies around the world. Nayak (2021), explained and analyzed the cyber law jurisdiction in India in the recent times. He also gave essential, relevant suggestions to increase cyber-security. Halder and Jaishankar (2021), emphasizes the limitations of the IT Act 2000 insisting on accepting only e-documents and concluded that the government must consider training and sensitizing data handlers and it is expected that if such suggestions are considered, the existing laws may be properly implemented and executed. Pujari et al., (2020), they ranged the knowledge of the crimes or violations that take place over and done with the internet or the cyberspace, alongside with the laws that are forced against those wrongdoings and offenders. They emphasized on the importance of cyber security. Malodia et al.,2020, conceptualized e-Government as a multi-dimensional construct with three underlying dimensions, namely empowered citizenship, hyper-integrated network, and evolutionary system architecture. Monika and Sahu (2019), gave literature review in electronic governance (e-governance) using classification approach is presented. The result shows that a cumulative volume of e-governance study has been accompanied for a diverse range of areas. The classification approach resulted in five numbers of sub-areas of e-government. The sub-areas are: (1) Awareness, (2) Literacy level, (3) Users' acceptability, (4) Legal and (5) Digitalisation. Anjali Jolly (2019) explained and highlighted the prevalent cyber laws in India and their importance and shortcomings. Singh and Singh (2018), their research paper highlights the main challenges regarding implementation of E – Governance in India. We have also given some important suggestions and scope for future study. This paper is briefly described impact of e-governance, challenges & opportunities, why need for present research, objectives of research study. As a result, data privacy by electronic means should be established not only on traditional jurisdiction, but also on soft law, such as self-binding rules like the existing data privacy standards. Hard legislation may not be as effective as soft law. The second issue with data protection is that these standards are not internationally harmonized, resulting in significant cross-border issues (particularly between the United States and the European Union), which is the rule rather than the exception in modern business. Data privacy legislation, particularly in Europe, tend to rely on a traditional human rights approach, ignoring the fact that data is now typically given out voluntarily in exchange for a contract. Users agree to the terms and conditions of corporations like Google, and Facebook when they use their services. Data privacy should consider not only data protection but also contractual norms, which refers to a contract in which there is a particular balance between what is given and what is received.

Security Issues with Big Data

While individuals appreciate the convenience that big data provides, they also face a number of drawbacks. Big data will directly endanger user privacy and data security if it is not effectively protected for user data in the process of use. It can be split into anonymous identifiers, anonymity protection, and privacy protection based on the distinct protective content. People's data security challenges in the era of big data are more dependent on the analysis and research of people's data, and the focused prediction of people's condition and behaviour, rather than the traditional issues of personal privacy.The reality is, however, that privacy protection cannot be properly achieved just through anonymous protection. For example, during three months, a corporation may use some of its search history records in an anonymous manner for consumers to use. The contents of many of the records contained therein can be correctly characterised, despite the fact that the identity information contained therein has been carefully handled. Although data can explain some problems to some extent, it is widely assumed that data is a fact in and of itself. However, the reality is that if data cannot be successfully vetted, individuals will be fooled by data. One is that criminals can use big data to create and fake data. These data are the foundation of big data analysis, and incorrect data will certainly lead to incorrect outcomes.Since the birth of the big data era and the explosive growth of the Internet, this type of network environment has become increasingly crucial for the security of mobile data and intelligent data terminals. China has surpassed the United States as the world's largest market for smart mobile terminals. These vast numbers of mobile terminals not only take up people's energy and time, but also allow them to store more personal data. People are currently concerned about the security of big data and believe that it is unsafe. Big data isn't the only source of problems. The security issues with personally carried intelligent terminals are also a major source of concern. The numerous privacy violations that we have witnessed in recent years indicate that, on the one hand, a significant amount of research on privacy protection has yet to make it into products, and, on the other hand, a solution to the problem of privacy appears to go beyond the implementation of an effective technique.

Technical Challenges

- **Transparency and monitoring tools.** In terms of what is required, very little effort has been made in this direction. However, we are unlikely to see effective tools that can combine and show information on an individual stored by many sources until new regulations are in place, as detailed in the legal elements below.
- **Combining several ways** to establish a good balance of privacy, efficiency, and service quality. We feel that combining current improvements in cryptography (e.g., efficient private set intersection and private set union) with obfuscation-based methods, with the goal of balancing efficiency and efficacy, is a promising direction.
- **The use of data.** Any privacy-preserving system has a substantial issue in reconciling users' privacy preferences with the data utility required by service providers. Only the data that is absolutely necessary to offer a decent level of service should be disclosed, preventing the release of extraneous data to untrustworthy parties.
- **Accurate modelling of adversary knowledge,** which in some situations is hardly predicted, remains a big difficulty. Overprotective strategies with large costs and insufficient service accuracy might result from very conservative assumptions, whereas privacy violations can occur if the adversary has access

to more external knowledge than thought. There are numerous examples of this last scenario in the literature.

Aspects of the User Experience and Problems

Both the definition of what is considered sensitive information and the actual adoption of privacy-enhancing technology are heavily influenced by user experience. Individuals' perceptions of what can be shared and with whom vary depending on their current situation, social standing, and a variety of other circumstances.

Legal Issues and Difficulties

Based on what has happened in the last ten years, privacy protection technology alone is unlikely to be able to win the struggle against the uncontrolled huge release and misuse of personal data that technology is enabling.

Protection of Big Data Security and Privacy

In Social Networks, fully supervise data information. Online media, which arose during the Big Data era, has emerged as the most essential avenue for interpersonal contact. The importance of improving data information oversight cannot be overstated. First and foremost, it is necessary to improve data supervision and management, as well as anonymously protect network data for anonymous social media; second, it is necessary to conduct social information supervision and management to ensure that personal information security is not exploited by criminals, resulting in greater losses. Furthermore, self-prevention awareness and vigilance pitfalls are required to raise users' understanding of safety precautions and to reduce the filling of personal critical information. Finally, the government should establish more stringent laws and regulations for the use of big data as soon as feasible, as well as reinforce the legal framework. Most western countries have established special privacy protection agencies to protect citizens' privacy and information. By establishing a privacy protection agency, not only can people's online behaviour be effectively monitored, but also the purpose of popularizing the law. Therefore, it is necessary to establish a professional privacy protection agency for privacy affairs protection, so that it can fully play its role, protect the privacy of citizens, and effectively crack down on infringement of citizens' privacy and build a safe and harmonious life. A legal action roadmap in the field of privacy and identity management must begin with a brief description of the current situation. The current section summarises the current legal drivers in the realm of privacy protection and identity management for governments and businesses. Governments have a dual role in privacy protection, which is why it is constantly confusing. Governments must ensure that the rule of law is upheld, but they must also take an active part in the establishment of a welfare state. Finding a proper balance between these two functions of the modern state will always be one of the most difficult challenges in developing a regulatory framework in this field. In a democratic society, the right to privacy is seen as a fundamental principle. It is recognised as a fundamental right in all major international human rights treaties and agreements, as well as in the constitutions of most countries around the world, whether officially or indirectly. Privacy regulation is, without a doubt, a major motivator for businesses in terms of privacy and identity management. A key concern is how legal rules should be framed to encourage businesses to develop strong privacy policies and identity management schemes that can be seamlessly integrated into their operations. Regular surveys and polls show that legal laws alone are insufficient to ensure adequate compliance and implementation of data privacy regulations by businesses [particularly small and medium-sized businesses].

Following big court cases involving leading corporations such as GeoCities and Microsoft, larger companies have finally understood that not complying with data protection standards carries an inherent danger. Despite this, most businesses treat data security as a compliance issue rather than a commercial concern.

DATA ANALYSIS AND INTERPRETATION

The research method used to derive this research paper was secondary method of research methodology. Hence the data is collected from various sources and interpreted according to the topic of this research.

In today's digital age, where large amounts of data are recorded in big data, database analysis might provide opportunity to solve major societal issues such as healthcare and others.

We prepared **Data Privacy and Data Security statistics for 2020**, including statistics, consumer research, ROI, data breach statistics, and more, to offer you a better picture.

However, it appears that these numbers reveal **trends and positive changes in younger generations' privacy awareness (61 percent** of individuals who are active about their privacy are under the age of 45).

One of the most major developments will be privacy awareness, which will put **pressure on governments** to enact data protection regulations, regulating how firms will manage individuals' data and what values they must include in order to compete in the market.

Companies that have engaged in privacy initiatives, on the other hand, appear to be reaping benefits such as operational efficiency and agility. At least

Figure 1. Big data life cycle stages, i.e., data generation, storage, and processing
Source: CISCO CYBERSECURITY SERIES 2020 -Consumer Privacy Survey

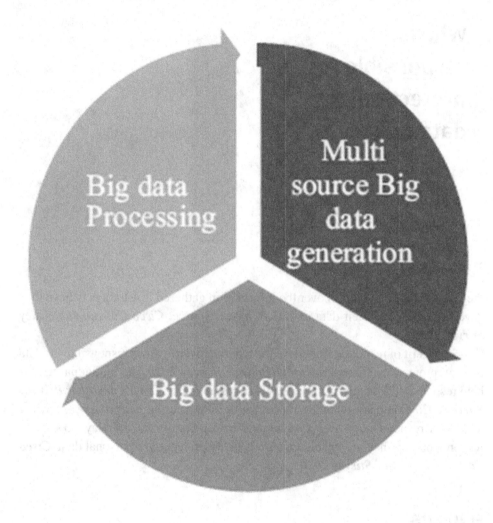

twice the value of their privacy investment is reaped by 40% of respondents.**84 percent** of respondents said they are concerned about privacy, their own data, the data of others in society, and that they want more control over how their data is used. **Eighty percent** of this group also stated that they are willing to take action to safeguard if. Because of their data rules or data sharing practises, **48 percent** of privacy-conscious respondents said they had already switched firms or providers. **79 percent** of respondents indicated they are very or somewhat concerned about how businesses use the information they acquire about them, while **64 percent** are concerned about government data collecting.**81 percent** of those polled believe

Figure 2.

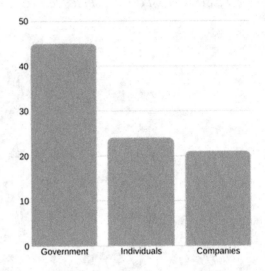

Who is responsible for protection of data privacy?

they have little or no control over the information gathered. Customers believe they have lost control of their data in **46%** of cases (Source: ***Cisco Consumer Privacy Survey 2020)***

    45 percent of respondents believe the federal government is responsible for data privacy protection. ***Cisco Consumer Privacy Survey 2020***.The individual user is held responsible for data privacy by **24%** of respondents. ***Cisco Consumer Privacy Survey 2020***.Companies should be accountable for protecting data privacy, according to **21%** of respondents. ***Cisco Consumer Privacy Survey 2020***.Today, **43%** of all respondents say they are unable to appropriately protect their personal data. ***Cisco Consumer Privacy Survey 2020***

FINDINGS

The dawn of the big data era has brought with it not only significant prospects for societal advancement, but also a slew of new information security dangers, making the protection of personal data privacy a concern. Not only will many professional private information security technologies be required to ensure the security and privacy of big data information, but citizens' awareness of privacy protection in our country will also need to be raised in order for privacy information security to be implemented.

CONCLUSION

An examination of the existing state of play in the field of privacy and identity management is the best place to start when considering prospective legal challenges. Defects in current types of regulation are frequently identified, prompting the question of whether an altogether new strategy should be taken to ensure effective influence on practises, or whether a simple assessment of the existing legal framework would enough. In this report both approaches are explored. The core concepts of the general data protection directive are systematically screened in this study. The key legal issue, in our opinion, is the necessity to develop an appropriate combination of various sorts of regulatory tools and processes for privacy protection. The formulation and application of rules are the two most important aspects of this analysis.

The relationship between legislation and technological advancements is a second major area of potential legal action. Previous workshops in the field of privacy technology have repeatedly concluded that technology and regulation have little or no impact on each other's development, and that ways to bridge the gap between technology and regulation should be devised. As a result, a key research challenge for the future is to increase multidisciplinary participation in order to avoid a situation in which technology de facto rules privacy concerns in the absence of suitable regulation, or vice versa. Any future legal action, in our opinion, should be inextricably related to technology.

Furthermore, in order to promote transparency and legal security, suitable legal support for the "free" use of privacy technologies will need to be developed. For the time being, this appears to be lacking, which may explain some of the apparent challenges in increasing demand for certain technologies. Finally, technological advancements that facilitate the use of online identities have yet to find an adequate legal response, particularly in terms of basic concepts of online identity, online anonymity, the use of multiple identities, identity manager regulation, and identity holder control instruments.

To sum up, the proposed legal problems must be open and adaptable in order to be directly linked to and regularly examined against ever-changing socio-economic and technical advancements.

FUTURE RECOMMENDATIONS

We've touched on the obstacles posed by the many inter-disciplinary components of data privacy that must be considered in order to come up with a viable solution: they include pertinent social, economic, and legal issues. Due to the enormous existing literature on data privacy and security, the multi-faceted problem of data privacy, and, most crucially, the rapidly changing world of ubiquitous apps, which we are all watching in its early stages of evolution, our work will necessarily be imperfect.

REFERENCES

Bettini, C., & Riboni, D. (2015). Privacy protection in pervasive systems: State of the art and technical challenges. *Pervasive and Mobile Computing*, *17*, 159–174. doi:10.1016/j.pmcj.2014.09.010

Boerman, S. C., Kruikemeier, S., & Zuiderveen Borgesius, F. J. (2021). Exploring motivations for online privacy protection behavior: Insights from panel data. *Communication Research*, *48*(7), 953–977. doi:10.1177/0093650218800915

Chen, D., & Zhao, H. (2012, March). Data security and privacy protection issues in cloud computing. In *2012 International Conference on Computer Science and Electronics Engineering* (Vol. 1, pp. 647-651). IEEE. 10.1109/ICCSEE.2012.193

Dumortier, J., & Goemans, C. (2004). Legal challenges for privacy protection and identity management. *Nato Science Series Sub Series III Computer And Systems Sciences*, *193*, 191–212.

Edwards, L. (2004). Reconstructing consumer privacy protection on-line: A modest proposal. *International Review of Law Computers & Technology*, *18*(3), 313–344. doi:10.1080/1360086042000276762

Feng, D., Min, Z., & Yu, L. (2014). Big Data Security and Privacy Protection. *Chinese Journal of Computers*, *37*(1), 246–258.

Huo, H. (2016). Exploration of Security and Privacy Protection Technology in the Big Data Era. *Cyber Security Technology and Applications*, *11*(5), 79–88.

Jain, P., Gyanchandani, M., & Khare, N. (2016). Big data privacy: A technological perspective and review. *Journal of Big Data*, *3*(1), 25. Advance online publication. doi:10.118640537-016-0059-y

Lee, W. W., Zankl, W., & Chang, H. (2016). An ethical approach to data privacy protection. *Isaca Journal*.

Oomen, I., & Leenes, R. (2008). Privacy risk perceptions and privacy protection strategies. In *Policies and research in identity management* (pp. 121–138). Springer. doi:10.1007/978-0-387-77996-6_10

Peng, L., & Fang, W. (2015). Heterogeneity of Inferring Reputation of Cooperative Behaviors for the Prisoners' Dilemma Game. *Physica A*, *433*, 367–378. doi:10.1016/j.physa.2015.03.053

Romanosky, S., & Acquisti, A. (2009). Privacy costs and personal data protection: Economic and legal perspectives. *Berkeley Technology Law Journal*, *24*, 1061.

Schilit, B., Hong, J., & Gruteser, M. (2003). Wireless location privacy protection. *Computer*, *36*(12), 135–137. doi:10.1109/MC.2003.1250896

Shin, S. Y. (2021). Privacy protection and data utilization. *Healthcare Informatics Research*, *27*(1), 1–2. doi:10.4258/hir.2021.27.1.1 PMID:33611870

Singh, N., & Singh, A. K. (2018). Data privacy protection mechanisms in cloud. *Data Science and Engineering*, *3*(1), 24–39. doi:10.100741019-017-0046-0

Wei, K., Jian, W., & Kui, R. (2016). A Survey of Big Data Security Protection Technology. *Journal of Network and Information Security*, *2*(4).

Yan, F. (2016). Big Data Security and Privacy Protection. *Electronic Technology and Software Engineering*, (1), 227.

Yang, P., Xiong, N., & Ren, J. (2020). Data security and privacy protection for cloud storage: A survey. *IEEE Access: Practical Innovations, Open Solutions*, *8*, 131723–131740. doi:10.1109/ACCESS.2020.3009876

Ying, L. (2016). Research on Big Data Security and Privacy Protection. *Information Communication*, (1), 162–163.

Zhang, D. (2018, October). Big data security and privacy protection. In *8th International Conference on Management and Computer Science (ICMCS 2018)* (Vol. 77, pp. 275-278). Atlantis Press.

Chapter 7
Smart Healthcare and Digitalization:
Technological and Cybersecurity Challenges

Navita Mahajan
https://orcid.org/0000-0002-2291-313X
Amity University, India

Seema Garg
Amity University, India

Shreyas Pandita
Amity University, India

Geetansh Sehgal
Amity University, India

ABSTRACT

The study focuses on some technological cyber security challenges that are prevailing. It covers the technologies that are used in healthcare and how digitalization has given a new regime to it. The challenges from the perspective of cybersecurity that are poised to digitalized healthcare have been covered in the study as cyber threats and security vulnerabilities can jeopardize patient protected health information and distract healthcare professionals. At the end, the study covered solutions to handle the technical and cyber-related problems, which can be considered one of the possible solutions.

DOI: 10.4018/978-1-6684-3448-2.ch007

INTRODUCTION

Enhancing the fantastic of health care and improving ease of access to fitness archives whilst keeping practical costs is challenging for health-care businesses globally. The hassle is similarly exacerbated by the swiftly growing world population, specifically the price of enlarge of senior human beings (65 years old and higher). According to the World Health Organization (WHO, 2018), the number of senior human beings will enlarge to about 1.5 billion via 2050. An getting older populace implies extend in persistent diseases that require prevalent visits to health-care providers, as properly as elevated hospitalization needs. The upward push in the quantity of patients requiring constant care substantially increases scientific treatment costs.

Over the previous few decades, Information and Communication Technologies (ICT) have been broadly adopted in the health-care surroundings to make health-care access and shipping less complicated and most cost-effective. When considering technology's future role in digital healthcare, it's important to weigh the benefits of better patient outcomes against the risks of increased physician burnout due to poor implementation and increased complexity[Agrawal and Prabakaran,2020) The use of ICT has led to the development of digital fitness document (EHR) systems. EHRs incorporate complete patient fitness history (current medications, immunizations, laboratory results, modern diagnosis, and so on) and can be without problems shared among a number providers. They have proven to enhance patient-provider interaction. The adoption of ICT in the fitness region is typically referred to as digital health care. Some clinicians, patients, and healthcare providers are wary of the sudden influx of technology, which is compounded by a lack of solid control(Duggal and Bagenal,2018).

Over the years, digital fitness care has prolonged from in particular preserving digital affected person information and offering patient Web portals, to permitting in addition flexibility and comfort in health-care management, and is often referred to as related health. Consumption of self-healthy foods and body image management is rapidly growing(Shen, Y. 2019) Connected health makes use of smart phones and cellular applications, together with wi-fi technologies (such as Bluetooth, Wi-Fi and long-term evolution) to permit patients to join easily with their providers barring touring them frequently. For example, a standard hypertensive patient would see his/her doctor as soon as in six months to file everyday blood strain readings. With a monitoring application, the affected person can transmit daily, or weekly blood strain readings thereby enabling his/her physician to realize a hassle and intervene earlier. Connected fitness has developed into smart fitness whereby conventional cell gadgets (such as smart phones) are used together with wearable clinical units (such as blood pressure monitors, glucometers, smart watches, clever contact lenses, and others) and web of things (IoT) devices (such as implantable or ingestible sensors) to enable continuous patient monitoring and treatment even when sufferers are at their homes. Smart health is expected to maintain hospitalization fees low and supply timely treatment for a range of medical stipulations through placing IoT sensors on health monitoring equipment. The information accumulated by using these microchips can then be sent to any faraway destination. For example, wearable sensors (such as a temperature sensor and the heartbeat sensor) can act as information accumulating units, accumulating the physiological alerts from the patient's body. The collected facts are then forwarded to a local gateway server by means of a Wi-Fi community such that end-systems (such as a physician's laptop) can retrieve the accumulated facts from the gateway server. Regular server updates allow docs get admission to real-time affected person data. These devices work collectively to create a unified scientific document that can be accessed through a number of providers. This statistic is not solely beneficial for the patient, however can be pooled collectively to find out about and predict healthcare traits throughout cultures and countries. While recent lockdowns and business closures have heightened the need for digitized fitness resources, disabled people have always needed safe digitized fitness resources that can be easily accessed from home, and would have benefited from a wider range of and easier access to exercise resources long before the COVID-19 outbreak(Stratton et al, 2020)

The quantity of information that may be generated as a result of combining clever fitness devices with IoT sensors is massive. Such records are often referred to as "big data." Application of fine analytic technologies to Big Data can assist supply significant data to medical practitioner which would help them make greater timely, knowledgeable decisions as nicely as take proactive measures for better fitness management. Healthcare providers must be fully equipped with adequate infrastructure to systematically create and analyse big data in order to give relevant solutions for improving public health. Big data management, analysis, and interpretation that is effective can change the game by allowing modern healthcare to explore new possibilities(Senthilkumar et al, 2018)

Artificial Genius (AI) purposes and cybersecurity threats in healthcare are all the rage now. Cyberattacks have become more sophisticated using AI to get past cyber defenses. The AI is also being used to constantly manipulate and tightly closed the growing range of healthcare Internet of Things (IoT) sensor nodes and Cyber Physical Systems (CPS) devices as they connect and disconnect from hospital networks. The CPS is sensible device consisting of cyber and physical elements which is managed and monitored with the aid of AI algorithm. With the development of clever multisensory systems, sensorial media, smart things, and cloud technologies, "Smart healthcare" is getting terrific interest from academia, government, industry, caregivers, and healthcare communities. During COVID-19, international and national regulatory agencies have emphasized the critical necessity for healthcare providers and universities to protect themselves from cyber-attacks, realizing that an increasing number of cyber-criminals are looking to exploit the healthcare sector's weaknesses(Muthuppalaniappan,2021).

With the ever-increasing world population, the conventional patient-doctor appointment has misplaced its effectiveness. Hence smart healthcare becomes very important. Smart healthcare can be applied at all levels, beginning from temperature monitoring for toddlers to monitoring fundamental symptoms in the elderly. The complexity and cost of implementation varies based totally on the required precision of the character devices, functionalities and sophistication of the software for which they are used. 5G networks are being conceived and built to address the different communication needs of Internet of Things health-care applications (IoT). Smart health-care networks that use 5G are made up of IoT devices that require better network speed and cellular coverage. Current IoT connectivity solutions confront difficulties such as supporting a large number of devices, standardization, energy efficiency, device density, and security(Ahad et al,2016)

IOT IN HEALTHCARE

By introduction of 'IoT' it has been feasible to distinguish between 'health data' in the analyzing and diagnostic of a health practitioner after systems of physical sensors. The largest gain of the 'IoT in healthcare' is to minimize upkeep burden, followed by means of an enlarge in the danger of healthcare. Many IoT-based smart healthcare gadgets and systems are already available for purchase. These devices have made a significant contribution to duties such as patient monitoring, maintaining touch with doctors, and enhancing rehabilitation performance, among others(Yuehong,2020) The addition man or woman and on-line fitness care community was once top notch gaining knowledge of experience and anticipated that cell information and regularly occurring technology killing purposes would lead to the development of cloud health services. IoT is already offered as a principal platform for neurological cognizance monitoring. Because effective surveillance devices are not available, it is feasible to take many greater risks. Technologies such as IoT are performed here. The first-class interest of the affected person is such caution. Multiple sensors are used to analyze patient details. The caregiver can grant enough guidance on health care. Increased monitoring is required for IoT units regularly used for disabled patients. Monitoring strategies, via the assistance of the sensors, have been accumulated to preserve a constant fabric motion by using the patients referred to there for caregivers. In turn, this enhances care quality. In the end, this leads to care costs.

The Architecture of IoT in HealthCare

IoT is a network of physical object-linked gadgets that allow remote gadgets to hear, analyze, and monitor. The computational mechanism for linking pc hardware to permit communication between sensors and smart sewing equipment. IoT implementations in IoT records processing remember closely on the middleware layer.

1. **Perception layer:** The sensory and bodily contraptions are identified in the cognitive layer. The perceptual layer sensor device points to and then detects an object and collects object information. Information on temperature, mobility, position, moisture, vibrations, distance, speed, chemical modifications and many others can be collected in accordance with the variety of sensor. The records is then handed to the next processing layer.
2. **Broadcast Layer:** The "Broadcast Layer" is often named, with its key motive being to connect quite a number waiters, sensible objects and community devices. After network layer coating, the records from the core is then moved to the middleware layer, which transfers the statistics from the core to the front of the working layer.
3. **Middle wave Layer:** Experiencing the enormous amount of data got from the community layer is the massive processing layer that stores it. The data base communication and useful resource administration are responsible, due to the fact it is in the center layer and presents the lower layers with a provider layer
4. **Application Layer:** An quintessential thing of this layer is to supply end-users with application-oriented services. That is because the layer explicitly interacts with the end user by using having utility layers. When the statistics has been got on the jewelry of a lady, inform you that you have fever and you can contact the woman in question on the software form. This is a layer that communicates with the user by way of sending a smart phone message about the flu.
5. **Business Layer:** The corporate layer controls the whole eco-business mannequin of IoT. It helps stop customers figure out extra efficiently.

Applications of IoT in Healthcare

Applications to healthcare allow sufferers and adults to stay independently. IoT sensors are used all through this length for diagnosing and second look of their wellness and sending indicators in illegal circumstances. Sustainable development, energy efficiency, and public health are all interconnected characteristics that can change a system or ecosystem for the betterment of people and the world. Sensors and smart devices should be integrated to increase energy efficiency and ensure that sustainable development targets are reached(Ahmadi et al,2019)

Glucose Sensitivity: Diabetes is a metabolic circumstance if the sugar level at a long-term period is above average. The blood sugar manipulate machine generates blood glucose of some type and helps to prescribe a wholesome diet, appropriate checks and medications. It is presently proposed an m-IoT configuration procedure that is not approved primarily based on glucose.

To this end, extraordinary sensors are linked in sufferers thru the right provider of IPv6 connectivity. In the running system, it creates an IoT-based conversation unit that transmits the records gathered to the level of blood sugar. A collector of glucose, a computer or a smart telephone and the processor is blanketed in this package. A trendy IoT based totally detector for glucose degrees is also proposed.

- **Blood Pressure Monitoring System:** High blood strain suggests the heart pumping thru the body powerfully. The method of IoT promotes the prognosis and remedy of health problems, which includes blood stress (BP), hemoglobin (HB), tiers of blood sugar and bizarre mobile growth. An IoT device for blood pressure, diabetes and obesity treatment.

- **Body Temperature Monitoring:** Body temperature control and monitoring is an integral component in fitness applications. The homeostasis alternate depends on the temperature of the body, based totally on the m-IoT principle. Telos Bmote software body-sensor sensors have clear and efficient inner performance. On the pinnacle of an IoT unit, the physique temperature manipulate gadget is founded on the home port. It supports the manipulate and calculation of the temperature infrared detection and RFID module.

- **Oxygen Saturation Monitoring System:** The Pulse oximeter is used to measure oxygen in the blood continuously. The use of IoT with pulse oximetry is beneficial for technical applications. The advantage of IoT-based pulse oximetry is addressed via coAP-based fitness care machine studies.

- **ECG (Electrocardiogram) Monitoring System:** The ECG monitoring unit has the option of displaying the consumer / affected person ECG waves. A patient's clinical file is published by means of gathering ECG alerts and importing facts to the cloud network. Provides user input on the groundwork of the gathered information.

- **Wheelchair Management System:** Comfortable wheelchairs are suggested by using specialists to keep the lives of the elderly and individuals with disabilities. IoT performs a widespread role in rushing up this method in this region. Smart wheelchairs are outfitted with one-of-a-kind sensors to music seat motion and additionally to show the repute of patient / user.

- **Rehabilitation System:** The method of regenerating population boom problems and a lack of life skills can be extended with the aid of IoT. The competencies of physically disabled people can be strengthened. In order to make stronger the recovery mechanism, the Body Sensor Network was once introduced.

- **Healthcare Solutions Using Smartphone:** The digital machine manage gadget with sensors has so a ways been seen on the Smartphone. Specific cell applications are offered in the healthcare quarter to help patients, supply medical coaching and provide preliminary training. A range of software program and hardware merchandise that portray the Smartphone as a useful device in healthcare are being developed. Another technology contributing to the future of IoT in healthcare is the introduction of 5G networks, which provide one hundred instances quicker speeds for connectivity than normal 4G networks. Although 5G has features that can meet the needs of the future IoT, it also introduces a new set of exciting research difficulties, such as 5G-IoT architecture, trusted communications between devices, security issues, and so on(Li et al, 2018)

IoT units be counted on connectivity to communicate and switch statistics between patient and care provider. Faster cell data transfer provides IoT flexibility in terms of the volumes of statistics it can trade and at a great deal faster rate. With these improvements, new healthcare IoT uses encompass gadgets that help sufferers with their medicinal drug adherence at home; sleep monitoring devices that can tune heart rate, oxygen tiers and moves for high-risk patients; far flung temperature monitoring tools; and non-stop glucose monitoring sensors that connect to cell units and alert sufferers and clinicians to changing blood sugar levels.

Key Applied Sciences of Smart Healthcare

Smart healthcare consists of multiple participants, such as medical practitioner and patients, hospitals, and research institutions. It is an organic total that involves a couple of dimensions, including disorder prevention and monitoring, diagnosis and treatment, hospital management, fitness decision-making, and clinical research. Information technologies, for example, IoT, cellular Internet, cloud computing, massive data, 5G, microelectronics, and artificial intelligence, together with cutting-edge biotechnology represent the cornerstone of clever healthcare. These technologies are widely used in all components of smart healthcare. From the standpoint of patients, they can use wearable units to screen their fitness at all times, are searching for clinical assistance thru virtual assistants, and use far flung houses to put into effect far off services; from the point of view of doctors, a variety of sensible clinical selection help systems are used to aid and improve diagnosis. Doctors can manage medical data through an integrated information platform that consists of Laboratory Information Management System, Picture Archiving and Communication Systems (PACS), Electronic Medical Record, and so on. More unique surgical procedure can be executed through surgical robots and combined fact technology. From the viewpoint of hospitals, radio-frequency identification (RFID) science can be used to control personnel substances and the provide chain, the use of integrated management platforms to accumulate records and assist decision-making. The use of cellular clinical platforms can enhance patients' experiences, From the standpoint of scientific lookup institutions, it is possible to use methods such as laptop mastering instead of guide drug screening and to locate appropriate topics using massive data.4 Through the use of these technologies, clever healthcare can efficaciously minimize the value and hazard of scientific procedures, improve the utilization effectivity of scientific resources, promote exchanges and cooperation in different regions, push the improvement of telemedicine and self-service clinical care, and in the end make personalised clinical services ubiquitous.

CHALLENGES IN DIGITAL HEALTHCARE ADOPTION

Digital health-care structures that leverage EHRs and use technologies such as IoT and big information are predicted to seamlessly join sufferers and providers across diverse health-care systems. These systems are additionally being more and more connected by using the Internet to more than a few types of medical wearable technologies that are being worn for real-time health-care monitoring.

However, quite a few challenges want to be addressed earlier than digital health care can improve stable, flexible and interoperable systems.

Security and Privacy

IoT gadgets can pose a chance to users' security and privacy. Unauthorized get right of entry to of IoT units ought to create a serious chance to patients' fitness as properly as to their non-public information. Denial of provider (DoS) assaults can have an effect on health-care structures and have an effect on affected person safety. While a frequent protection to DoS is redundancy (the use of more than one gadgets on the network), in a health-care surroundings the duplication of resources may also not always be possible due to the fact some of the devices are implanted life-critical systems. The fast detection of practicable protection threats remains a project because of the quantity and complexity of rising software and hardware vulnerabilities. This issue is getting worse as growing variety of gadgets are being related to the Internet.

Today, default authentication stays prevalent, and insecure Web-based interface get admission to further will increase the attack surface. Healthcare professionals have numerous reasons to distrust the cloud, including the inability to relinquish control over their medical records. Many security vulnerabilities are connected with the use of the cloud, including failure to separate virtual users, identity theft, privilege abuse, and insufficient encryption(Al-Issa et al,2018)

Recently, many wireless networking applied sciences have additionally been deployed in the healthcare environment and these encompass Wi-Fi, BLE and ZigBee that are being used to furnish connectivity to exclusive sorts of clinical units and sensors. Security protection of these wi-fi and sensor applied sciences towards eavesdropping, Sybil attacks, sinkhole attacks, and sleep deprivation attacks should be enforced. Centralized statistics sets of non-public information, household history, electronic medical files and genomic data, must also be blanketed from hackers and malicious software program to enforce safety and privacy.

Confidentiality and privacy are essential worries for medical doctors as well. Patients may also not desire to share their clinical files due to the fact of the sensitive nature of the fitness data (for example, most cancers or HIV take a look at results). Concerns exist that the integration of connected science into cutting-edge clinical statistics structures might also compromise the confidentiality of fitness data. These privacy concerns stem from the worry that digital and connected technological know-how may additionally appeal to hackers. Furthermore, researchers every so often argue that connected health technological know-how would be implemented imperfectly, permitting for safety vulnerabilities to be exploited

Health Statistics Alternate Barriers

Health Information Exchange (HIE) enhances health-care delivery through providing the ability to electronically share health-care data among diverse health-care groups in a reliable and impervious manner. Currently, HIE is carried out through using one of the following methods: consumer-mediated exchange, directed exchange, and query-based exchange. Consumer-mediated change affords patients with get right of entry to their own digital records, for that reason permitting them to music their health conditions, determine whether there is faulty billing or clinical data, and replace their self-reports. Directed alternate is carried out when a health-care organisation transfers such imperative information such as laboratory test outcomes and remedy dosage to other experts involved in the care of the same patient. Query-based exchange usually takes place in unplanned medical care when a health-care enterprise needs the preceding health data of a new patient. This is carried out by way of soliciting for get admission to these documents through the HIE system. Data from health-care partners is crucial for public health, and information technology has made this easier than ever. Data, on the other hand, is frequently structured using a number of terminologies and formats, making data interfaces complex and costly(Shapiro et al,2011)

Impediments in the deployment of HIE systems are typically owing to security and privacy concerns. Some of the troubles related with present day HIE systems are as follows: First, abuse of access rights by using approved insiders. This usually happens when health-care businesses share medical documents of their patients with unauthorized individuals, either out of irresponsibility, for non-public reasons, or in alternate for some form of gain. For instance, clinical information of celebrities and politicians frequently leak out of Healthcare Information Management Systems (HIMSs) into the media. Second, violation of regulations through unauthorized insiders, who may have get entry to the machine itself however not to the records. For instance, health center personnel who do not supply direct patient care or former personnel who have not yet been electronically confined from data retrieval. The former crew can use the existing get entry to hack the personal informational database whilst the latter might also figure out to are trying to find vengeance on their former employers with the aid of undermining the HIMS's security. Third, unauthorized intruder attempts to enter the device both by means of attacking it without delay or by pretending to be phase of the health-care team. Despite the abundance of health-related material on the Internet, nothing is known regarding its accessibility, quality, or reading level(Cline and Haynes, 2001).

Device Communication

One of the important challenges to enforcing clever or linked fitness is communication. Many units now have sensors to gather records and they frequently talk with the server in their personal language. Each producer has its own proprietary protocol, which potential sensors made by using one-of-a-kind producers cannot always speak with each other. This fragmented software program environment, coupled with privateness concerns, frequently isolates valuable records on information islands, undermining the main idea at the back of IoT.

The presence of quite a few devices also opens up issues associated to connecting clinical units using wireless community technologies. For instance, people using a Wireless Personal Area Network (WPAN)-enabled machine are predicted to pass freely however mobility can result in collisions when WPANs that function in comparable frequency channel are within shut range. Collision in WPANs has quite a few disruptive outcomes because it reduces performance and might also lead to disastrous conditions specially when health-care delivery is concerned. Therefore, it is imperative to make positive that medical units function precise when connected the usage of a variety of kinds of wi-fi verbal exchange technologies.

Smart health structures are no longer continually convenient to use with the aid of physicians. The presence of a giant range of aspects ought to now and again make a gadget complicated which in turn demotivates health-care workers in mastering how to use it. Users and provider providers both require interoperability inside individual IoT domains and amongst themselves. This creates complex challenges due to the fact the various disciplines captured by way of IoT are regulated by way of a various team of regulatory agencies. This complexity is similarly exacerbated in related fitness situations wherein clinical requirements require particularly strict regulations. Companies that desire to construct clever health purposes in the clinical vicinity should consider the policies imposed with the aid of Food and Drug Administration, the Centers for Medicare and Medicaid Services, and the Federal Communications Commission.

A truly interoperable linked health system is one in which information flows with each one to-one and one-to-many connections, leading to the alternate of facts amongst more than one interfaces which require systems to cooperate with one another. In health-care environments, it is important for units to be compatible with many transmission formats and protocols for authentication and encryption. Device administration will require directories of devices' functionality, protocols, terminologies and standards compliance. The level of "plug and play" interoperability now common in non-health areas remains a undertaking for clinical devices.

Collection and Administration of Data

Digital health care that leverages IoT sensor gadgets faces various information administration challenges. The information originates from clinical sensors, which are worn or implanted inside the human body. Because the kingdom of the human physique is continuously changing, there is a continuous inflow of statistics that is being produced. Furthermore, the captured data are heterogeneous.

Digital health systems want to be designed the use of appropriate data-driven learning strategies to handle its continually varying cyber-physical components. Proper analysis of information can supply precious records about patients' health conditions. When a lot of patients' facts are not analyzed and understanding is now not extracted from it, we do no longer reap the most usefulness of this data, and its collection additionally wastes computing resources. Several challenges exist due to the fact of the absence of standardized information series codecs as nicely as the extent and velocity of data generated in health-care settings. Integrity is additionally indispensable with recognize to big data. Inaccurate statistics can lead to unsuitable decisions and lengthy term strategic planning. Because health-care information regularly comes from a number sources, robust authentication systems are needed to make sure that health-care statistics are submitted from actual registered clinics, hospitals, and scientific institutions.

Collecting statistics that is clean, formatted, thorough, and specific in a health-care device is Challenging. In addition, health-care definitions are complex and metrics are continuously changing in the health-care industry. The complexity of records in the health-care industry makes integrating massive data challenging. While some information, such as fitness variables, have to be up to date frequently, greater passive facts such as geographic vicinity and contact facts want now not be up to date that often. Data integrity have to be maintained whilst updating information. Inappropriate report control may additionally pose a hazard to data integrity. Maintaining these databases is challenging because of the charges of maintenance.

Design and Implementation Based Totally on Multi-Disciplinary Knowledge

Digital fitness (including related and smart health) is developed using understanding in many fields inclusive of embedded systems, network design, data analytics and bioengineering. The design and implementation of such a heterogeneous device requires significant expertise in multi-disciplinary areas. The device also desires to evolve consistently to tackle continuously changing needs. For example, presently there is constrained integration of smart health systems with some scientific systems such as ultrasound and CAT scan imaging.

HEALTHCARE CYBERSECURITY IN TECHNOLOGICAL ERA

Healthcare is one of the most inclined industries when it comes to cybersecurity. The healthcare machine around the globe has emerge as extra prone to cyber assaults in technology era. Many cyber-security corporations are reporting a rapid enlarge in cyber attacks on the grounds that the begin of the COVID-19 pandemic. The healthcare system, including nursing home, has always been one of the key target of cyberattacks. Recent string of attacks in numerous principal hospitals and healthcare systems, have exposed the security vulnerabilities of most depended on healthcare institutions. The technology is characterized via a steep rise in cyber attacks, from one of a kind perpetrators and for different motivations, and the healthcare zone has now not been secure. Cybersecurity events have become a growing problem for the healthcare business as a result of the widespread integration of technology into the healthcare system(Tully,2020)

Security and privateness in the healthcare industry are very fundamental as they involve a patient's/user's personal records and non-public clinical records. During the final few decades, the healthcare provider has extended the use of superior technologies, like Artificial Intelligence (AI), machine learning methods to impervious patients' fitness profiles, storing statistics in the cloud, superior clinical devices, etc. These technological developments have reduced the work of healthcare vendors and have led to a paperless environment. But in return, the chance of cyber-attacks has increased. In most of the cases, there are no suitable safety structures set up to protect the clinic database, and the healthcare provider are regularly unaware of the cybersecurity threats lie in the shadows. Information Technology (IT) in healthcare structures is vulnerable to the factor that it can take even various weeks earlier than a cyberattack is acknowledged. Industry 4.0 is a new phenomena that has evolved in the contemporary period as a result of rapid technological advancements. The convergence of information and operational technology creates new issues, particularly in the area of cyber security(Ervural, and Ervural,2018) The healthcare companies proceed working with a hacked machine without having any knowledge of the attacks. This ought to end result in spending billions of dollars and affect thousands and thousands of patients every year. The unforeseen COVID-19 catastrophe has wreaked havoc on medical education and patient care. Despite the difficulties, the health-care system and patients have been resourceful and resilient in devising solid "temporary" remedies. It's unclear if some of the COVID-era transitional processes will be kept in medical education and telemedicine in the future(Shah,et al,2020).

Internal Threats

Besides exterior cybersecurity threats, healthcare companies every so often have to face internal threats as well. These inside threats to the agencies are either due to human error or as a end result of a breach of an employment contract. According to various case studies, there are three sorts of interior attacks: the carelessness/negligence of employee or contractor, the criminal or malicious insider, and the credential thief (imposter risk).

Medjacking

Medjacking is the exercise of attacking and manipulating a scientific device and instrument with the intent to damage a patient. The malfunctioning of any scientific gadgets at hospital and/or clinic is very distressing and would possibly have severe deadly consequences. The erroneous diagnostic consequences from any clinical instruments could lead to the incorrect prescription. If any medical gadgets are no longer running properly, it may purpose harm to patients that lead to death, rather than help.

Artificial Intelligence

Artificial Intelligence (AI), the place computers operate duties that are typically assumed to require human intelligence, is currently being discussed in nearly each and every area of science and engineering. Major scientific competitions like ImageNet Large Scale Visual Recognition Challenges are providing proof that computers can reap human-like competence in image recognition. AI has additionally enabled huge growth in speech awareness and natural language processing. All of these advances open questions about how such abilities can support, or even enhance, human decision making in fitness and fitness care. Most stakeholders in most sectors withstand disruption because they like the status quo. Healthcare, on the other hand, currently needs disruption. With hovering fees and wasted time in each section of the ecosystem, the healthcare zone wishes to evolve to deliver top notch constant care and value. Hence, many one of a kind sorts of AI functions have emerged, which include drug discovery, discovering sufferers for scientific trials, transcribing notes for digital fitness information (EHRs), providing pre-primary care records to patients, predicting worsening heart conditions, apnea or allergies and alerting clinicians to possible 'code blue' emergencies hours earlier than they occur.

Artificial talent (AI) can furnish a device or software program the ability to interpret complicated data, inclusive of images, video text, and speech, or other sounds and to work on that interpretation to acquire the goal. Since AI-driven computers are programmed to make selections with little human intervention, some wonder if machines will soon make the difficult selections we now entrust to our doctors.

AI has been employed in applications in a number domains of healthcare such as most cancers research, cardiology, diabetes, mental health, identification of Alzheimer's disease, stroke-related studies, identification of cardiovascular disease, etc. Rather than robotics, AI in healthcare typically refers to physicians and hospitals having access to extensive information sets of potentially life-saving information. The healthcare sector must protect patients' personal information since hackers can access it and exploit it to commit clinical fraud and other crimes. Monetary gains Cybersecurity helps you to keep your data safe. For criminal purposes, the affected person's information is kept private. Additionally, cybercrime prevention is a priority(Thyagarajan,,2017) The recent advancement of computing power can analyze the distinct elements from the multisensory information for predictive analytics to discover the conceivable fitness consequences via the desktop learning techniques. The artificial Genius and machine studying methods use statistical methods to analyze incoming sensory and community statistics to identify patterns and safety hazard and make a selection with a minimal human interaction.

Internet of Things (IoT) and Cyber-Physical System (CPS) in the Generation of AI

Healthcare systems in hospitals/clinics are one of the key goals of attackers for carrying out Internet-of-Things (IoT) and Cyber-physical System (CPS)-focused cyberattacks. The most necessary endpoints from the medical institution security standpoint are patient health monitoring, ventilation, anesthesia, infusion pumps, etc. A Cyber-Physical System (CPS) is a collection of physical world systems or devices that interact and communicate with one another in order to perform their functions. For operations and control, CPS combines the principles of computing, communication, and control. Physical systems are monitored. Cyber-physical systems may be dynamic and interactive. Dispersed subsystems with the capacity to auto-connect and self-operate(TR, R. (2021) There is growing use of IoT in healthcare settings, consisting of cell devices, wearables, robots, drones, and contactless devices. IoT is enabling the control of coronavirus.

Early detection of Covid-19, isolation of contaminated people, and tracing possible contacts are necessary to stopping the unfold of the virus. IoT and CPS protocols, GPS, and Wi-Fi are presenting options to the challenges that distance and accessibility would have posed. Using the IoT to combat virus outbreaks has been advantageous at some point of Covid-19. Interconnected tech devices, such as smart thermometers to check a patient's temperature, are used to construct up unique datasets for more correct analysis and diagnosis. Quarantine compliance is additionally substantially assisted by using the use of IoT. By the use of a patient's existing smartphone or wearable devices, it is less complicated to make certain compliance with quarantine policies and establish patterns by way of track-and-trace methods.

Challenges in Wise Cybersecurity

Cybersecurity is the principal problem of the nation's standard cyber-physical protection and economic interests. The safety analysts in each organisation are going through many challenges associated to cybersecurity along with securing federal and nation exclusive data. One wishes to distinguish between the instant dreams and long-term desires when coming up with the long-term analysis, development, and software of AI in cybersecurity. There are a range of methods AI can be without delay applied in cybersecurity. Currently, there are on the spot cybersecurity troubles that want a lot of shrewd solutions. In the future, customers will see the promising views of the software of entirely new concepts of information handling. A key application area of AI is the information administration for cyber threats. AI-based systems are already getting used in several applications, like the protection measures hidden inside the software. However, AI will get a wider application as massive databases for healthcare systems are developed. Many technologies are normally referred to as most of the healthcare databases are incorporating AI for cybersecurity. However, there are many exclusive applied sciences that, if they reach a excessive degree of sophistication, would deliver about the introduction of smarter-than-human intelligence.

How to Enhance Cybersecurity for AI

The improvement of AI and machine mastering applied sciences will have an impact on cybersecurity in numerous ways. the security industry has successfully adopted some AI-based techniques. (Bertino et al, 2021). Cyber attackers can assault any community systems from somewhere in the world, at any time. It is observed that cybersecurity purposes have acquired large technological development over the closing few years. There are many approaches to enhance cybersecurity for AI, like improving cyber threat detection with machine learning, AI and laptop learning plays an necessary role in mitigating phishing attacks, automated community security, strong behavioral analytics, etc. AI and computing device gaining knowledge of make smarter cybersecurity feasible and these rising applied sciences have great possible applications in healthcare, finance, retail, etc. There are several comparable troubles to deal with the question of how AI systems are invulnerable when they are used to augment the safety of the accrued healthcare facts and pc networks. The application of AI security options to respond to rapidly evolving threats makes the want to invulnerable AI itself even more pressing. It is all the extra necessary that those algorithms be protected from interference, compromise, or misuse if we depend on laptop mastering algorithms to observe and shield from cyberattacks. Increasing dependence on AI for critical functions and offerings will no longer solely create greater incentives for attackers to target these algorithms, however also the potential for each profitable assault to have extra severe consequences.

The enchancment of cybersecurity and security for AI is one of the key challenges. AI has turn out to be greater popular and extensively used technology in many different sectors along with the healthcare industry. The policymakers locate it more and more indispensable to consider the intersection of cybersecurity with AI. Recently, several researchers working on to decrease the opportunity for adversaries to get right of entry to private AI education information or fashions in healthcare structures throughout the era of Covid-19.As noted above, one of the key safety threats to AI structures is the opportunity for adversaries to compromise the integrity of their decision-making processes. The way to attain this when adversaries take the direct manage of an AI device so that they can figure out the outputs the gadget generates and the choices it makes. An attacker may try to affect these selections directly by way of delivering malicious inputs or education records to an AI model.

IMPROVING THE ADOPTION OF DIGITAL HEALTH CARE WITH INTERNET OF THINGS AND HUGE FACTS TECHNOLOGIES

Evidence-Based Care

The exponential amplify in the extent of health-care data generated by way of IoT gadgets makes information processing very challenging. Big records can grant evidence-based care through aggregating data units from diverse sources. Analysis of information can grant useful insights into detecting anomalies and offering appropriate redress to patients. Intelligent analysis the use of new strategies can supply significant financial savings on the order of countless hundred billion dollars, which quantities to about eight per cent of the countrywide health expenses.

The learn about of health-related data with environment friendly strategies promotes early identification of ailment patterns, which expands public fitness surveillance. This ensures that gorgeous and well timed selections on the treatment of a unique disorder are taken thereby decreasing patient mortality. Big records enhances the kind of care sufferers obtain as remedy choices are primarily based upon information gathered from analyzing massive records sets. The areas of computer science and electronics have united to produce one of the most significant technical breakthroughs in the shape of the Internet of Things' reality (IoT). (Yeole, A. S,et al,2016) Although still in its early stages, the Internet of Things has had a significant influence on healthcare.

The early phases of development have proven crucial.

Self-Learning and Self-Improvement

IoT sensors allow records collection, but IoT on my own cannot grant rehabilitation treatments. Accurate and well timed treatments can be made based totally on fast patient evaluation, and the improvement of rehabilitation processes corresponding to the clinical investigation. Many elements need to be regarded to provide a unique treatment. Computer equipment purely matter on the statistics accrued by means of the sensors and past case studies, whilst self-learning strategies can adaptively analyze and propose new remedy options. A few self-learning algorithms, are appropriate for information analysis and mining. Topology primarily based and ontology-based heuristic algorithms can assist in discovering most effective options for a large-scale health-care system.

Standardization

Standardization goes to the heart of the mission in reforming healthcare: reaching fee besides compromising patient outcomes. The argument is now not about results versus efficiency, on the grounds that the two are no longer opposing forces. Our assessment of the current literature affords proof that standardization works, however only if implemented properly. In order to facilitate this, we advocate the following recommendations:

1. Healthcare authorities respond to the language of evidence, so make certain that an evidence-based process is used to guide the standardisation process, and describe it.
2. Make positive nearby healthcare experts are consulted as quickly as feasible and have the opportunity to take ownership.
3. Focus on implementation and shared learnings. Authors ought to file now not only the standardisation protocol but additionally the implementation challenges and how they were overcome.
4. Ideally, alongside a description of the standardisation protocol, a local customization implementation guide need to be provided.
5. Future researchers should collect information on a range of consequences that will be essential to all stakeholders, including patients, payers and providers.
6. More and better-quality research is needed around ICT, body of workers issues and procurement.

Safety and Risk

The fast development in Internet of Things (IoT) related with biosensors affords many benefits to the humans, such as clever healthcare structures (SHS). SHS provide plenty of possibilities to the healthcare experts and hospitals to display the patients' health in a remote basis. The aggregate of IoT gadgets with the increasing networked nature of the healthcare surroundings permit the healthcare experts to supply emergency and precautionary scientific services to their patients extra efficiently and effectively. SHS collected fitness facts are especially sensitive in nature. However, SHS are rendering the patients' fitness records inclined to more than a few attacks. Maintaining the security and privateness of the patients' health data are the largest challenges in clever healthcare systems.

IoT-based structures are beneficial as long as its customers stay safe. In IoT systems, all kinds of statistics series and mining are performed over the Internet. Thus, personal records can be accessed at a number of ranges (during collection, transmission and so on). Patients' safety must be taken into consideration by means of stopping any form of tracking or unlawful identification. The greater the level of autonomy and intelligence of the IoT devices, the harder the protection of identities and privateness becomes. IoT-based functions are also prone due to the fact of wireless verbal exchange which makes eavesdropping easier. Additionally, IoT gadgets typically have low strength and low computing energy which makes it tougher to implement complicated algorithms to assurance security. As big statistics turns into extra ubiquitous in the health-care system, more safety challenges will emerge. Rigorous lookup is needed to make certain privacy, trust, and protection during the health-care environment.

Interactive Reporting and Visualization

The world is full of facts which is increasing with the aid of leaps and bounds. From local weather exchange to area science to economics, large facts has turn out to be necessary now not solely to a number of corporations of professionals but additionally to folks and communities. Big statistics is beneficial in grasp the situation, identification of underlying problems, planning to overcome those problems, and comparison of implemented plans in every field. At the man or woman level, large records is developing consciousness about extraordinary matters and giving readymade solutions to the things to do in their daily life. The health quarter too has seen phenomenal boom in data gathered from hundreds of thousands of people, every uniquely identifiable or anonymized and pooled together. When proper geared up and analyzed data uncovers unseen problems, relationships, trends, and reasons that lead to solutions. It empowers specialists such as researchers, administrators, policymakers, public fitness agencies, and clinicians to make higher decisions.

Big information purposes want to distinguish between analysis and reports. Big records functions will no longer succeed if data are absolutely written to reports. Applications need to derive treasured insights from a bulk of information and only point out particular highlights. It is also quintessential to train algorithms to generate unique insights based on accessible information except which the credibility of the report comes into question. Reports can be made attractive and useful with the aid of which include graphs and statistical information.

Applications ought to additionally center of attention on developing visualizations that would make it effortless to derive insights from a file and enable effortless identification of tendencies and challenges in a health-care segment.

FUTURE DIRECTIONS

Needle-less and low-cost healthcare solutions have constantly been on excellent demand. With vast funding and growing interest in the direction of the smart healthcare domain, there are numerous merchandise and functions accessible for users. As smart healthcare has multi-dimensional applications, it presents a lot of scope for researchers to constantly innovate new products and enhance the already present architectures. The transition closer to smart healthcare services, is a sluggish and steady process. This is by and large due to the fact healthcare professionals want to be constantly trained and satisfied to adapt to the digital era. By bridging the hole between researchers and healthcare professionals, greater lookup troubles and illnesses can be addressed and smarter existence can be adapted. Though the clever healthcare options backed by using the IoT can improve revenue, and make bigger quality of life, the benefits can be without difficulty overshadowed, if safety is compromised. Additional measures want to be taken to take care of threats and securing the practicable facts at each the consumer and developer ends. Thus, the vision and long-term success of this dynamically developing enterprise lays in the synergy of researchers, healthcare authorities and the public. Future smart healthcare networks are likely to be made up of a mix of 5G and IoT devices that will improve cellular coverage, network performance, and solve security problems. (Tian,2019)

Technology is altering continuously, and it is vital to remain on the slicing edge. In the future, incorporating hybrid software program would be a true thinking to impenetrable the health data. Cybersecurity professionals intelligently manage the machine due to the fact AI and machine getting to know are still inclined to attacks. It is encouraged that in the future records governance and compliance techniques be a pinnacle precedence with more protection and privacy legislation on the horizon. Many cybersecurity purposes can be made less difficult and more efficaciously with machine learning algorithms. In the future, this technological know-how will lighten the weight of a heavy cybersecurity workload and will limit human error.

That equal reduction in human error is also relevant to fitness diagnoses. Medical errors, some of which are improper diagnoses, may additionally end result in approximately 251,000 deaths each and every year according to. Additionally, many greater die each and every year because they do not get therapy rapidly enough. Healthcare systems that contain AI into the prognosis process, as nicely as the smart health sector, may want to see a drop in these deaths due to the AI extra precisely diagnosing a patient, as nicely as figuring out the trouble sooner.

CONCLUSION

In sum, the prospects for clever healthcare are vast. For man or woman users, smart healthcare can facilitate better health self-management. Timely and gorgeous medical services can be accessed when needed, and the content of medical services will be greater personalized. For scientific institutions, smart healthcare can limit costs, relieve personnel pressure, acquire unified administration of substances and information, and enhance the patient's medical experience. For lookup institutions, clever healthcare can minimize the price of research, reduce research time, and enhance the general effectivity of research. With regard to macro decision-making, smart healthcare can enhance the status quo of clinical aid inequality, push the system of clinical reform, promote the implementation of prevention strategies, and limit social clinical costs.42 However, there are still some issues in the development process. The answer to these issues relies upon no longer solely on technological progress, however additionally on the joint efforts of patients, doctors, fitness institutions, and technology companies.

We are currently witnessing speedy advances in information conversation technologies. It is a accepted fact that the implementation and deployment of these technologies in the health-care region bring about enormous benefits (affordable fitness care, within your means fitness services, and many others) to all health-care stakeholders. In this work, we mentioned some of the foremost impediments that are slowing down digital health-care adoption nationally and internationally along with some viable solutions to allow quicker digital health-care deployment. While the health-care sector is more and more involved in leveraging IoT and massive facts applied sciences to emerge as extra efficient, there are various challenges that want to be addressed earlier than digital fitness care can come to be a great reality.

Artificial Intelligence is fast, developing field with broad applications. Recent cybersecurity occasions that targeted healthcare structures have highlighted cybersecurity vulnerabilities that have compromised the confidentiality, integrity, and availability of data for the affected institutions. Further, these events have proven that even with care, it only takes one slip up to value a commercial enterprise or corporation millions of bucks and numerous years to get to the bottom of the issue. Additionally, the COVID-19 pandemic has shown the want for enhancements in the healthcare sector that can make diagnoses extra correct and extra efficient. One proposed method is to integrate AI into both cybersecurity and healthcare. AI is already used in the medical area to diagnose many types of cancer, as properly as many other illnesses. Further integration of AI into the clever health discipline can lead to faster treatment, as well as make the diagnosis manner extra efficient. AI is additionally already discovering use in the cybersecurity discipline to discover threats or to help resource professionals in figuring out and dealing with threats.

Continued integration of AI in the cybersecurity field will lead to more refined, and robust structures that are capable of dealing with ever-changing cyber threats.

In the age of large data, public health have an effect on and implementation needs can be assessed in one of a kind ways the usage of different interactive visualization techniques. When visualized well, huge records can become aware of implementation gaps and disparities and speed up implementation techniques to reach population organizations in most want for interventions. For precision public fitness to succeed, advances in predictive analytics, and realistic equipment for data integration and visualization are needed. As Health Administrators may also come from various specialties and most, consisting of those from public health, will now not be well versed in big records science, strong coaching, and career development for big statistics in public health is the need of the hour.

REFERENCES

Agrawal, R., & Prabakaran, S. (2020). Big data in digital healthcare: Lessons learnt and recommendations for general practice. *Heredity*, *124*(4), 525–534. doi:10.103841437-020-0303-2 PMID:32139886

Ahad, A., Tahir, M., Aman Sheikh, M., Ahmed, K. I., Mughees, A., & Numani, A. (2020). Technologies trend towards 5G network for smart health-care using IoT: A review. *Sensors (Basel)*, *20*(14), 4047. doi:10.339020144047 PMID:32708139

Ahmadi, H., Arji, G., Shahmoradi, L., Safdari, R., Nilashi, M., & Alizadeh, M. (2019). The application of internet of things in healthcare: A systematic literature review and classification. *Universal Access in the Information Society*, *18*(4), 837–869. doi:10.100710209-018-0618-4

Al-Issa, Y., Ottom, M. A., & Tamrawi, A. (2019). eHealth cloud security challenges: A survey. *Journal of Healthcare Engineering*. PMID:31565209

Bertino, E., Kantarcioglu, M., Akcora, C. G., Samtani, S., Mittal, S., & Gupta, M. (2021, April). AI for Security and Security for AI. In *Proceedings of the Eleventh ACM Conference on Data and Application Security and Privacy* (pp. 333-334). 10.1145/3422337.3450357

Cline, R. J., & Haynes, K. M. (2001). Consumer health information seeking on the Internet: The state of the art. *Health Education Research*, *16*(6), 671–692. doi:10.1093/her/16.6.671 PMID:11780707

Duggal, R., Brindle, I., & Bagenal, J. (2018). Digital healthcare: Regulating the revolution. *BMJ (Clinical Research Ed.)*, 360. PMID:29335296

Ervural, B. C., & Ervural, B. (2018). Overview of Cyber Security in the Industry 4.0 Era. In *Industry 4.0: Managing The Digital Transformation. Springer Series in Advanced Manufacturing*. Springer. doi:10.1007/978-3-319-57870-5_16

Li, S., Da Xu, L., & Zhao, S. (2018). 5G Internet of Things: A survey. *Journal of Industrial Information Integration*, *10*, 1–9. doi:10.1016/j.jii.2018.01.005

Muthuppalaniappan, M., & Stevenson, K. (2021). Healthcare cyber-attacks and the COVID-19 pandemic: an urgent threat to global health. *International Journal for Quality in Health Care, 33*(1).

Senthilkumar, S. A., Rai, B. K., Meshram, A. A., Gunasekaran, A., & Chandrakumarmangalam, S. (2018). Big data in healthcare management: A review of literature. *American Journal of Theoretical and Applied Business*, *4*(2), 57–69. doi:10.11648/j.ajtab.20180402.14

Shah, S., Diwan, S., Kohan, L., Rosenblum, D., Gharibo, C., Soin, A., ... Provenzano, D. A. (2020). The technological impact of COVID-19 on the future of education and health care delivery. *Pain Physician*, *4S*(23), S367–S380. doi:10.36076/ppj.2020/23/S367 PMID:32942794

Shapiro, J. S., Mostashari, F., Hripcsak, G., Soulakis, N., & Kuperman, G. (2011). Using health information exchange to improve public health. *American Journal of Public Health*, *101*(4), 616–623. doi:10.2105/AJPH.2008.158980 PMID:21330598

Shen, Y. (2019, July). An Empirical Study on the Influential Factors of User Loyalty in Digital Fitness Community. In *International Conference on Human-Computer Interaction* (pp. 550-559). Springer. 10.1007/978-3-030-22219-2_40

Stratton, C., Kadakia, S., Balikuddembe, J. K., Peterson, M., Hajjioui, A., Cooper, R., Hong, B.-Y., Pandiyan, U., Muñoz-Velasco, L. P., Joseph, J., Krassioukov, A., Tripathi, D. R., & Tuakli-Wosornu, Y. A. (2020). Access denied: The shortage of digitized fitness resources for people with disabilities. *Disability and Rehabilitation*, 1–3. doi:10.1080/09638288.2020.1854873 PMID:33305961

Thyagarajan, C., Suresh, S., Sathish, N., & Suthir, S. (2020). A typical analysis and survey on healthcare cyber security. *Int. Journal of Scientific & Technology Research*, *9*(3), 3267–3270.

Tr, R. (2021). Internet of Things (IoT) and Cyber Physical Systems (CPS) for Smart Applications. *International Journal of Sensors, Wireless Communications and Control*, *11*(3), 262–262. doi:10.2174/221032791103210310141755

Tully, J., Selzer, J., Phillips, J. P., O'Connor, P., & Dameff, C. (2020). Healthcare challenges in the era of cybersecurity. *Health Security, 18*(3), 228–231. doi:10.1089/ hs.2019.0123 PMID:32559153

Yeole, A. S., & Kalbande, D. R. (2016, March). Use of Internet of Things (IoT) in healthcare: A survey. In *Proceedings of the ACM Symposium on Women in Research 2016* (pp. 71-76). 10.1145/2909067.2909079

Yuehong, Y. I. N., Zeng, Y., Chen, X., & Fan, Y. (2016). The internet of things in healthcare: An overview. *Journal of Industrial Information Integration, 1*, 3–13. doi:10.1016/j.jii.2016.03.004

Chapter 8
Internet Banking Safety Framework:
An Evaluation of the Banking Industry in Bangladesh

Ayon Dutta
University of Dhaka, Bangladesh

Partho Ghosh
North South University, Bangladesh

Avishak Bala
North South University, Bangladesh

ABSTRACT

The internet is part and parcel of our everyday lives. Internet banking is playing a major role. But the risk is always there: malpractitioners always ready with their unethical and illegal ways of making crimes. Internet banking is the updated medium of communication to serve customers. Recently, the use of the internet in the banking sector of Bangladesh has increased rapidly. Through the internet banking system, banks have made a consequential growth and the number of frauds also has increased. Like other countries, Bangladesh is facing security problems. It is not totally free form risk and fraudulent activities. This chapter unveils internet banking crimes methodology and the limitations of existing security systems. To mitigate the internet security problems, manifold-layered security systems should be ensured among the clients and the banks. The internet banking security structure and its manifold-layered security systems have been developed and evaluated through an expert evaluation method.

DOI: 10.4018/978-1-6684-3448-2.ch008

INTRODUCTION

Internet Banking is the fastest and cheapest service system for the banking industry. But, the internet is also a new cause of risk. The internet is making the banking system user-friendly and efficient. The banking industry has been facing Internet banking problems, threats and attacks now a days, and critically discussed the importance of strong security implementation in the Bangladeshi banking industry by recommending security enforcement and measures, that should be established based on bank site as well as customer site perspective. The authorities should take some initiatives to make the service system safe and secure (Milic, 2016). Nowadays internet is the part and parcel of our everyday life. Modern world can be imagining without internet. Now a day, internet has a substantial impact in banking industry (Josanov, 2011). It can make the banking activity easy, cheap and cost effective. Because of the rapid development in the internet system, there is no specific control measure to mitigate the risk.

Technology is giving us so many choices to operate financial activities. It's making the banking sector cost-efficient and fastest. With the help of the internet, Banks are offering different types of online services, such as paying a bill, checking the account balance, opening an account, applying for a loan, and so on. Internet banking is playing a major role. But, nothing is except its demerits. So the risk is always there: hacker always ready with their unethical and illegal ways of making crimes. Entire banking industry is at the risk of online fraudulent activity, which may cause harm to the banks, its clients and it's the entire economy (Worobec, 2021).

Besides the technical advancements, the internet is also creating new challenges for the banking industry. The modern banking system in Bangladesh with the help of the Internet banks started introducing ATMs, Internet banking, SMS, Call center, and Mobile Banking.

In short, maximum research shows that most of the attacks in Internet banking systems target the customers' personal information with the use of social engineering and install malware that compromises a Clint's Internet banking access device and executes bank transactions without the authority of the client. Each bank has typically been found to focus on Information Tech resources on the server, strictly protect network boundaries, and maintain an inner layer of security around the server (Scarfone, 2009). Because of that, the invaders are closely monitoring customers' platforms. So it is essential to create a proper security framework with a view to making a proper safeguard form online malpractice and threat. This study illustrates a security framework that is able to provide proper safeguard and safety in this regard. Like other countries, Bangladesh is also facing security problems. It is not totally free form risk and fraudulent activities. It is essential to create a proper framework to save Bangladesh banking industry from the risk of online fraudulent engineering.

DISCUSSION

This paper pays concentration on client-side susceptibility; this is usually occurred by unauthorized software on devices. Internet banking is the updated medium of communication to serve customers (Danaiata, 2014). Recently the use of the internet in the banking sector of Bangladesh has increased rapidly. Through the internet banking system, banks have made a consequential growth and the number of frauds also has increased. The use of the unsafe application is another customer-side risk. The invaders take the opportunity of using unsafe applications to access or manipulate clients' sensitive information and hack users' application sessions.

Both client-side and server-side manifold-layered security can reduce the risk. It can protect sensitive information from hackers. This research paper unveils internet banking crimes methodology and the limitations of existing security system by construct a manifold-layered security system framework.

The multiple options of Internet banking are a threat to both the bank and the clients. An effective security system is a must to secure their financial and non-financial resources.

Through the legal framework (policies, structure, and process) internet banking security has gained a suitable set of controls. To meet the banking security goal, the manifold-layered security outlook must be initiated, monitored, maintained, implemented, controlled, reviewed, and updated.

Study shows that the internet banking system is emphasizing network security and server-side. (i.e., initiate secure medium between the bank's servers and user's computers)

Most threats on Internet Banking are by stealing user id and data generally termed as social engineering of fishing.

To mitigate the internet security problems, manifold-layered security system should be ensured among the clients and the banks. The Internet Banking security structure and its manifold-layered security systems have been developed and evaluated through an expert evaluation method.

To achieve proper and appropriate Internet banking security goal, the banking industry needs a coordinated and synchronized outlook or point of view of the banks, financial institutions, service providers, authorities, regulatory bodies, customers, and other relevant shareholders to apply encyclopedic chambers (implement properly) of appropriate internet banking security stricture under one framework.

This paper consists of six parts. The very first part introduces the idea by representing an overview of the study history, background and present situation. The second part clarifies the objective of the Research. The third part provides a brief representation of present adjacent literatures in the relevant field, part four analyses the existing limitation or research gap and illustrates solution of such limitation or research gap. Part five makes a details discussion and interpretation of the framework and finally part six (the last part of the paper) illustrates conclusion of the research.

The main objective of the research is to develop a proper security framework with a view to making a proper safeguard form online malpractice and threat. This research paper unveils internet banking crimes methodology and the limitations of existing security system by construct a manifold-layered security system framework. It illustrates an effective security system is a must to secure their financial and non-financial resources. To meet the banking security goal, the manifold-layered security outlook must be initiated, monitored, maintained, implemented, controlled, reviewed, and updated. To mitigate the internet security problems, manifold-layered security system should be ensured among the clients and the banks.

Many works have been done to find out an effective banking system. We would like to mention some of them so that we can do a comparative analysis. From the existing theories, knowledge and ideas of reviewed literature and conducted surveys, this study has been able to draw a new stricture of the framework that is applied in the banking industry for practicing Internet Banking security implementation in a safely manner. Study shows that the internet banking system is emphasizing network security and server-side. (i.e., initiate secure medium between the bank's servers and user's computers). Most threats on Internet Banking are by stealing user id and data generally termed as social engineering of fishing. To mitigate the internet security problems, manifold-layered security system should be ensured among the clients and the banks.

Stawowski has done a study focusing on client-side threats. This study indicates some testing tools such as Apache Tomcat, SSl-explorer etc. This research is similar to ours, though it primary focus was only on testing and checking guidelines and standards for client-side threat. They suggest that, security framework that is able to provide proper safeguard and safety in this regard.

Thorsten and Weigold have done extensive research on Safe and Secure Online Banking Authorization. They conclude that, malpractitioners are always ready with their unethical and illegal ways of making crimes. Entire banking industry is at the risk of online fraudulent activity, which may cause harm to the banks, its clients and it's the entire economy. The main purpose of this study is to explain authentication and authorization threat. It also suggests two organized solutions to create a safeguard form possible future attack although it was a superficial idea to face corresponding attacks. Also there is lack of designing the security structure portrait. There is no analysis for risk and vulnerability from the client-side;

Concludes "potential threats to online banking" in which he identified that at present the amount of harmful malicious software and applications attacking internet banking transactions has enhanced noticeably and represent the idea that malicious harmful applications conduct two kinds of attack (Wüeest, 2005). The internet banking system, banks have made a consequential growth and the number of frauds also has increased. The internet is also creating new challenges for the banking industry. The use of the unsafe application is another customer-side risk. One is vector-local attack, happens on the local computer. The other is remote attack, which re-conduct the victim to another site.

Since this study mainly pointed on characterizing attack vectors as local type attacks or remote type attacks, this may bolster our research work in concentrating prime threats in analyzing the Online banking security risk but wouldn't properly and wholly satisfy the main conclusion of our study.

Gemechu have done a survey investigating the establishment of Electronic-banking and the barriers it identified adoption of Electronic banking are Security risk, luck of trust, lack of regulatory framework and IT expertise. It is not totally free form risk and fraudulent activities. Since they mainly identified the security risk of E-banking is the major reason for less adoption, hence, it will not fulfill our core and specific objectives. It emphasizes that, internet banking system is emphasizing network security and server-side. Through the internet banking system, banks have made a consequential growth and the number of frauds also has increased. The use of the unsafe application is another customer-side risk. The invaders take the opportunity of using unsafe applications to access or manipulate clients' sensitive information.

Moreover, Reba has found that most of the attacks in Internet banking systems target the customers' personal information with the use of social engineering and install malware that compromises a Clint's Internet banking access device and executes bank transactions without the authority of the client. Each bank has typically been found to focus on Information Tech resources on the server, strictly protect network boundaries, and maintain an inner layer of security around the server. The cyber security research and policies are not running appropriately in the absence of specified rules, regulations and policies suggesting formulations of strong security principles.

Entire banking industry is at the risk of online fraudulent activity, which may cause harm to the banks, its clients and it's the entire economy. So it is essential to create a proper security framework with a view to making a proper safeguard form online malpractice and threat. This study illustrates a security framework that is able to provide proper safeguard and safety in this regard. It is essential to create a proper framework to save Bangladesh banking industry from the risk of online fraudulent engineering. The multiple options of Internet banking are a threat to both the bank and the clients. An effective security system is a must to secure their financial and non-financial resources. This research paper unveils internet banking crimes methodology and the limitations of existing security system by construct a manifold-layered security system framework.

Our paper indicates that the holistic manifold-layered and integrated security system for the bank of Bangladesh is inevitable to ensure secured Internet Banking Channels and included the involvement of key stakeholders such as the bank, clients, authority, regulatory bodies, organization and service providers to adopt the suggested manifold-layered security emancipation framework. Through the legal framework (policies, structure, and process) internet banking security has gained a suitable set of controls (Khatri, 2019). To meet the banking security goal, the manifold-layered security outlook must be initiated, monitored, maintained, implemented, controlled, reviewed, and updated.

From the result of the survey and reviewed literature, we can suggest a framework that realizes a holistic approach to IB security for the Bangladeshi banking industry and in that case, we consider the major stakeholders are the government and private banks, authority and regulatory bodies.

Our new version of the Internet Banking security framework is designed in such a way that it's started from the general framework and then gone on proper components structure.

The Internet Banking security structure and its manifold-layered security systems have been developed and evaluated through an expert evaluation method (Desisa, 2013). To achieve proper and appropriate Internet banking security goal, the banking industry needs a coordinated and synchronized outlook or point of view of the banks, financial institutions, service providers, authorities, regulatory bodies, customers, and other relevant shareholders to apply encyclopedic chambers (implement properly) of appropriate internet banking security stricture under one framework.

Moreover, the suggested framework has consists of two layers; Inside layer and Outside layers. Inside layer comprises five major models and fifteen additional sub-components which were denoted during the study as equally important for a holistic manifold-layered security approach. The key models in inside layer that are elements of the Internet Banking security framework guild lined in this study are Internet Banking Client Site Safety Model, Net Banking AAA Model, Net Banking Risk Management Model, Internet Banking Security Defend & Offend Model, and Internet Banking Security Checklist. However, the outside layer comprises national regulatory bodies. Manifold-layered security system to outweigh the limitations currently identified that has been denoted by security experts and analysts through viva-voce and conversation (Luckham 2012). The suggested manifold-layered internet banking security framework, therefore, formed of the attachment of outer-layer security (consist of national fraud protection organization/institutes/department) and inner-layer (consist of bank and client site security) ensuring governance and transparency by combining and coordinating different security layer system from different perspective. From the bank side, this study we suggest proper security approaches and authentication of transaction based on monitoring through SMS,

Phone and Email. All of this should be performed in cooperation and observation from national Financial Intelligence Center (FIC) and Cyber Emergency Response Team (CERT).

The new version of the manifold-layered Internet Banking Security Framework shown in the figure (1) is designed based on net banking security framework and with egg shape anatomy and structure. Though the eggshell security has soft smooth middle part, it has a strong and hard outer shell part that is depicted in manifold-layered Internet Banking Security Framework (ie; Outer-layer part and Inner-Layer part. Once the shell is broken, the whole system is effectively and efficiently being alert.

In this study, it is notified that, banks in Bangladesh initiated internet banking service designing their security steps focused on only the perspective of bank site security and believing and assuming that client site security is on the hand of the client to secure or not. Both client-side and server-side manifold-layered security can reduce the risk. It can protect sensitive information from hackers (Geek 2014). This research paper unveils internet banking crimes methodology and the limitations of existing security system by construct a manifold-layered security system framework. However, it has been detected as the main probable security threat in the field of social engineering and its limitations is customer site security. This paper unveils internet banking crimes methodology and the limitations of existing security system by construct a manifold-layered security system framework. The Internet Banking security structure and its manifold-layered security systems have been developed and evaluated through an expert evaluation method. To achieve proper and appropriate Internet banking security goal, the banking industry needs a coordinated and synchronized outlook or point of view of the banks, financial institutions, service providers, authorities, regulatory bodies, customers, and other relevant shareholders to apply encyclopedic chambers (implement properly) of appropriate internet banking security stricture under one framework.

. This study potentially recommends that Bangladeshi Banking Industry to adopt the manifold-layered and integrated security system in providing net banking services through public network. Inner part-layer of manifold-layered Internet Banking Security system is formed by five major models (Montagna, 2016). Internet Banking Client Site security model, Risk Mitigation Model, Internet Banking Verification, Delegation, Authorization and Auditing model, Internet Banking Protective model, and Internet Banking security verification checklist while the outer-layer consists of the Financial Intelligence Center (FIC) and Cyber Emergency Response Team (CERT). Manifold-layered Internet Banking Security Framework is designed based on net banking security framework and with egg shape anatomy and structure. Though the eggshell security has soft smooth middle part, it has a strong and hard outer shell part. Once the shell is broken, the whole system is effectively and efficiently being alert.

Figure 1. Internet banking security framework (INSF)

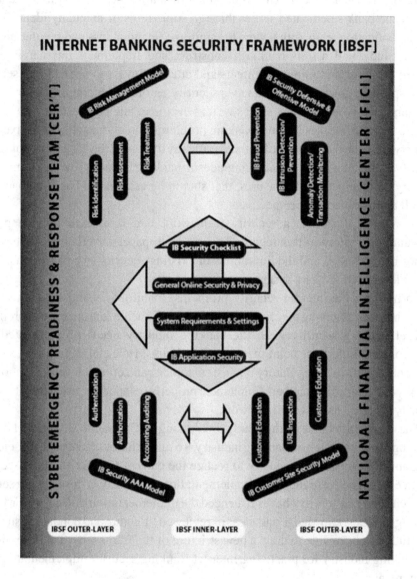

From the reviewed of literature we found that, the security system of the banking sector focused on only the perspective of bank site security. Banking industry needs a coordinated and synchronized outlook or point of view of the banks, financial institutions, service providers, authorities, regulatory bodies, customers, and other relevant shareholders to apply encyclopedic chambers (implement properly) of appropriate internet banking security stricture under one framework. Exceptional program should be developed which will redirect the message sent from intruders to customers (Kok 2016). This program will automatically identify fake URL against the bank's dedicated server through some tools or manually identified by the authentication team with a view to minimize financial loss and reputation loss.

The study will assists banks to construct and implement Internet Banking security to lower and minimize threats and attack relevant to net banking service. To be specific, this study recommends security enforcement and measures should be established based on bank site as well as customer site perspective.

This paper addresses Internet banking problems, threats and attacks the banking industry has been facing now a days, and critically discussed the importance of strong security implementation in the Bangladeshi banking industry by recommending security enforcement and measures, that should be established based on bank site as well as customer site perspective.

This study illustrates a security framework that is able to provide proper safeguard and safety in this regard. This research paper unveils internet banking crimes methodology and the limitations of existing security system by construct a manifold-layered security system framework.

To mitigate the internet security problems, manifold-layered security system should be ensured among the clients and the banks. To achieve proper and appropriate Internet banking security goal, the banking industry needs a coordinated and synchronized outlook or point of view of the banks, financial institutions, service providers, authorities, regulatory bodies, customers, and other relevant shareholders to apply encyclopedic chambers (implement properly) of appropriate internet banking security stricture under one framework.

The prime objective of this study was to suggest a manifold-layered Internet Banking Security system in banking industry. To fulfill this motive, this study selected the Bangladeshi banking industry to realize the current Internet Banking security practice through investigating the implementation of security in this banking service and identifying factors that have influenced the implementation of security. From the existing theories, knowledge and ideas of reviewed literature and conducted surveys, this study has been able to draw a new stricture of the framework that is applied in the banking industry for practicing Internet Banking security implementation in a safely manner.

So this study draws a manifold-layered security system to outweigh the limitations currently identified that has been denoted by security experts and analysts through viva-voce and conversation. The suggested manifold-layered internet banking security framework, therefore, formed of the attachment of outer-layer security (consist of national fraud protection organization/institutes/department) and inner-layer (consist of bank and client site security) ensuring governance and transparency by combining and coordinating different security layer system from different perspective.

Inner part-layer of manifold-layered Internet Banking Security system is formed by five major models. (ie. Internet Banking Client Site security model, Risk Mitigation Model, Internet Banking Verification, Delegation, Authorization and Auditing model, Internet Banking Protective model, and Internet Banking security verification checklist while the outer-layer consists of the Financial Intelligence Center (FIC) and Cyber Emergency Response Team (CERT).

Undoubtedly, this structure of framework makes it possible for the banks to have an appropriate approach to mitigate Internet Banking security risk by realizing the manifold-layered security system

From the bank side, this study we suggest proper security approaches and authentication of transaction based on monitoring through SMS, Phone and Email. All of this should be performed in cooperation and observation from national Financial Intelligence Center (FIC) and Cyber Emergency Response Team (CERT).

Additionally, clients Uniform Resource Locator evaluation instruments should be upgraded for ensuring authenticity. Adequate testing should be done regarding the usability issues.

A program should be developed which can redirect the message sent from intruders to customers if fake URL against the bank's dedicated server to be automatically identified through some tools or manually identified by the authentication team with a view to minimize financial loss and reputation loss.

REFERENCES

Al-Sharafi, M. A., Arshah, R. A., Abu-shanab, E., & Elayah, N. (2020). The Effect of Security and Privacy Perceptions on Customers Trust to Accept Internet Banking Services, An Extension of TAM. *Journal of Engineering and Applied Sciences, 10.* doi:10.3923/jeasci.2016.545

Bultum. (2017). *Adoption of Electronic Banking System in Ethiopia Banking Industry: Barriers and Driver.* Academic Press.

Jolly, V. (n.d.). The Influence of Internet Banking on the Efficiency and Cost Savings for Bank's Customers International. *Journal of Social Sciences and Management, 3*(3), 163–170. doi:10.3126/ijssm.v3i3.157

Khrais, L. T. (2019). Highlighting the Vulnerabilities of Online Banking System. *Journal of Internet Banking and Commerce, 20*(3).

Kleemans, E. R., & Stol, W. P. (2016). Cybercriminal Networks, Social Ties and Online Forums: Social Ties Versus Digital Ties Within Phishing and Malware Networks. *British Journal of Criminology*, 1–19. doi:10.1093/bjc/azw009

Konstantin, B. (2017). Phishing Threat Avoidance Behavior, an Empirical Investigation. *Computers in Human Behavior, 60,* 185–197. https://doi.org/10.1016/j.chb

Peotta & Holtz. (n.d.). A formal Classification of Internet Banking Attacks and Vulnerabilities. *International Journal of Computer Science and Information Technology, 3*(1).

Reba. (2018). *State of Cyber Security in Ethiopia.* Ethiopian Telecommunications Agency, Standards and Inspection Department, Standards Division.

Safeena, R., & Hema, D., & Abdullah. (2019). Customer Perspectives on E-Business Value, Case Study on Internet Banking. *Journal of Internet Banking & Commerce, 15,* 1–8.

Stawowski. (n.d.). *Client side Vulnerability Assessment.* Retrieved from http://www.clico.pl/services/Clientside_Vulnerab ility_Assessment.pdf

Thorsten & Weigold. (n.d.). *Secure Internet Banking Authentication.* Academic Press.

Wong, D., Kuen, H., Loh, C., & Randall, B. (2015). *To trust or not to trust, the consumers dilemma with e-banking.* Academic Press.

Wüeest. (2015). *Threats to Online Banking, Symantec Security Response.* Academic Press.

Chapter 9
Data Privacy Policy:
Cyber Security Implications on Retail Operations

Rabinarayan Patnaik
ⓘ https://orcid.org/0000-0003-2246-0174
Institute of Management and Information Science, India

ABSTRACT

In an era dominated by technology and trade, the business processes have started looking forward to innovations and ever-changing applications. This paradigm shift in the thought processes is not limited to any industry per se. Thus, the cyber practices have developed various tools, practices, as well as avenues for applications in real-time situations. With the advancement of these technological platforms, various gadgets in the form of smart phone, etc. have also complimented to the use of the same. Retail processes like any other business practices have also seen the changes due to these technological interventions. As a process responsible for creating direct customer touch points, retail at its operational level needs to be vigilant about the threats, insecurity, loss of privacy, and challenges coming because of the technological adoptions. Therefore, a systematic and well-designed data privacy policy with all possible components incorporated can lead to a secure environment.

INTRODUCTION

In the ongoing digital world, the information flows at the fastest speed from one source to the other without considering the limits or boundaries of framework. Any individual irrespective of profession or expertise encounters volumes of data

DOI: 10.4018/978-1-6684-3448-2.ch009

be relevant or unnecessary every now and then. Therefore, in such a dynamic environment, the organisations need to take care of the authenticity, relevance and confidentiality of data pertinent to its stakeholders. In order to safeguard the data against any emergencies arising naturally or intentionally, the companies need to have proper facility (be in the form of hardware or cloud) of collection, storage, retrieval as well as usage of data in proper quantity as well in the proper channels. Thus it asks for a systematic configuration of a framework ensuring the privacy of data kept intact which over a period of time translates itself into a policy. This data privacy policy has got various dimensions to consider depending upon industries and individuals it comprises of.

While the security of data and subsequently that of the information is concerned, the prime concerns of 'how much' and 'whose responsibility' need to be answered (Kang, 1998). Thus the data to get quantified and protected asks for cyber interference. The support of cyber data is not limited to this only. In the times of damages or vulnerability to undue theft or counterfeiting, a proper data privacy policy can be of immense help to the organisations. The extent of information related to any individuals (e.g. consumers) can be sometimes dangerous looking into the degree of exposure it gets to the outer world let's say from public to private (Gordon & Loeb, 2002). Mostly the service industries or the business practices like retail operations are coming under such frequent unwanted and unexpected situations because of data breaches and so on. Proper assessment of any type of threats and subsequent mitigation can be analysed for effectiveness of data usage and protection of its privacy (Hoo, 2000).

Coming to the retail operations front, as we understand retailing to be the final stage of any economic activity and operations in a retail framework indicate the front end activity. The very nature of the process comprises the individual as well as intersecting activities of customers, employees, inventories and transactions considered to be the dipstick parameters of store operations. Each of these parameters needs special attention to protect the sensitive characteristics attached to them. For example, the private data of customers as well as employees, the authenticity of stocks/inventories, the secure environment created for payments by both physical and digital modes and so on. The necessity of maintaining privacy and the subsequent security has become more intensified because of the rise in organised retail as well as ecommerce as in these modes of retail operations, the vulnerability of data mishandling and mismanagement naturally becomes more. In this recent decade, the addition of multiple and sophisticated supply chains and logistics modes have created scope for application of technology and asked a robust system of securing the data of products as well as vendors. There will be four key enablers of this digitally enabled retail operations whose privacy will become utmost important.

i)   Organisational structure
ii) IT Infrastructure
iii) Data and Decision
iv) Financial Status

Even there is a significant increase in the online businesses or e-retailing, there is still a substantial business coming from the physical store base privacy and protection of consumer data has been a major concern for the brick and mortar retailing for many reasons containing fraudulent activities in the context of payment through credit/ debit cards to malware affected payment devices used by retailers (Alberts & Dorofee, 2002). Formulating a data privacy policy becomes more important in today's context of retailing because of several natural and system made reasons like customer tracking and so on. Thus it is important to understand the various facets of cyber security in the context of robust retail operations and suggesting a framework containing general guidelines to abort any kind of possible threats to the privacy and security of data points. The present study focuses on several dimensions of these issues and attempts to formulate a framework of policy points.

BACKGROUND

As we are in the transition of a brick and mortar world to click and pay world of retailing, there are many changes which will mark the future of retail process as a whole. Convergence of technology- enabled systems like payments, e-commerce, logistics etc. in retail have started rewriting the business. Customer centricity and collaboration have redefined the way retailing happens worldwide (Deloitte, 2017). There will be tremendous shift in the future of retail operations and maintenance of data security and privacy in various dimensions (Table 1)

Primarily there are two dimensions of any kind of data privacy policy related to cyber security, viz. laying down the standards and protecting the data. These two dimensions are equally applicable to retail operations as well. Before creating a framework of this Data Privacy Policy, there are certain preambles which need to checked and ensured (Figure 1).

Top Management Intervention

This typically includes a note of effective leadership and solid commitment from the top management for smooth implementation of information security management. This should focus on the objectives of privacy and security policy synchronizing with the organizational strategies. This integrates the resources as well as the processes

161

Table 1. Cyber shift in retail operations

Paradigm shift in KRAs (Key Resource Areas)	Intervention of Cyber Data
Precise Customer Base The population based marketing will be moving towards customised propositions thereby value-added services will hold the key.	Segments will become further small and more focused with the use of Artificial Intelligence and experience creation will be based on real time customer data.
Strategic Formats Consumer territory or the trade are will not be definite. Rather the business strategy will be based on reaching far and wide by the uniquely designed delivery systems.	Voluminous data collected by the use of registration and subscription of customer will become the enabler of operational effectiveness.
Experiential Shopping The focus will be shifted from physical store layouts and visual merchandising to building up of digitalized customer experience based on trend and contemporary styles.	Designing digital experience based on customer feedback data on various stages of shopping, e.g. planning, trial and real time purchase.
Payment and Promotion Traditional promotional tools like loyalty card programs etc. and the physical payments at the POS will be made easy by the use of electronic gadgets and advanced apps.	The physical windows for collecting customer data will become more technology based and the entire purchase cycle will be as per the customer data.

Source: compiled by the author

underlying the information privacy and security. It also communicates and promotes the importance of the policy and system related to data and information privacy.

Managing Information Risk

This requires continuous identification, assessment and evaluation of information risks. This will also execute mitigation measures and evaluate the effectiveness of the same in accordance with its efficiency, feasibility and economic aspects. In this process there is a requirement of appointing Information Owners (after due consultation with Business Heads). Within the organizational framework, the Information Owners periodically monitor and implement control measures of all information assets belonging to the company.

Securing Human Resources

Creating a standard for Data Privacy and Security, it's essential that the human resources infused into the organizational set up, must be integrated into the information system framework starting from their prior employment till leaving the organisation. Certain security policy tools like employee engagement, duly signed

Figure 1. Organisational Requirements for Setting up Data Privacy Policy
Source: compiled by the author

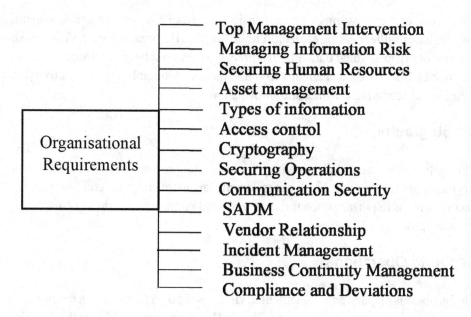

confidentiality agreement (containing proprietary as well as trade information) and so on come in handy.

Asset Management

This process requires identifying and making lists of all types of information assets as cited by various Information Owners. Over a period of time the seriousness and sensitivity of these information must be examined in order to understand the value of these and subsequently safeguard the same against any kind of miscarriage.

Types of Information

This is a kind of requirement for any organization (including retail companies) to create various hierarchy of information depending on the degree of confidentiality required to protect the safety and privacy of the same. This will in other way help the policy makers to conclusively take decisions on certain aspects like cost and feasibility of keeping them.

Access Control

This is one of the most important dimensions to make a secure data environment. This includes authenticating each individual (user) in the organization trying to take the help of organisational data. For example, the users can be given unique IDs and passwords, biometric mechanisms to make them accountable for each activity or theirs while accessing the data and information.

Cryptography

This is typically maintaining security protocols by proper and authorized use of Cryptographic algorithms, key lengths, key management protocols etc. This process becomes more important once the data is shared on various verticals of the same business group.

Securing Operations

The business is planned and implemented vis-à-vis the data points with a focus on the trade secrets and privacy of the same. The IT Heads are responsible for the security of various servers, networks and end points. This needs a continuous monitoring of the entire system and provides safety against threat, vulnerability, and malware and so on. It also effectively carries out change management, logging and monitoring, security analytics and assurance.

Communication Security

This is a multi-dimensional process wherein all kinds of Network communications are protected with right kind of security control levels thereby protecting the information as well as the system. Based on the degree of risks associated with various networks, this also makes a communication security control mechanism at various service levels. This also provides protection while the information exchange happens among different business verticals of the company.

SADM

An acronym for System Acquisition, Development and Maintenance, this implements appropriate security controls at various stages of acquisition, development and maintenance of information. This removes the negative impact of unauthorized and undue access of confidentiality and integrity of privacy.

Vendor Relationship

This is one of the important areas which ensures monitoring and reviewing of access to information provided to vendors. The degree of access and the control mechanism in case of any undue practices are always taken care by proper assessments of the risks associated as well as the class of vendors under consideration.

Incident Management

This calls for creating a framework securing situations or events on time through identifying, documenting as well as recovering the same properly. This framework should work as an enabler for various users like employees, contractors, third party users etc. to understand the various types of data and their subsequent impact on the privacy concerns.

Business Continuity Management

During any crisis or adverse situation, the continuation of business processes should not be hampered. There has to be a mechanism of documenting, implementing and maintaining processes for information privacy and security. This needs to be done in proper intervals to ensure continuity of processes.

Compliance and Deviations

The employees of various functional areas in the organisation or different business verticals of the group must be ensured of security compliance as applicable under the policy considering the level of risk associated with the respective departments or employees. The role of control and audit department in this regard become more important as they need to ensure the operational integrity and subsequently make it actionable in case of deviations. However, there needs to be sufficient and relevant reasons behind deviations and the provision of appropriate control mechanism of the same.

TECHNOLOGICAL TOUCH POINTS

As we have understood the dynamism of data privacy and subsequent protection of the same, we also need to agree to the fact that the environmental changes (to a retail process) in technological innovations and trade practices can continuously challenge and influence the policy as well. On the light of developments in ICT,

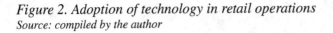

Figure 2. Adoption of technology in retail operations
Source: compiled by the author

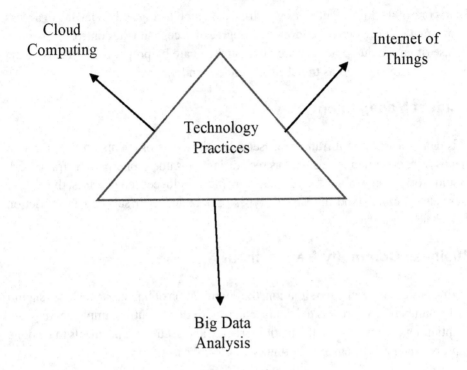

the emerging technologies need to be understood and comprehensively practised for data privacy protection. The big three in the technological world who have been significantly changing the other business practices are equally responsible for the changes in retail operations as well (Figure 2). Use of each of these technologies has got the underlying challenges in the defining the data privacy and subsequent protection of the same (Roberts & Grover, 2012).

Cloud computing

This is typically a kind of technologically enabled service which can be provided to the clients at any time of their demand as well as requirement. Generally, this technology users (for example, the retailers) with connected devices can access the network containing measurable data repository with flexibility. This data can also be shared within various user groups with a proper administration of the same. Currently standing at $150 billion dollar, this cloud computing industry has promises to grow rapidly and having a significant impact on client industries like retail and all. However, there are certain challenges which exist with the use of this technology presently in relation to the data protection. For example, there are less number of legal watchdogs to take care of lapses arising out of the usage of these kinds of services across a bigger geographical territory. Certain countries have also put localized restrictions on the free use of this technology and service obtained and conveyed through cloud in their respective trade areas. The degree of surveillance has also been in the upswing which has triggered the companies to think and act on formulating a broader and more strategic data privacy policy. The other side of these challenges has resulted in a better understanding of the technology and refining the components thereby setting up better and higher standards of cyber security in the years to come.

The Internet of Things

The Internet of Things, popularly abbreviated as IOT is typically a facilitating technology to connect multiple components and devices to the internet for the purpose of data communication. The execution of this technology covers various dimensions like visualization, monitoring, analytics, storage and above all connecting with various networks. The very nature of this technology asks for understanding the process and formulating means to manage the same (for example, the data). The scope of this technology covers applications in the field of security gadgets, various domestic products like automobiles, home appliances, cell phones, personal computers etc. in its current practice typically for the retail operations, the technology supports logistics and supply chain functions. This technology-based industry is growing really fast and can be a game changer for the user industries like retail (for example, in the areas of digital payment, protection form shoplifting and so on) in the years to come as well (Bandyopadhyay & Sen, 2011). However, various studies have shown that the challenges in using this technology are gigantic and the present cyber security legal frameworks are finding it tough to address the issues to the fullest (for example, the challenges coming due to the decrease in consumer confidence related to privacy and security concerns in the connected gadgets and components).

Big Data Analytics

This technological platform helps in understanding various patterns, trend factors as well as associations among several business components. This works on collection and storage of data for future uses. The scope of using this technology has been wide-spread providing solutions to economic and societal problems as well. However, there are certain challenges while adopting and using the technology. The volume of data collected is so high that it creates a real time effort to ensure the privacy of the same. At the same time, certain data sources and data are public in nature and cannot be kept really secure. Along with that the Big Data Analysis certain specific algorithm and decision making tools which are not comprehensive enough to ensure the data transparency while required. Thus it creates a real time problem for the decision makers at the retail operation front and very often at the time of data mining.

Apart from all these, certain other latest technological tools like Augmented Reality can also be handy while maintaining data privacy and creating a framework for this. However, the limitation of these tools is because of the rare usage of the same at the retail operation level. But given the proliferation of increased use of advanced networks and digitally abled innovations in the processes, there is a great promise for these tools to be used in the years to come. Along with these advancements of technology and the application of the same in business processes including retail operations, there will be proportionate challenges in mitigating the risk and augmenting the benefits to the users as well as the organisation as a whole. So the requirement is always creating a benchmark of the same and ensuring the privacy of the data to be protected.

In a retail environment, the technologies adopted have to be used in securing three operational dimensions, viz. 1) Securing the System, 2) Securing the Network and 3) Securing the Data. The processes, product and people configure the retail operation environment. On the other hand, Network refers to all possible networks the company uses starting from LAN and moving to Internet. Data refers to all possible documentable elements which can be collected, stored, analysed and retrieved as and when required for decision making. This can be more visible and prominent in the retail operations involving the chain of stores. Therefore, the emerging and recent changes in technological environment must be compatible to the organizational policies and goals of securing private data.

Point of Sale (POS)

In organised form of store based retailing, POS is a common junction, where the technology based systems help in recording sales based information. Due to the compulsory use of bar codes various retail organisations irrespective of their size and products offering are taking the help that coded number to ascertain the product specifications. The laser scanners are used to read the bar code on the product for recording the data related to product and transaction. In addition, at the POS or more specifically EPOS (Electronic Point of Sale), the recorded information can also be printed to produce the receipt of the transaction. This entire exercise is controlled by the centralized system of the store and the privacy of data related to promotional planning, inventory management, and advertisement expenses and so on becomes really important (Jones, 1985). This system apart from transactions can be equally helpful in creating a data repository of customers as the transaction details contain relevant customer information. In the recent times, many retailers have started using EPOS systems in combination with technologies related to self-service. This has led to the focus on data privacy more intensified as the transactions are solely made by the customers with the data of theirs as well the transactions being transmitted automatically. So if properly used, this EPOS can help retail operations being conducted more precisely and efficiently with proper analysis of customer data stored in high volumes.

Gadgets, Apps and Digital Payments

Almost for more than a decade, the electronic gadgets mostly in the form of smartphones have changed the shopping styles of customers. Packed with various latest technologies the smartphone industry has created several interactive points between the retailer and the customers. The customers are able to take the help of several features like browsing, messaging, editing, using video camera and so on. With the inclusion of several Apps, these gadgets have further changed the shopping behaviour of customers to a visible extent. The customers are given the opportunity to compare the pricing, offers and reviews and so on because of these advents (Taylor & Levin, 2014). However, with these advancements, the flow of data and information has almost crossed all boundaries. The retail operations have become so much sophisticated and most importantly so much visible to the outer world, the retailers need to do all possible provisions to safeguard the confidentiality of data in such a volatile situation.

Adding to this fact is the payment systems enabled through these Apps. Due to the digital payment processes, the customers' payments are following a wireless communication technology which asks for significant security of data in terms of banking and individual details. Use of QR codes has added to this technical process of retail payments. As QR codes contain information like location, web-links etc., the use of this by scanning the codes transmit the information to a different place and through a different route. By the use of QR codes, the customers can be easily aware of various trade practices of retailers like that of country or place of origin of products, thereby making the information sensitive for the retailers to protect. The review, rating and sharing of information of competing brands have become almost a regular practice of customers. Though the benefits of this process are numerous, like paying with due reviews and analysis of prices and all, the dangers of misuses of technology still remain a concern. Because of its robustness, this can also add to the cost and maintenance budget (in regard to the IT systems) for the retailer. Appropriate security policies can act as a safeguard (to retailers and customers) for such technology enabled process and at the same time can put the retailer on an advantageous position over the peers, e.g. creating a trust factor for retailers (Tarjan *et al.*, 2014).

RFID Tags

An acronym for Radio-frequency identification, RFID has been extensively used in the retail operation in tracking and with the help of a microchip, reader and an antenna. This technological tool is of great use to the retailers for locating an object as well as collecting data related to price, transaction date etc. These tags can be used for some protective processes like Electronic Article Surveillance (Roberts, 2006). However, as this can be used at the time of sharing information among various components like system and other tools like goods, vehicles and so on, the sensitiveness of using human factor creates a scope for data privacy. At the time of updating, the user must be very much responsible about information related to counts, item number, destination etc. The data security even becomes more important at the time of distortion or natural destruction of the tag by moisture etc.

E-Commerce

Again in the latest form of data security importance is because of shopping through online space. The shopping is done via electronic mode taking the help of mobile devices (a laptop/tablet/smartphone/personal computers). Due to the requirement of customer's location and requirements to start the process, this form of retail operations facilitate the same information to various stakeholders like, the vendor, the e-commerce site and the logistics provider. Though there is no physical involvement of customers at the shopping place, the information becomes moves in bulk and in authentic way (Burt & Sparks, 2003). The necessity of protecting the information becomes more essential again because of the payment made by the customers be it any form, COD (Cash on Delivery) or Debit/Credit cards/through Net Banking. The safety and security of the financial transactions need to be ensured. In addition to that the cookies (small files and programs) tracing the customers (visiting the webpage) are a threat to the privacy, more specifically when the cookies are responsible for collection of customer information (third party cookies) by the company. Very sensible information related to the geographical presence, income etc. can also be traced further by this mechanism (Kaplan, 2012).

PROLIFERATION OF SOCIAL MEDIA

The traditional or mass media has been slowly and steadily getting replaced by social media quite recently thanks to the various interface points. This media makes the things go viral at the fastest speed possible in different shared ideas, opinions, writings, events and so on. The retailers are no exception to these as being a business entity the retailers also take the help of different tools used traditionally, e.g. blogs, podcasts, social sites etc. for various reasons of theirs like product launching, promotional offers, celebrations, achievements, customer connect programs and so on (Drury, 2008).

In the last decade or so various social media companies have started growing at an exceptional rate thanks to the increase in the active internet users. Certain prominent social media sites like Facebook, YouTube, WhatsApp, Instagram etc. have been attracting active users over few years and are ranked as global leaders in the field of social media (Figure 3). The biggest benefit of these using these media sites by various business houses lies in the fact that these sites are capable enough to create a powerful interface for the companies to connect, communicate as well as start conversation on various business values as well as uniqueness of theirs with the customers and prospects alike (DREAMGROW Report, 2021). At the same time retailers can connect with various other stakeholders of the company like the vendors, business associates and so on. Creating a relationship and maintaining the same over the social media becomes easy for a retailer. However, all these processes sound encouraging, the pitfalls remain there in the form of data and information duplicity and hacking. At the same time any lapse in the company brand management and public relationship can backfire if not put and maintained in almost a virtual or a digital platform. As the information can be easily made available and accessible by the social media sites, the companies must have a protection technique to secure the privacy of customers, employee etc. information from being tracked unduly by the competitors with the use of advanced technology. In addition to that the anti-campaigns (as perceived by the respective governments) created by certain media sites in the name of liberty of expressions (as in the case of Twitter refusing to comply with the regulations of Indian Government) might act as detrimental to the popularity of sites and thereby can cause the reputation of the subscribes (both buyers and sellers) as well. There can be instances wherein the tussle arising between the privacy policies maintained by the social media platforms and the localized rules of cyber security for example the recent case of WhatsApp challenging the customer protection rules of Government of India. Therefore, the retail companies before deciding their effectiveness in customer creation and retention processes being promoted on social media sites need to evaluate the pros and cons of the same.

Figure 3. Leading social media sites and the active users
Source: compiled by the author

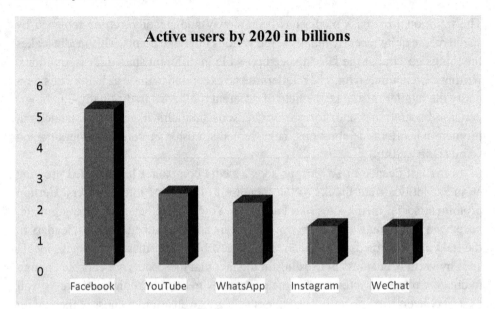

STANDARD FORMULATION

In every retail organisation, the privacy and security of personal information covers various stakeholders like employees, customers as well as vendors. Different functions/tasks to safeguard the privacy of theirs can be done as per the following flowchart.

Task 1: Identification of organisational privacy objectives (This will include define personal information and underlining the level of importance each data element carries)

Task 2: Collection of Data (This has to be done in a fair and legal manner under the due knowledge of the source and provider)

Task 3: Obtaining Consent (While collecting, using and subsequently disclosing of any personal data the prior or spontaneous consent from the information provider needs to be taken)

Task 4: Notification (Proper and timely notice needs to be sent to the concerned stakeholders about the privacy policy and procedures of the company in regard to the data security and so on)

Task 5: Data Warehouse (There has to be provisions of storage of data components in regard to its importance and privacy)

Task 6: Disclosure (Upon the prior consent of individuals, the personal information to any third-party can be provided or disclosed)

Task 7: Framework Maintenance (Creation of a framework keeping in mind the objectives of data security and privacy ensures practices, standards and policies at place. It asks for protection from unauthorized access and review at proper intervals)

Task 8: Training and Updating (From time to time to ensure adequate understanding of privacy requirements, principles and implications, there has to be arrangement of trainings and workshops related to the same targeted to various stakeholders)

POLICY FRAMEWORK AND GUIDELINES

With due identification of the requirement and applications of data privacy, the retailers must come up with a framework which constitutes several components for systematic construction and subsequent maintenance of the same. Broadly, it can be containing the following procedures to make a systematic framework.

1) Information Coverage

Mostly personal in nature, the framework is configured on the volume and nature of information with due identification can be collected, stored, transmitted or processed. This can consist of password, financial information like bank account, credit card etc. This can also include information related to physical as well as mental conditions, sexual orientation, medical records, and biometric information and so on.

2) Information Collection

To be used for specific purposes, minimum information required are generally collected which falls under the framework. This has to be as per the requirement of the company. For example, in case the company requires the list of vendors providing wedding collections, this should be collected keeping an eye the reason and the time horizon to use the information. The information collected must be communicated to the user in the organisation itself for maximum benefits, with the authenticity checked before transferring the same.

3) Information Correction

While there is a requirement of updating or modifying certain information, there has to be provisions of access by the System Administrator or any one authorised to do the same. This will also remove certain personal and sensitive information raised by any individual from different places, like company intranet and so on.

4)   Information Processing

In order to comply with the legal procedures and mandatory requirements, the framework should be processed in the way the data has been stored and retained for that specific time period only. The information assets must be ensured of obtaining managerial, technical, operational as well as physical security control measures. In order to ensure the speed of data processing these cleaning and maintaining measures must be done and evaluated periodically.

5)   Information Disclosure

The policy must framework must have an arrangement of disclosing only those type of information which had been collected for the same reason. Before disclosing the degree of legal and statutory requirement of the disclosure must be evaluated and monitored. For example, while passing the information related to vendors to the peer group of vendors, it must be examined the pros and cons of the same.

Thus the requirements of several guidelines for users can create a framework for Data Privacy Policy and can cover the various information assets and safeguard of the same. Primarily this information contains the security and privacy aspects of all possible stakeholders and company dimensions.

Password Security

- Logging on must be done by using own user ID and Password only and shall be accountable for all actions performed on company's information systems using their credentials.
- Strong & complex and not easily guessable passwords must be set to login to the corporate applications.
- None share their passwords, PINs/OTP, etc. that protect company's information systems with anyone else and shall not write them down in easily discoverable place.
- Company's domain credentials (username and passwords) for any other online/public accounts must not be used. Using unique passwords for different accounts is a preferred choice.
- Multifactor authentication for applications (wherever applicable) using the own mobile number or email ID address through own mobile devices needs to be practised.

Anti-Virus

- None should disable the installed anti-virus software or change the settings of the scheduled scans.
- Installing any other virus other than the company approved Anti-virus on the system by the users must be prohibited.
- It has to be ensured that the licensed anti-virus installed on the systems and is kept updated with latest signatures.

Internet Usage

- Access to Internet shall be allowed through organisational channels to all users. Users must not bypass the enterprise proxy or use proxy avoidance websites to browse the Internet.
- Using the internet for the purposes of harassment, abuse, anti-social or illegal activities should not be entertained.
- None should violet any copyright or license agreement by downloading or distributing protected or copyrighted material.
- Illegal or unethical activities including gambling, accessing obscenity material or misinterpreting the company policies should not be permitted.
- Downloading and installing unauthorized, pirated or copyrighted software from the Internet need to be stopped.
- None should offer opinions on behalf of the company unless they are specifically authorized to do so.
- Clicking ads or pop-ups on the online websites should be restricted as these could be malicious.
- Using online text format converters such as PDF-to-doc converters, to change the format of confidential files should be avoided.
- In case where such misuse of internet is detected, user should be solely responsible and accountable and may face disciplinary action.
- Users should ensure that they do not install or integrate unknown or unnecessary browser extensions as it may lead to deploying spying tools, malware in the systems.

Email and Messaging Usage

It is the users having a company Email/messaging account who should be liable for the content of message originating from their account within or outside the company.

- It has to be ensured that the company provided email/messaging facility is used only for business purposes. Personal use is permitted where such use does not affect the individual's business performance, is not detrimental to the company in any way, not in breach of any terms and condition of employment and does not place the individual or the organisation in breach of statutory or other legal obligations.
- The organisation reserves the rights to monitor emails/messaging activity of users.
- None should send chain or spam mails to other users using their company/ official email accounts
- Emails and messages should not be sent with any defamatory, offensive, racist or obscene remarks/content from the corporate Email ID.

Safeguards against Phishing Attacks

- Every user needs to verify the sender's address for all emails originated from an external domain (which has an external tag).
- Users need to ensure that they do not click on links or open attachments in email sent by unknown senders.
- None should disclose sensitive information such as passwords, bank account information, etc. by clicking on a link provided in an email from unknown sender.

Usage of Devices

- The privileged rights such as local admin, USB, MTP, rights, privileged Internet access, etc. provided for the business purpose on the users' official laptops should not be misused.
- Users have to ensure that they do not modify or remove pre-installed security functionality or alter hardware / software configurations, operating system settings or any application installed on their desktops / official laptops.
- The security software/agents installed on the devices for performing unethical activities should not be bypassed.
- Unauthorized, illegal, pirated, illicit or obscene content or personal content on official laptops should not be stored.
- While travelling additional physical security of the devices that holds information must be ensured.
- Theft or unauthorized access to the company managed devices shall be reported to the appropriate team immediately.

- In case of a suspected security incident, the company should always reserve the right to confiscate the device for forensics investigation purpose.

Social Media

- None should reveal confidential or proprietary information, trade secrets, or any other material of the company on social media, comment section websites or on blogs.
- It should be avoided posting photographs clicked at work areas & sensitive information processing facilities on social media.
- It has to be made clear that expressing own beliefs and/or opinion in blogs shall explicitly mention that the statement is personal and do not present the view of the company.

Maintaining a Clear Desk and Screen

- It is required that users must lock their systems when the system is left unattended.
- None should leave confidential information on their desks.
- Company business confidential information should be securely stored in a locked cabinet when not in use.
- Users must need to prevent company information on their screen from being visible to unauthorized users.

DATA PRIVACY LEVEL AT RETAIL OPERATIONAL LEVEL: AN ILLUSTRATION

A general practice of data security and privacy at the store operation level of any retail process can be containing various components. A flow chart of the same is given in Figure 4.

At the *Protection Zone – I,* there are several windows which come into picture at the operational levels of any retail process, for example POS Window, Inventory Window and Consumable Window.

POS Window as the name suggests is responsible for all types of transactions and payments done and recording of the same. It also ensures the transmission of the same to processing window of the data point.

Inventory Window records all types of stocks, their receiving and reordering details. It also keeps a track of the vendors and manufacturers as well as other stock details. The information stored here is directed to the processing window of the store.

Figure 4. Data privacy process at store operational level
Source: compiled by the author

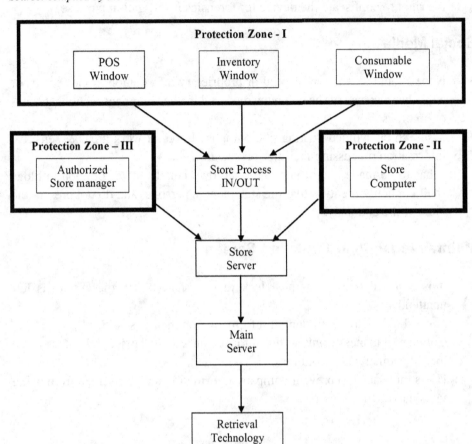

Consumable Window ensures the products which have been either sold off or meant or ready to be sold. It stores the information of those merchandises which the retailer is asking from the entire lot to make a sale. The information like other windows pass on to the processing place as well.

At the *Protection Zone – II,* the respective store manager only has got the authorization to use and access data at the store server. In fact, the information contained at the store manager's scope itself is protected and secured as the value of these information is very strategic for the retailer.

At the *Protection Zone – III,* the store computer placed at the store itself has been disconnected from various devices for any kind of information retrieval and protected from other systems by the use of firewall and so on.

The flow of information is from the store server to the main server from where subsequently it is retrieved as and when necessary by the use of certain tools like Tableau and others. However, the retrieval process is authenticated at the head office and the operational levels don't have the capacity to do it at their own capacity. Of course based on specific requests and requirement only the store level people may get the permission to do that. The situations like this are very few in nature.

CONCLUSION

It is quite transparent that the retail operations require complex yet productive activities required at the several customer touch points. Because of this very nature, the technology perspectives at several areas of the business process require to be properly and systematically configured be in the processes like e-commerce, digital payments and customer tracking and so on. As we are on the crossroads of a paradigm shift in terms of mere transaction to experience building up process, the technology becomes an integral part in successful trade practice. Due to the intervention of technology, the various functional areas like supply chain and logistics, marketing and pricing etc. have been facilitated and made really efficient. Even with the increase in competition in retail business and models, the adoption of advanced and updated technology has created scope for innovations and development.

To make the technology infrastructure work, it is necessary to have a sound data privacy policy wherein all possible customer touch points along with the sensitive information related to other stakeholders as well as trade practices can be protected. It requires the changes and openness of various governments to support and formulate cyber laws for protection and privacy of several consumer and trade data. A sound policy will always be a bonus for the businesses, individuals as well as investors for adoption of newer and appropriate technology. It is required to create consensus among the nations, states and continents for creating enough flexibility to accommodate changes in technology and prepare the traders and business houses for the next big things.

Coming to the technology practices at the operational level, the employees and organization as a whole need to learn the consideration of accountability for effectiveness of any policy for that sense be it technological or non-technological. It becomes more essential when we talk about cyber security. The users must be learning the tenets of cyber changes and updating their information level before ensuring the effective and efficient practice of the same. Though it's a challenge till now for ensuring accountability at the operational level of retail space because of its very nature, the companies are giving their best to make it happen.

One more aspect which needs to be secured is the intellectual property rights related to the ownership of brands, labels as well as offerings. Due to the increased dependence of retailers on their own label popularly called as private labels, the data specific to these dimensions need to be protected at the highest level. This in turn will help the retailers to have an edge over their competitors and maintain a sustainable growth in the years to come.

A secured data privacy policy will contain all possible dimensions like gap in the technology, detection of nature of threats to data, existing legal and cyber protection available, impact of lapses on the success of trade practices and so on. Thus a framework will be of immense help in this regard provided enough real time research and study has been done on this time and again.

REFERENCES

Alberts, C., & Dorofee, A. (2002). *Managing information security risks: the OCTAVE Approach*. Addison Wesley.

Bandyopadhyay, D., & Sen, J. (2011). Internet of Things: Applications and Challenges in Technology and Standardization. *Wireless Personal Communications*, *58*(1), 49–69. doi:10.100711277-011-0288-5

Burt, S., & Sparks, L. (2003). E-commerce and the retail process. A review. *Journal of Retailing and Consumer Services*, *10*(5), 275–286. doi:10.1016/S0969-6989(02)00062-0

Deloitte & Indian Chamber of Commerce. (2017). *Disruptions in Retail through Digital Transformation Reimagining the Store of the Future*. Author.

Dreamgrow Report. (2021). *The 15 Biggest Social Media Sites and Apps*. Available at: https://www.dreamgrow.com/top-15-most-popular-social-networking-sites/

Drury, G. (2008). Opinion piece. Social media: Should marketers engage and how can it be done effectively? *Journal of Direct, Data and Digital Marketing Practice*, *9*(3), 274–277. doi:10.1057/palgrave.dddmp.4350096

Gordon, L., & Loeb, M. (2002). The economics of information security investment. *ACM Transactions on Information and System Security*, *5*(4), 438–457. doi:10.1145/581271.581274

Hoo, K. S. (2000). *How much is enough? A risk management approach to computer security*. Retrieved October 25, 2006. Available at: http://iis-db.stanford.edu/pubs/11900/soohoo.pdf

Jones, P. (1985). The Spread of Article Numbering and Retail Scanning in Europe. *Service Industries Journal, 5*(3), 273–279. doi:10.1080/02642068500000042

Kang, J. (1998). Information Privacy in Cyberspace Transactions. *Stan. Law Review, 1193*, 1198.

Kaplan, A. M. (2012). If you love something, let it go mobile. Mobile marketing and mobile social media 4x4. *Business Horizons, 55*(2), 129–139. doi:10.1016/j.bushor.2011.10.009

Roberts, N., & Grover, V. (2012). Leveraging Information Technology infrastructure to facilitate a firm's customer agility and competitive activity: An empirical investigation. *Journal of Management Information Systems, 28*(4), 231–270. doi:10.2753/MIS0742-1222280409

Tarjan, L., Šenk, I., Tegeltija, S., Stankovski, S., & Ostojic, G. (2014). A readability analysis for QR code application in a traceability system. *Computers and Electronics in Agriculture, 109*, 1–11. doi:10.1016/j.compag.2014.08.015

Chapter 10
Cyber Security at the Heart of Open Banking:
An Existing and Futuristic Approach

Lopamudra Hota

(iD) https://orcid.org/0000-0003-0581-9819
National Institute of Technology, Rourkela, India

Dhruba Charan Hota
Maharaja Bir Bikram College, India

ABSTRACT

During the last year, the pandemic prompted a heavier reliance on technology, as well as the adoption of interconnected devices and hybrid work settings. As a result, we are more vulnerable to cyber-attacks than ever before. The chapter introduces open banking and cyber security concepts briefly, presenting the reasons for rising of open banking. An insight to open banking in India is also presented. In India, the non-banking financial companies are intermediaries responsible for open banking and customer consent management. The trend of open banking systems is depicted from recent years. A short description of various threats and key security measures are discussed. Further, the need and implementation of cyber security in open banking are elaborated. Finally, future perspectives and research challenges are described to extend work on cyber security mechanisms in open banking.

INTRODUCTION

The advent of open banking has created a playing arena for FinTechs and other

DOI: 10.4018/978-1-6684-3448-2.ch010

financial service providers. With open banking, clients and providers can build more secure and convenient relationships. With the emergence of 'open banking,' which lets third-party financial service providers access consumer banking, transaction, and other financial information from banks and Non-Banking Financial Company (NBFCs) through Application Programming Interfaces (APIs), this latest trend in financial technology is catching on rapidly. This innovation offers several advantages, but it also entails a high level of risk since a vast amount of data must be shared and traded. In addition, the Covid pandemic has facilitated tremendous growth in financial technology in India over the past few years (Baret et al., 2020). UPI reportedly handled 4.3 lakh crores worth of transactions in January 2021, compared to 2.1 lakh crores in January 2020, illustrating the need to build a robust banking system that is open, efficient, and secure. The use of technology is extensive in every aspect of life, from education to real estate to travel. Apps, UPI, card transactions, etc., are becoming increasingly popular with banks, as well (Thomas & Chatterjee, 2017). Online banking was initially used for making and receiving payments, etc., but since the pandemic began, more and more people have taken to online/card banking systems in place of cash and cheque.

Further technological changes will undoubtedly drive the future of banking. 'Digital' banking is the way of the future. Currently, open banking serves 3-4 million customers and is expected to extend by 46 percent by the end of 2026 (Puppala, n.d.). In addition to powering FinTechs both nationally and internationally, it's on the rise. This is being referred to as the fintech revolution. Technology has changed the way we bank in the last 10 years. It is likely; however, that banking will be entirely digital by 2030. In the banking industry, APIs aren't new. They're used just like any other tool to delegate tasks to applications; however, they are a brand-new pathway for innovation since banks worldwide allow licensed third parties access to their APIs. The open banking module has already been adopted by many banks, such as Kotak Mahindra, SBI, ICICI, HDFC, and the country is now slowly adapting to the new technology (Premchand & Choudhry, 2018).

What exactly is Open Banking?

In open banking, third-party financial services have access to user data on transactions, banking, and other economic activities with the user's consent. Consumer activity data can be acquired from banks and financial institutions and shared via application programming interfaces (APIs) (Zachariadis & Ozcan, 2017). By allowing third parties to create tailored products and services that cater to customers' needs, open banking is set to drive serious innovation in the banking industry. It is generally believed that open banking will ensure an exceptional customer experience as it reshapes the competitive landscape. Financial service companies could use valuable customer data to target them with financial services, gather aggregated data to create segmented marketing campaigns, and assist with switching customers from one bank to another (Brodsky & Oakes, 2017). Despite this, it is imperative for banks and financial institutions, and third parties that adopt open banking to approach security from the very beginning.

Data breaches and human error are two of the primary risks associated with open banking (Mansfield-Devine, 2016). A data breach could occur, affecting the bank whose data has been shared with the consumer if the APIs of the third-party providers fail to meet security requirements. A third-party company's web or mobile application may contain vulnerabilities that hackers can exploit to conduct fraudulent activity. For example, hackers may pose as an individual user and request fake payments. Many individuals are unaware of the impact of their personal choices on their data security. Cyber-attacks are most often targeted at individuals, and 81% of them target weak or duplicate passwords. With 61% of users using the same password for all accounts, attacking data across many different digital locations is significantly easier. Through the Open Banking API (application program interface), third-party providers can access financial data. This helps to improve financial services for consumers [6].

Additionally, it allows companies to offer more tailored services and help leverage the power of fintech innovations and customer insights. Financial regulators and national authorities have acknowledged the need for financial data exchange via digital medium. Using customer permission, data can be collected and used to reduce system inefficiencies. As a result, new product and service models can be developed. As a result, digital applications that facilitate faster and more manageable payments have been built with this data.

SOME REASONS FOR THE RISE OF OPEN BANKING

Open-banking is growing at a breakneck pace since 2020, due to COVID outbreak and contact-less service. Figure 1 depicts a trend in rise of open-banking since 2020 and in years to come.

Escalating Customer's Expectation

Rising customer expectations have primarily driven finance industry innovations. Consumers expect service that is available 24x7. Innovative solutions can be provided at every stage of a user's journey. A seamless transactional journey can also be provided. In exchange for customized service, customers are able to trade personal data. Customer loyalty and trust can be increased by providing real value in return

Figure 1. Rise of trend in open-banking
(Data-source: eMarketer, March 2021)

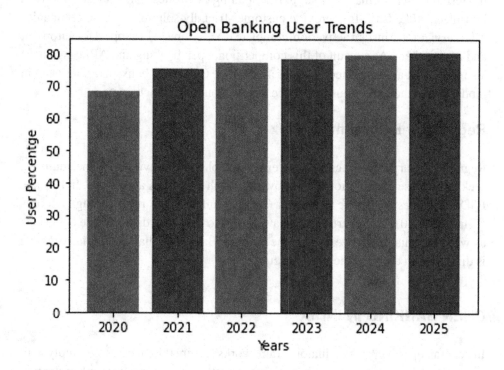

for customer data. According to a recent study, 48% of customers expect banks to provide them with product information after their actions on the app or website. Customer accessibility is also a necessity. 15% of banking customers prefer to do their banking on a mobile device, according to a PwC survey (Drigă & Isac, 2014). Banking and financial services are expected to be offered on these apps for these customers. An array of services can be offered, from fully-automated dashboards to real-time transaction status updates.

Fintech Competition

The existence of fintech providers is understood to be impossible without banks. These companies serve as intermediaries between banks and fintech firms (He et al., 2020). These firms enhance financial services through technology. Technology advances, however, will inevitably increase customer expectations. However, corporate banking solutions do not provide customer-friendly processes for bulk payments and are based on outdated systems. Offline processes and bank visits may be part of corporate banking solutions.

Furthermore, there might be technical limitations since they might not support modern browsers or may only support uploading excel files. The services provided by fintech's like Cash-free provide customer-friendly solutions. These companies offer services like instant activation, complete KYC online, API support for autopilot, and many others. As a result of this competition, open banking and API usage have also increased among fintech players and banks. Currently, banks are interested in modernizing their solutions to be able to reach out to more customers.

Regulatory Environment Flux

Regulations vary widely across different geographies, as is evident. Some countries seek to increase competition and innovation, such as the UK and China. In Europe, PSD2 regulates electronic payments. The EU enforces the rules through accords (Petrović, 2020). Third parties may have access to customer data in these countries, as well. In India, it is governed by the Reserve Bank of India. The initiative taken is discussed in detail in the below section.

OPEN BANKING IN INDIA

In general, open banking regulatory frameworks require third parties to comply with privacy and disclosure requirements, license or authorize third parties, and implement third party access to customer-permitted data. Additionally, many frameworks contain provisions on data sharing and reselling, using data for purposes beyond the initial consent of the client, and the possibility of third parties being compensated for sharing their data. In addition to expectations about data storage and security, open banking frameworks may contain requirements.

Open Banking in India has started with creating an intermediary, which will be responsible for managing customer consent. Such intermediaries can operate as NBFCs. The Reserve Bank of India announced in September 2016 that a new licensed entity called Account Aggregator (AA) had been created, enabling it to consolidate information about a customer spread across financial institutions. AA is a middleman between Financial Information Providers (FIP) like banks, banks companies, non-banking financial companies, asset management companies, depository participants, insurance companies, pension funds, etc., and Financial Information Users (FIUs). Applications Programming Interfaces (APIs) facilitate the exchange of information (Scraping, n.d.).

Appropriate agreements and authorizations bind the customer, AA, and financial information providers before transferring such information to them. The aggregator may not store or use any data other than that which is required to perform its functions.

Figure 2. Cyber-security threats in open-banking

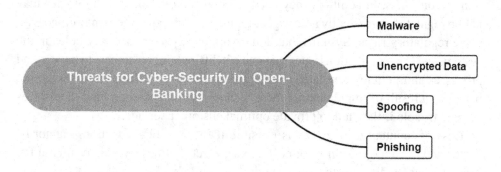

Account Aggregators are prohibited from engaging in any other activity, primarily to protect customers' interests, except for adhering to explicit and robust data security and grievance redressal measures.

RISKS FACED IN DIGITAL TRANSACTIONS

The objective of financial institutions' digital strategy is to ensure customer satisfaction while optimizing resources. Vendors like technology and software companies are outsourced to ensure customer satisfaction. Financial activities are ultimately managed by on-premises financial institutions or external organizations, both under their direct control. The financial institutions must ensure security, privacy, data governance, and organizational integrity are considered when selecting vendors for outsourcing services (Gozman et al., 2018). Some of the threats of open-banking is presented in figure 2.

In order to better manage various operational and security risks, financial institutions need to place adequate architecture and security protocols. Institutional risk can result in investment losses for banks and inefficient service for customers due to an inappropriate system design or technology. The popularity of online transactions can result in increased fraud and account takeover risks by making identity verification more difficult. In addition, financial institutions must keep updating their systems and train their personnel regularly to keep up with the rapid changes in the technology landscape to avoid exposing any gaps in their security system. It is the role of experienced institutions to make such a vision a reality. While low market barriers encourage innovation, they also place enormous responsibility on novice banks to reduce significant financial crime risks.

As part of their effort to digitize, banks use APIs, biometrics, AI, machine learning, Robo advisory, and blockchain to enhance their services. In addition, financial institutions are implementing open banking initiatives to facilitate faster transaction times. In addition, they need to be aware that these technologies may not be regulated consistently across geographies, so adopting them may come with some regulatory risks. Systems that don't work as expected, security holes in the system, and communication issues that make it difficult for customers to understand processes and policies can damage bank trust as well as a result in losses for the bank. As a result of implementing these technologies, banks may find themselves in legal trouble if they fail to provide optimal customer service.

Loss of reputation for banks is possible if these critical functions cannot be performed or diverge from what customers expect. Ultimately, this results in the loss of either funding, customers, or both. As mobile banking continues to expand, consumers will likely download unsecure third-party applications, use unsafe wireless networks, and click on links on their mobiles or emails that will invite trouble. They may even lose complete control of their mobile devices. The behavior leaves fraudsters with several vulnerabilities to exploit (Lynn et al., 2020). As more banks and financial firms move to digital, managing such risks has become critical to avoid being crushed by the competition in the second wave of the pandemic.

While digital banking is not without risks, it does allow for geographical expansion, perhaps even beyond national boundaries. Banks and financial institutions have a great opportunity here, but it is not without risk. A handful of factors exacerbate the above-mentioned legal, operational, and credit risks associated with cross-border business. Certain national laws and jurisdiction ambiguities may exist in certain countries. An overseas service provider can cause incorrect transaction processing, compromise the integrity of data, violate the privacy of customers, and otherwise expose the bank to any number of risky transactions. Considering customer applications from another country is complex, and the pandemic has made credit risks even more evident.

CHALLENGES FACED BY OPEN BANKING

Open banking can provide consumers with access to financial data and services while reducing some costs for financial institutions. The risks that might apply to open banking include:

Data privacy and security risks: In open banking frameworks, losses or theft of personal data can result from poor security measures, data protection violations, money laundering, or terrorist financing concerns. A strong data protection and privacy law should therefore precede a large-scale adoption of open banking frameworks. Data should be anchored in ownership rights, and its use should be governed by consent. Additionally, they should set limits on third-party use and down-streaming of data to third parties as well as the resale of that data. Indian law has already ushered in this development by introducing the Personal Data Protection Bill, 2019 (Datwani & Raman, 2020). By establishing a Data Protection Authority, the bill aims to protect the personal information of individuals.

Liability of customers: Without explicit arrangements for resolving customer grievances and for limiting a customer's liability in case of error or fraud, open banking frameworks are likely to remain unacceptably proprietary. Consequently, local governments should consider enacting laws that address the issue of third-party access to customer data. The RBI issued a Charter of Customer Rights in December 2014 that enumerates rights such as those to privacy and grievance redress. Unless they have provided the financial services provider with specific consent or the law requires such information to be provided or for a mandated business purpose, customers' personal information should be kept confidential (Stiefmueller, 2020).

Operational and Cybersecurity Risks: The use of open banking architectures, which entails enhanced data sharing, increases the potential for cyber frauds. In addition to giving customers unfettered access to all of their banking data, such as transactions and balances, the open API may also pose a series of serious cybersecurity threats. When financial institutions suffer losses from cyber events, they would be obligated to compensate customers. As well as account hacking, fraud, data breaches, and denial of service attacks, API use may cause operational and cyber security issues among institutions (Mohammed, 2015).

Reputational risk and compliance: Compliant Banking poses extreme responsibilities in terms of ensuring compliance with all applicable laws and regulations governing privacy and prudential regulations. While open banking extends vistas of traditional banking and has unique opportunities, it also poses extreme responsibilities with respect to compliance. A third-party service provider risks fines, penalties, or punitive damages resulting from supervisory actions and private settlements based on omissions or commissions.

Grievance Amendments: The open banking model makes it more difficult to assign responsibility for complaints due to the involvement of more parties and intermediaries. The national authorities may find it difficult to provide adequate levels of protection to the customers if the regulations governing customer grievance redressal are not updated to consider open banking business models. In January 2019, the Reserve Bank of India introduced a new Ombudsman Scheme for Digital Transactions in India. In recent years, the Ombudsman Scheme for Digital Transactions (OSDT) has seen an increase in complaints related to the adoption of digital banking (Pazarbasioglu et al., 2020).

Regulatory challenges associated with open banking frameworks are not limited to those mentioned above. The open banking model allows for the involvement of a broad range of third parties, including fintech companies, aggregators, and others that might lack contractual agreements with banks over which regulators can exercise jurisdiction. Furthermore, it's possible that some of these firms do not face regulation by any financial industry regulator. Regulatory bodies have a difficult time setting requirements, describing specifications, and exercising jurisdiction in such situations.

Banks and other regulated entities have explicit regulations governing outsourcing arrangements in most jurisdictions, including India. There is also some oversight by supervisors over these entities. Standards and prudential policies may have difficulty being enforced if the open banking relationships extend beyond the existing supervisory and regulatory boundaries.

CYBER-SECURITY WITH OPEN BANKING

Whether you enter your credit card info on a website or log into your online banking account, sharing sensitive information with a digital product will always be a risk. Despite these risks, most users of these platforms do not let them stop them from using them since they have a level of confidence in the product. Open banking must follow the same path. To realize the benefits of open banking, both financial actors and consumers should embrace it. Instead, they should educate themselves on the subject and put in place frameworks that promote safety and security (Nicholls, 2019).

Additionally, users ought to learn how to deal with their data responsibly and ensure its protection on the internet. To make sure that digital financial services are secure, strong passwords must be created and never shared, while Multi-Factor Authentication (MFA) should be implemented at every step. It makes no sense to disable MFA, as it prevents 99.9% of account takeovers (Mansfield-Devine, 2016). In addition to securing data when it is shared or stored, encryption technology is also vital. Machine learning (ML) algorithms, in addition, can further enhance the monitoring of suspicious activity by financial institutions and third parties. In the past, ML systems have been able to identify fraud instances, flag anything unusual, and suggest appropriate countermeasures. With blockchain technology stepping forward, it has been announced that banks and finance industries will see a transformation in the way they conduct business and form relationships with customers; providing high transaction security frameworks (Dong et al., 2020). Unlike previous manual methods, the rate of attempted attacks can be kept up with automated threat response systems. Rather than fixing problems post-mortem, cybersecurity policies must implement all of these measures proactively from the onset.

All third parties must follow data protection rules. As a matter of national security, regulators should step up and set standards that ensure open banking is not curtailed. Cohesive, strong frameworks and best practices will be developed only with communication between all parties, including banks, fintechs, and regulators. Furthermore, these organizations play a crucial role in providing consumers with assurances of the legitimacy of the services that collect their data. The open banking movement isn't going away, in fact, it's already rewriting the rules for the financial industry (Huang & Madnick, 2020). The promise of open banking is too big to ignore, with its potential to offer better value, services, and convenience to customers and to allow banks and third parties to innovate their products and services. All parties must commit to cyber security in order to create a secure ecosystem that keeps the financial information of everyone safe-from governments and regulators all the way down to the individual user. This is the only way open banking will gain support and play a significant role in building the financial world of the future.

DATA SECURITY IMPLEMENTATION IN OPEN BANKING

With the emergence of 'open banking,' which lets third-party financial service providers access consumer banking, transaction, and other financial information from banks and NBFCs through Application Programming Interfaces (APIs), this latest trend in financial technology is catching on rapidly. While this has several benefits, the innovation is also a high-risk practice as it involves sharing and trading a vast amount of data. India has seen tremendous growth in financial technology over the past few years; however, recent outbreaks of the Covid virus have facilitated an even greater surge. The UPI payment system was reported to account for 4.3 lakh crore of online transactions in January 2021, compared to 2.1 lakh crore in January 2020, illustrating the urgent need for the development of an open banking platform that provides robust data security protocols.

The Reserve Bank of India has released guidelines for digital banking and payments. These guidelines require regulated entities (REs)-scheduled commercial banks, small finance banks, payments banks, and NBFCs that regularly issue credit cards to evaluate apps and associated third-party services (Omarini, 2018). REs must also evaluate Cyber-risk parameters such as technology stack, operational risk, and storage. To manage cyber-risk effectively, REs will also have to hire trained personnel and adhere to policies regarding third-party engagement in the case of outsourcing. The REs will also be required to conduct rigorous third-party periodic testing, and are subject to penalties if they do not comply with the requirements.

The following are some of the most crucial Data Security processes that banks and other NBFC's must adopt immediately:

1. Security and access management of APIs: APIs or Application Programming Interfaces are ubiquitous today, and they play a crucial role in protecting app-

based transactions, access control, and the overall API security. API security aims to create a safe and secure API platform by implementing procedures such as API gateways, encryption, signatures, and using quotas. In order to ensure API security is successful and effective, APIs, their key functions, and their interactions on the web need to be considered, and security assessments need to be conducted timely to track and fix any vulnerabilities.

2. Stringent KYC and encryption: Data transparency is a prime feature of open banking. Customers can better understand how their data is being used when they have greater control over it. However, data transparency can also be a security risk, since it can lead to data theft and piracy. Secure transmission and storage of sensitive information require the use of encryption technology. This protects the data from hackers, as it is encrypted from end to end. KYC is also an important tool for banks to maintain updated data and to ensure that it is well encrypted and managed.

3. AI-based authentication protocol: Encrypting KYC information and conserving data are the first steps to ensuring data security. Authentication is an important step in the process. The use of AI and ML in data security and API security has been around for some time now. By using artificial intelligence-based techniques, KYC and authentication can be completed faster and more efficiently, resulting in a better user experience.

4. AI and ML based cybersecurity: Cyber threats have been targeting the baking industry for years, and open banking has its own vulnerabilities. By using AI and machine learning in cybersecurity processes, threats can be mitigated. A cybersecurity platform that takes advantage of AI and machine learning can make open banking one of the safest and most efficient channels for financial transactions (Wewege et al., 2020). In the event of a cyberattack, having more access to more data will enable banks to have more effective responses, since they won't be passively waiting for an attack to occur.

Risks and uncertainties are inherent in any new technology. It's also evident that open banking platforms can change the way banks and their customers interact. It is possible to ensure the smooth, safe, and customer-centric management of money with the help of data security technology. With open banking, customers and service providers can build a more reliable and secure relationship using technology.

MITIGATING CYBER-ATTACKS

Several fintech companies are expanding into the banking industry, forcing banks to rethink open banking in order to stay competitive with non-traditional players.

Non-traditional players offer tailored services designed to address the changing preferences of customers. Existing banks are developing new technologies and new approaches to business to cope with this type of digital disruption. Business models are being rethought, open technologies are being invested in, and data management is being redefined. Similarly, digital payments have become commodities as the most preferred way to transact in the current age. Consumer demand, new technology, market competition, and regulatory pressure have also boosted the electronic payments industry. On the one hand, banks are actively working on developing cross-platform device payment options through the use of open APIs in tandem with emerging technologies. On the other, banks are including products that integrate existing capabilities with FinTech partners (Nicholls, 2019).

Moreover, due to the rapid evolution of IT & Cyber risk landscape and its rapidly changing nature, the BFSI sector is exposed to a number of cyber threats as a result of the digital transformation, making it challenging for the CEO/CIO to identify IT security vulnerabilities (Kulkarni & Patil, 2020). As a result, they face a multi-dimensional environment that is constantly evolving with emerging technologies, such as adopting cloud infrastructure, signing up for a SaaS service, and allowing integrated analytics, machine learning, and other tools to become ancillary to their business process. To resolve these issues, an overview of bank resources and activities that encompasses all resources and activities is needed. Efficiencies in managing business risks and regulatory compliance will be shown through a holistic approach to managing risks. Banks can do this by building a strong cyber-security backbone and by training their personnel. In developed countries, numerous skilled professionals are employed by banks and financial institutions to prevent cybercrime. However, in India there is a significant need for improvement.

A detailed set of guidelines was published on 18th February 2021 by the Reserve Bank of India (RBI) to help strengthen India's booming digital payments ecosystem. Regulated Entities (REs), including scheduled commercial banks, small finance banks, payment banks, and credit card issuing NBFCs, will now be required to adhere to these new guidelines to ensure customers' more safe and secure environment use digital payment products. Currently, the majority of world currency has been converted into digital, so all of the money we earn and spend each and every day lives somewhere in cyberspace. Therefore, the new RBI guidelines will spur a new era of business growth in the digital economy, as they will establish customer confidence and speed up the adoption of digital payments in India, not to mention improve the overall data security posture of the payment industry. The recently released RBI guidelines are also a good opportunity to take a long-term look at how banks in India can maintain consumer trust even as they address emerging risks, we believe. Consequently, banks and financial institutions must leverage cross-functional coordination to develop a comprehensive cybersecurity system, ensuring consumer experience and preferences are protected while focusing on driving profitability by expanding digital payment protection (Laplante & Kshetri, 2021).

Below are Some Key Measures for Security

Standardization and Collaboration

In order for digital banking to flourish, open banking must be secured. The API (application programming interface) and VPN (virtual private network) are transforming collaboration for the end consumer, be it an individual or a business, and creating a safe ecosystem for them.

In addition to banks and their FinTech partners, government agencies and regulators also participate in this collaboration. In order to develop strong guidelines and best practices, communication between parties from across the ecosystem is key. Additionally, collaboration increases standardization, making it easier for everyone to follow the same rules. Security can be ensured by providing trusted services, such as KYC (Know Your Customer) standards and regulatory compliance tools. Moreover, it allows companies to focus on innovation and consumer-facing offerings by freeing their resources from noncompetitive activities.

Encryption and Transparency

The openness of open banking makes it a highly secure method of banking. Consumers better understand how their data is being used when they have greater control over it.

The key to building trust with consumers is transparency for service providers. In the FinTech market, it is a statutory requirement for companies and young brands to tell their customers how and why their data is being used, how it is controlled, how it is stored, and how the company is regulated and audited. Also, service providers may become more proactive about selling customers on increased transparency and encouraging customer engagement when dealing with this data. In order to encourage consumers to share their data, educating them about the value of openness will be crucial. Conversely, user data must be protected if it is to be shared. Data is often perceived as being in the hands of banks, but ultimately, consumers must be the ones in charge. When sensitive information is transmitted or stored, encryption technology is important to protect it from cybercriminals. Since open banking is all about giving customers control over their data, customers can decide at any time whether they wish to use these platforms: something that should also prompt banks to ensure strong data protection standards.

Improved Security with AI

Preventing illegal activity or money laundering through digital banking systems is one of the biggest challenges for financial institutions. By combining rigorous KYC controls with open banking processes, such as digital passports, the customer will be able to send and receive trusted KYC information. Banks and their partners often work together to find and flag suspicious acts in the billions of transfers worldwide every day through transaction monitoring. AI systems can benefit from open banking by gaining a broader view of a customer across institutions and a broader pool of data they can use. An anonymous 'profile' of users is usually built for monitoring, and the system flags anything unusual based on that.

Overall, this should result in better transaction monitoring, thereby making depositors, business customers, and the banking sector more secure, and giving banks greater confidence about the risks related to regulatory compliance.

Authentication and Authorization

A user usually clicks 'accept' when the terms and conditions are very long. In the future, consumers may be more careful when agreeing to share their financial data as they become aware they may have given apps access to more information than they realized. However, robust regulatory authorities can confirm the legitimacy of any app or service that requests personal data. The Financial Conduct Authority (FCA) is responsible for defining APIs, infrastructure, and governance in the UK, while the Open Banking Implementation Entity (OBIE) works on implementing them. Consumers can check the authenticity of data collection services through these regulatory bodies, thus helping to reassure them.

Consumers must also be confident that the companies and apps they allow to access their data are legitimate, as well as assurances that they are the only ones authorized to share it. Additional security and trust are increased with multifactor authentication. Biometrics technology connects security to the physical realm by letting consumers know they are in charge.

Proactive Cybersecurity

Industry-wide cybersecurity standards protect customers and businesses alike. In addition, companies will be able to share their intelligence and information more easily, and their automated threats will be able to react automatically to the latest attacks. Security has evolved from resilience to proactive threat detection, tracking down system vulnerabilities to address them before an attacker gains control. Through the use of collaborative intelligence across the banking ecosystem, banks will learn from each company's experience and implement necessary changes more broadly. With more data at their disposal, banks can make better insights, and by doing so, they can take on any hostile forces taking on their interests, instead of waiting passively for cyberattacks to happen.

Use of Blockchain

Blockchain technology has been gaining popularity as a dominant force in the industrial revolution, and its prominence is not by accident. Besides resolving these issues, blockchain technology also paves the way for a next-generation digital financial system based on trust and transparency. Blockchain technology is used to layer distributed ledger technology over legacy banking APIs and create a new digital financial ecosystem. By creating this platform, third parties are able to securely interact with banks and their data without gaining direct access to the core banking systems. Transacting securely within a trustless environment can be done by financial institutions on the platform. A shared platform also allows teams to collaborate, build networks, and exchange information. By using blockchain technology, we are able to aggregate and store industry-wide data from which we can develop new products and services such as loans, investment packages, pensions plans, etc., tailored to the customer's financial situation.

Banks benefit from blockchain technology's enhanced data security and protection, which minimizes their risks of hacking and data breaches. A distributed ledger is a system based on only transactions and records. The data in blockchains can be organized and managed hierarchically. This data is classified into highly classified, private, banking sensitive, and third-party use data. By establishing access and disclosure controls for each category, smart contracts enhance data security and minimize risk. Using this technology, users can generate a single digital ID that they can use through their banks, without disclosing their personal data to third parties, to access the digital banking ecosystem. At the same time, blockchains allow for customer privacy disclosure schemes. Parties can specify how their user information is to be used and how it is to be shared across different apps, ensuring customers are informed about how their data is being used. By controlling data privacy through the blockchain, the open banking policy enshrines users' right over data. This allows the customer to control how their information is used and to authorize access based on given conditions.

FUTURE PERSPECTIVE

There are always risks and uncertainties associated with new technologies. However, the potential of open banking platforms is so great that it's impossible to ignore the opportunity to change the relationship between banks and their clients completely. Money management could become more convenient, more secure and more cost-effective. By offering new channels for engagement, banks will be able to build relationships with their customers, opening the way for innovation and services that will be at the heart of open banking. All participants of an open banking ecosystem must understand that open banking is not an attempt to introduce new technology into existing customer-bank relationships randomly. The goal is to make the relationship between customers and service providers more intimate, responsive, transparent, and secure based on the use of the technology.

A gist of competitors, regulators, customer demand and recent technologies is depicted in figure 3. Competitors such as Big-Tech like Apple Pay, FinTech and other insurance and finance companies are challenging competitors for open-banking services. Regulatory bodies like Payment Services Directive 2 (PSD2), provides exclusive data access by banks; General Data Protection Regulation (GPDR), gives data protection to users; and electronic IDentification, Authentication and trust Services (eIDAS), provides electronic verification standard. Customer demands includes product and service development like instant loan, providing centralized platform for trading etc, single contact for digital services. Applying recent technologies for security, automation, and enhanced services.

Future Research Scope and Challenges

Data theft, corruption, or breach must be prevented in banks' networks and customer records. In the event of a regulatory breach, there can be severe consequences for failing to properly secure customer data (Hsiao, 2021).

1) Digital Competition: Financial companies are using software to provide core banking functions without requiring any human interaction. Third party innovators, whose technology is leading in the financial sector, can compete more directly with traditional financial institutions using open banking. Banks and financial institutions grant access to their financial information to third parties through open banking.

2) Big-Data: An enormous amount of data is generated by financial services firms, which is often siloed and underused. Data from enterprise systems can help improve product design, underwriting margin management, and resource allocation. Banks with legacy systems and siloed data are at a disadvantage to

smaller firms with systems that support better data management (Hassani et al., 2018). These huge data volumes are a challenge for maintenance as well as security.

Figure 3. Open-banking at a glance

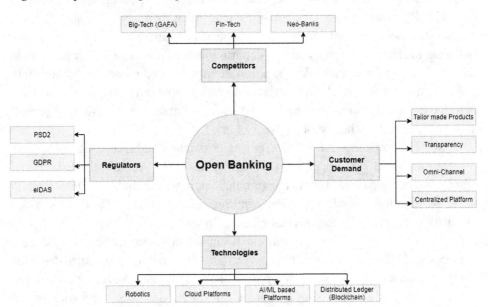

3) Regulatory Body: The regulatory landscape has evolved into one where regulation has become bolder and interventionist, introducing initiatives like open banking, know your customer (KYC), and customer authentication. Regulatory burdens are increasing, which makes it easier for non-compliance to occur. Regulatory changes that keep pace with technology are mirrored in the evolution of technology, from data sharing liability models to sustainability principles incorporated into regulatory guidance. It can also harm a bank's reputation if it does not adhere to initiatives.

4) Authentication Mechanisms: Monitoring personal information, passwords, alerts on breach information are one of the prime challenges, along with the design of efficient encryption-decryption technique during the transaction. The use of new security mechanisms like that of blockchain and its implementation is challenging and is one of the most focused research areas (Zhang et al., 2019). Security mechanisms by AI technology like threat recognition, security detection, and predictive analytics are also a booming area of research, remediating security

in real-time. These mechanisms prevent third-party intruders and hackers from exploiting vulnerable attacks.

CONCLUSION

Open banking is still a valid aspiration. Competitive markets are good for consumers and banks that can offer competitive financial products and up-and cross-sell new customers. By fostering new choices while preserving traditional banking security standards, a "beyond banking" environment will enhance trust. In fact, open banking is already poised to rewrite the financial sector's rules. In addition to delivering better customer value, experience, and convenience, open banking allows third-party companies and banks to drive innovation in their services and products. All parties - from governments and regulators all the way down to the individual user, need to commit to cybersecurity to build a secure financial ecosystem. This chapter describes cybersecurity issues, challenges, and future directions for open banking in context. In addition to this, a brief description and detailed insight to open banking and cybersecurity are presented. Open banking will reap the benefits it deserves and play an essential role in building the financial world of tomorrow, if it receives the support for enhancement and implementation of latest technologies.

REFERENCES

Baret, S., Celner, A., O'Reilly, M., & Shilling, M. (2020). COVID-19 potential implications for the banking and capital markets sector. *Maintaining Business And Operational Resilience*, *11*(8), 74–88.

Brodsky, L., & Oakes, L. (2017). Data sharing and open banking. McKinsey & Company.

Datwani, L., & Raman, A. (2020). *India's New Approach to Personal Data Sharing.* Document de travail. Washington, DC: CGAP. https://www. cgap. org/research/publication/indiasnew-approach-personal-data-sharing

Dong, C., Wang, Z., Chen, S., & Xiang, Y. (2020, September). BBM: A Blockchain-Based Model for Open Banking via Self-sovereign Identity. In *International Conference on Blockchain* (pp. 61-75). Springer. 10.1007/978-3-030-59638-5_5

Drigă, I., & Isac, C. (2014). E-banking services–features, challenges and benefits. *Annals of the University of Petrosani. Economics*, *14*, 49–58.

Gozman, D., Hedman, J., & Olsen, K. S. (2018). *Open banking: emergent roles, risks & opportunities*. Academic Press.

Hassani, H., Huang, X., & Silva, E. (2018). Digitalisation and big data mining in banking. *Big Data and Cognitive Computing, 2*(3), 18. doi:10.3390/bdcc2030018

He, Z., Huang, J., & Zhou, J. (2020). Open banking: credit market competition when borrowers own the data (No. w28118). National Bureau of Economic Research.

Hsiao, Y. (2021). *Opportunity Exploration and Evaluation: in the Trend of Open Banking*. Academic Press.

HuangK.MadnickS. (2020). Cyber securing cross-border financial services: calling for a financial cybersecurity action task force. Available at SSRN 3544325.

Kulkarni, M., & Patil, K. (2020, March). Block Chain Technology Adoption for Banking Services-Model based on Technology-Organization-Environment theory. In *Proceedings of the International Conference on Innovative Computing & Communications (ICICC)*. 10.2139srn.3563101

Laplante, P., & Kshetri, N. (2021). Open Banking: Definition and Description. *Computer, 54*(10), 122–128. doi:10.1109/MC.2021.3055909

Lynn, T., Rosati, P., & Cummins, M. (2020). Exploring open banking and banking-as-a-platform: Opportunities and risks for emerging markets. In *Entrepreneurial finance in emerging markets* (pp. 319–334). Palgrave Macmillan. doi:10.1007/978-3-030-46220-8_20

Mansfield-Devine, S. (2016). Open banking: Opportunity and danger. *Computer Fraud & Security, 2016*(10), 8–13. doi:10.1016/S1361-3723(16)30080-X

Mohammed, D. (2015). Cybersecurity compliance in the financial sector. *Journal of Internet Banking and Commerce, 20*(1), 1–11.

Nicholls, C. C. (2019). Open banking and the rise of FinTech: Innovative finance and functional regulation. *Banking & Finance Law Review, 35*(1), 121–151.

Omarini, A. E. (2018). *Banks and FinTechs: How to develop a digital open banking approach for the bank's future*. Academic Press.

Pazarbasioglu, C., Mora, A. G., Uttamchandani, M., Natarajan, H., Feyen, E., & Saal, M. (2020). *Digital financial services*. World Bank.

Petrović, M. (2020). PSD2 influence on digital banking transformation-Banks' perspective. *Journal of Process Management. New Technologies, 8*(4).

Premchand, A., & Choudhry, A. (2018, February). Open Banking & APIs for Transformation in Banking. In *2018 International Conference on Communication, Computing and Internet of Things (IC3IoT)* (pp. 25-29). IEEE. 10.1109/IC3IoT.2018.8668107

Puppala, V. K. (n.d.). *Digital technology–The 4th industrial revolution & beyond.* Academic Press.

Scraping. (n.d.). *Open Banking, APIs, and Liability Issues.* Academic Press.

Stiefmueller, C. M. (2020, July). Open Banking and PSD 2: The Promise of Transforming Banking by 'Empowering Customers'. In *International Conference on Applied Human Factors and Ergonomics* (pp. 299-305). Springer. 10.1007/978-3-030-51057-2_41

Thomas, R., & Chatterjee, A. (2017). Unified payment interface (UPI): A catalyst tool supporting digitalization–utility, prospects & issues. *International Journal of Innovative Research and Advanced Studies*, *4*(2), 192–195.

Wewege, L., Lee, J., & Thomsett, M. C. (2020). Disruptions and Digital Banking Trends. *Journal of Applied Finance and Banking*, *10*(6), 15–56.

Zachariadis, M., & Ozcan, P. (2017). *The API economy and digital transformation in financial services: The case of open banking.* Academic Press.

Zhang, Q., Zhu, J., & Ding, Q. (2019, October). OBBC: A blockchain-based data sharing scheme for open banking. In *CCF China Blockchain Conference* (pp. 1-16). Springer.

Chapter 11
A Study on the Perceptions of Internet Users With Respect to Information Sensitivity in Delhi

Shivani Choudhary
Amity School of Economics, Amity University, India

Neeru Sidana
Amity School of Economics, Amity University, India

Richa Goel
Amity International Business School, Amity University, India

ABSTRACT

The study aims to examine internet users' perceptions of information sensitivity, as well as to assess individuals' privacy attitudes, experiences with privacy violations, and risk factors that can influence internet users' privacy concerns. The topic of whether the information is considered sensitive by an individual and what influences this perception of sensitivity emerges since each person perceives information sensitivity differently. This study used an online survey method to collect data utilizing a structured questionnaire, and 385 internet users of Delhi participated in the study to assess their perceived sensitivity through 39 different categories of data. The findings of this research can contribute to a better understanding of how online websites can construct their privacy policies without infringing on individuals' rights to privacy and additionally develop innovative communication strategies to educate customers about the importance of responsible data sharing on websites.

DOI: 10.4018/978-1-6684-3448-2.ch011

INTRODUCTION

Consumer privacy concerns are one of the key impediments to participating in electronic commerce (e-commerce) activities that require customers to share personal information such as address, personal number, credit card information, and so on (Raja, 2016). Therefore, protecting consumers' privacy is an important factor for the success of e-commerce (Liu, Marchewkab, Luc, & Yu, 2004). However, acquiring customer data is also required for e-commerce to get insights of consumer preferences. The act of selective disclosure (of oneself) in an online context is referred to as online privacy. Online privacy is generally characterized as Internet users' concern about their control over the gathering of information during online activity and control over the use of that information (Buchanan, Paine, Joinson, & Reips, 2007).

Many people underestimate the importance of online privacy, but they should be aware of how much information they are revealing - not only on popular social media platforms but even just by browsing. In other cases, users do not become aware that information about them was collected until after the information is collected. Consumers generally become aware when they receive some type of marketing communication from an entity that has collected information about them (Sheehan & Hoy, 2000). Some internet users, on the other hand, are concerned regarding privacy online and are totally unaware of the risks (Mekovec, 2010). Not only is your privacy threatened, but so is personal safety, especially when you utilize the internet to perform vital and secret tasks such as internet banking and transferring critical business information. According to the studies, users are aware of the growing amount of data collected about them, as well as the potential threats associated with data processing. Customers, on the other hand, are vulnerable in this situation because they have little control over how information is acquired and used by e-marketers beyond the original purpose for which it was collected.

Users perceive items that are more personally identifying as more sensitive (Malheiros, Preibusch, & Sasse, 2013). However, as technology advances, it cannot be assumed that the majority of users comprehend how data might be linked to identify a person. The level of concern that users have regarding data collection is driven not just by which person or organization is collecting their data, or what is their purpose of taking the data, but concerns also arise by the sort of information that is at stake (Ortlieb & Garner, 2016). The topic of whether the information is considered sensitive and what influences this perception of sensitivity emerges, because each individual perceives information sensitivity differently.

Therefore, this research study examines the consumers on an individual level to ascertain their perception of the sensitivity of information shared during online activity. The primary data collection method was used to collect the data with the help of a structured questionnaire, with a focus on the Delhi region's population.

The researchers chose Delhi as their study area because it has the greatest percentage of internet access in India. According to the Telecom Authority of India's (TRAI) report, Delhi's internet subscriber base stood at 40.242 million in March 2020, making it the country's largest urban internet subscriber base. When it comes to internet subscribers per 100 people, Delhi ranked first, with nearly double the users at 199.88, compared to the rest of India.

With the digital surge and the massive amount of data generated every day, privacy violation is inevitable. Data breaches have soared across the country, and data protection is becoming a primary concern for both consumers and organizations (De', Pandey, & Pal, 2020). According to a study by a top VPN service company, India is listed third globally in terms of privacy breaches, with 86.63 million victims up to November 2021.

The findings of this research, therefore, can contribute to a better understanding of how online websites can construct their privacy policies without infringing on individuals' right to privacy, and additionally develop innovative communication strategies to educate customers about the importance of responsible data sharing on online websites.

The researcher is also attempting to assess individuals' privacy attitudes, experiences with privacy violations, and risks that can influence Internet users' privacy concerns. Furthermore, the identification of factors influencing Internet users' privacy concerns allows for a detailed study of their interdependence. Companies that sell their services or products online may be able to improve or adjust their offers based on the findings of such evaluations. Finally, public and private policymakers can get a rudimentary understanding of the elements that influence consumer's online behavior.

REVIEW OF LITERATURE

Numerous organizations are conducting studies on the influence of online privacy on consumers, including the Federal Trade Commission (FTC). In a prior study conducted in this field, the researchers (Sheehan & Hoy, 2000) examined and analyzed the influence of the criteria reviewed by the FTC on customers' online privacy concerns. The researchers discovered that there are three main characteristics that raise privacy concerns among online users, as well as there are other factors that influence or moderate privacy concerns. The study's findings indicate that people's privacy concerns are influenced by the type of information collected, the organization collecting it, and the purpose for which it is collected. The marketers who recognize internet users' privacy concerns and work to alleviate them through their marketing communications have had success with e-commerce.

Despite the repercussions concerning e-commerce, consumers' perceived risks linked with online retailing have gotten little attention. (Miyazaki & Fernandez, 2001) In their study have tried to investigate the perceptions of internet users in regard to risk in online shopping and how the risk perception with respect to the different internet experiences. The findings show a correlation between the levels of experience online, the methods used for purchasing such as mail-order, risks perceived by consumers while online shopping, and their purchasing activity. The results of the study evaluate that consumers' perceived online risk tends to be lower if they have a high level of online experience and they are less concerned about security and fraud.

(Belanger, Hiller, & Smith, 2002) Examined the relative importance of four commonly used trust indices while conducting online transactions: third-party privacy seals, privacy declarations, third-party security seals, and security features. According to the findings, consumers valued security aspects substantially more than the other three trust indices. The study also looked into the connection between these trust indices and consumers' judgments of a marketer's trustworthiness and how ready consumers are to give private information to online and offline shops. The findings demonstrated that when deciding whether to share their personal information, users depend on their views of trustworthiness, regardless of whether the merchant is electronic exclusively or both land and electronic.

Despite the necessity of gaining a better understanding of internet users' issues regarding data privacy, this issue has gone unnoticed in the field of information systems. This study (Malhotra, Kim, & Agarwal, 2004) focuses on the multidimensionality of Internet users' information privacy concerns (IUIPC). Authors have tried to propose a causal method to explain the relationship between internet users' concerns and their behavioral intention in regards to disclosing private information to the web marketer. This paper developed a ten-item IUIPC scale that was found to accurately represent the dimensions of privacy concerns, which were classified as collection, control, and awareness. Using this measure, the authors were also able to explain how customers' privacy concerns affect their willingness to establish partnerships with online companies.

Over the years, Internet users have consistently identified privacy as a primary concern. A more comprehensive, psychologically informed assessment of consumer perceptions of privacy concerns is required. (Ashworth & Free, 2006) Have made two significant contributions to the debate over digital privacy. To begin, the authors used theories of justice to gain a better understanding of how customers perceive and react to privacy concerns. They conclude the study with a set of suggestions addressed to firms and government agencies, based on the idea that customers react similarly to perceived privacy infractions as they do to unfair trade. According to the findings of this study, businesses should be proactive in drafting their privacy policies. Consumers are not only growing more aware of internet privacy breaches, but they're also becoming more empowered to avoid privacy invasions and retaliate against corporations that are considered to have acted unfairly.

For policymakers, online privacy is becoming a "hot" concern. Commercial interests want to maximize and then enhance the significance of consumer data, while consumers express worries about the marketplace's violation of rights and ability to govern their personal information. Despite the criticisms, it indicates that consumers freely supply personal information. This study (Norberg, Horne, & Horne, 2007) investigates the "privacy paradox," or the relation between consumers' intentions to release personal details and their true personal data disclosure behaviors. The author conducted two experiments, both using a repeated-measures design, to compare disclosure intentions to actual disclosure.

(Castañeda & Montoro, 2007) Investigated how user behavior can get influenced if the user is familiar with the site sponsors, the extent of control the customer has over the information requested, and then the sensitivity of the data requested. The findings indicated the different significance and extent of the impact that various aspects of information privacy have on bringing customers to a website. Individuals with strong privacy protection requirements may be appealing targets for e-businesses.

Some authors (Mekovec, 2010) have presented an overview of various elements of Internet users' perception of privacy across several privacy dimensions. Furthermore, since online shopping and e-banking are two of the most popular e-services, the researcher conducted an examination of the privacy perceptions of users of e-banking/online shopping services. The findings of the study show that internet users' perceptions of online privacy are influenced by various factors such as their control over the information that is collected during online activity, the type of information requested in order to complete a transaction, concerns about improper access to information collected, users' perception of data collected during the use of banking services or on online web site, and users' perception of online privacy rules and regulations set by the government.

Internet users often disclose information about their health on online healthcare websites with the intention of earning benefits such as receiving healthcare advice, or personal health evaluation. (Bansal, Zahedi, & Gefen, 2010) Has discussed the role of disposition of personal information during the disclosure of health information online. Individuals' intentions to share such information, according to the conceptual model, are determined by various personal dispositions which act as fundamental trust antecedents. The data gathered and the analysis focuses on the importance of personal dispositions which could be used to improve healthcare websites and increase the success of online health service delivery. The findings contribute to the privacy and trust literature by demonstrating that personal dispositions should be considered when assessing privacy concerns and behavioral intentions to reveal health information online.

Consumers' perceived sensitivity is influenced by the level of Internet knowledge and perceived control over the information and its use. (Bandyopadhyay, 2011) Investigated the elements that influence internet users' online privacy concerns. Indian customers' privacy concerns have been found to have a detrimental impact on both their desire to disclose personal details to Websites and their desire to indulge in e-commerce activities. According to the report, there is a need to investigate the negative effects of Indian customers' internet privacy concerns on digital marketers. Digital marketers addressing the Indian market must identify and handle the influencing variables so that consumers' online privacy issues are addressed and the internet users are not hesitant when it comes to sharing their personal information online and partaking in e-commerce activities.

Past researchers have tried to identify and investigate online privacy issues, and their impact on Indian customers' emotions and online purchase behavior. These findings are encouraging for online businesses who want to collect personal information from Indian customers in order to provide more personalized services (Kansal, 2014). According to the findings, Indian consumers prefer to express their online privacy concerns, and if they are not heard, they will hesitate from making purchases. As a result, companies targeting Indian customers have to build a marketing strategy for advertising the security of their e-commerce platforms. The study discovered a link between consumer behavior and their online privacy concerns. Businesses must invest in recovery methods as according to the study, Indian consumers choose to express and complain about privacy concerns.

A lot of prior studies have been conducted with respect to East Asian students' perceptions of e-learning privacy. (Yang & Wang, 2014) Held a survey for the first time in Japan in 2009. In 2012, the same study was conducted in these two countries, but with different participants, to explore if cultural factors influence e-learning privacy attitudes. The study will be repeated every three years to assess if opinions on e-learning privacy have evolved with time. Although students are concerned with personal data being revealed online, the findings reveal that they prefer their professors to acquire and share their personal info for instructional purposes. East Asian students consider their personal photos, cell phone number, and street address to be highly private, and they are unwilling to provide these details also in e-learning platforms.

There is a need to address the necessity to provide a clear distinction between privacy and security issues and to provide an integrative framework that incorporates security and privacy concerns, (Raja, 2016) tried to answer these research questions like how are privacy and security concerns are related to the consumer's attitude and how these factors affect the intention of consumers to be a part of the e-commerce

207

world. The management aspect of this study is that the website's usability features can be improved not only aesthetically, but also by incorporating security aspects.

A prior study (Anica, Škareb, & Milakovićc, 2019) presents a model that connects individual variables and government legislation with online privacy concerns, also referred to as OPC in short, and investigates customer perceptions of privacy concerns in Croatia, where online privacy is still a relatively unexplored problem. Structural equation modeling is used to examine the provided hypotheses. According to the findings, respondents prefer to have more control over the personal information they are sharing, and government online regulation is viewed as weak, which enhances the OPC. This study indicates that OPC is associated with personal information theft and has a negative impact on willingness to disclose information.

The authors of this study (Wirth, Maier, Laumer, & Weitzel, 2019) expanded the idea of information sensitivity that includes adverse consequences for other people. The findings show that extending the idea of information sensitivity resulted in a greater grasp of privacy-related concepts, particularly in an interconnected privacy context. Researchers attempted to advance the theory by establishing the broad idea of information sensitivity and developing conclusions about how to apply it in future privacy research projects

It is necessary to examine the relationship between modern digital-age technologies and the concepts of information security, privacy, and personal data protection. (Romansky & Noninska, 2020) talk about the information security and protection of data with respect to the organizational and structural components of the digital era and its existing problems and risks. Furthermore, the research sheds light on the primary risk problems of the digital era for user privacy, particularly with regard to modern technologies, and proposes specific measures to reduce their negative influence on users.

(Wang, Zhang, & Wang, 2021) Underlines the interdisciplinary character of privacy-related issues of users and sets the framework of a unified viewpoint focusing on solutions. An ontology of online privacy is proposed, and emerging research fields are described, on the basis of a thorough study of the literature in several domains. Finally, the authors provide a few observations, such as the necessity to examine the broader consequences of digital tech on protecting space and privacy. The purpose of the study should be to get a more comprehensive and scientific understanding of the long-term behavioral and economic consequences of privacy concerns.

BACKGROUND

In this section, privacy concerns, information sensitivity, demographic differences, and their potential relationship with each other are outlined.

Information Privacy

Privacy has garnered considerable attention in the research, with a special emphasis on its causes and ramifications, and its complex character (Castañeda & Montoro, 2007). User engagement with e-commerce entails making judgments even in the case of conflicting variables such as privacy and its related risks and trust concerns. It is necessary to examine the impact of these factors on customer decisions as they engage in e-commerce activities on a daily basis (Raja, 2016).

Information Sensitivity

The perceived information sensitivity influences privacy concerns as one major contextual aspect. The more sensitive the data is believed to be, the bigger the worries are for users. It has been shown that people are especially concerned about medical data and that people who view health data to be more delicate are also more concerned about health data. Furthermore, when highly sensitive data is at stake, privacy concerns have a bigger adverse influence on willingness to give information than when the data is less sensitive. But what exactly is sensitive information? One's point of view has a large influence on this.

Users perceive things that are more individually identified as more sensitive. However, as technology progresses, it is unrealistic to anticipate that every user will grasp how data might be linked to identify people. Additionally, risk evaluation by consumers is highly subjective. The usage environment has a considerable impact on the perceived dangers and the perceived need for Internet security. Similarly, defining data sensitivity as the potential loss connected with its disclosure underscores the complexities of determining sensitivity.

(Markos, Milne, & Peltier, 2017) In their research examined how consumers perceive the sensitivity of data and how their willingness to provide information is affected by various factors like the country of the user, their age and perceived control on the privacy, the type of information provided, and their data relationship. The researcher has conducted a cross-national survey among the U.S and Brazilian consumers to understand their perceptions. According to the findings, Brazilian consumers are far less sensitive to their data getting collected and are more willing to disclose their information as compared to the U.S. sample. The most sensitive information is that which is in the high-privacy section and is shared with unknown marketers. When researchers compared the individual data items between both the countries, the rankings on the sensitive items came out to be similar.

Furthermore, different forms of data are associated with various types of hazards. Credit card numbers, for example, are more related to monetary hazards, but social network profiles are more associated with social and psychological dangers

(Markos, Milne, & Peltier, 2017). Established an information sensitivity continua by experimentally rating 52 types of information kinds based on how the consumer perceives the overall sensitivity and linking that impression of sensitivity to readiness to disclose that information. In conclusion, the sensitivity of information is critical when it comes to online privacy perceptions and is dependent on the nature of information as well as individual characteristics.

Demographic Differences

There is no single sort of customer with a set of qualities. Users differ, for example, regarding their perception of the value of privacy, their level of trust in the entities who manage their personal data, and how they assess threats. These personal attributes, as well as prior experience or even current mood, could have an influence on sensitivity evaluation.

Privacy disposition shows an individual's necessity for privacy and is a personality trait that has a major influence on the perception of privacy and perceived information sensitivity. The propensity toward privacy impacts whether a venture into private space is perceived as an invasion or not. Furthermore, prior exposure to online privacy breaches and risk perceptions are substantially connected to privacy perceptions.

In the framework of privacy behavior and attitudes, trust has a vital complex role. Beliefs in trust alleviate privacy worries about information. However, trust has been proven to be a predictor of behaviors, also be influenced by user privacy, and act as a moderator between attitudes and behaviors.

It can be concluded from prior research that demographic factors such as age, education qualifications and gender influences the perceptions of privacy. Although some research indicates that there is no obvious effect of age on attitude towards the sensitivity of data and privacy (Markos, Milne, & Peltier, 2017), the majority suggests that young age groups disclose a lot of information and are less worried about information privacy. Researchers have also found that young adults discern between different sorts of information, being cautious about revealing personally identifiable information but not anonymous information. One study found that in the medical setting, both age sensitivity positive and negative findings exist: highly intimate data, such as data on mental diseases, should not be disclosed in any situation. Older users, on the other hand, were more willing to disclose data about general health and bodily ailments whenever it contributed to societal wellbeing.

Most studies show that women are more cautious about personal information than males. Other research, however, has found that gender variations in perception of sensitivity are only present in certain circumstances and information kinds. If we talk about the educational aspect, the results are mixed: Although a review study found no variations in privacy concerns based on education level, other research shows that consumers with lower educational levels are less concerned. Thus, changes in sensitivity perception due to education and gender could explain some of the disparities across empirical studies on privacy concerns.

RESEARCH METHODOLOGY

Method

This study used an online survey method to collect data utilizing an experimental questionnaire and 385 Internet users of Delhi participated in the study to assess their perceived sensitivity through 39 different categories of data. This study statistically assessed the data and compared them to the results of American, Brazilian, and German users.

The survey was conducted online and was divided into three sections. In the first section, demographic factors such as age, sex, level of education, and social status were considered. In the second section, participants assessed the perceived sensitivity of 39 different forms of information. Respondents were asked "How sensitive are the following data types to you?" and were required to grade the sensitivity with the help of a 6-point Likert scale ranging from "not at all sensitive" (1) to "extremely sensitive" (6). To avoid sequence effects, all the data types were presented in a randomized manner. The final section of the questionnaire assessed individuals' privacy attitudes, experiences with privacy violations, and risks. Table 1 has a list of the things. Again, all items were graded on a 6-point Likert scale, with 1 being "I do not agree at all" and 6 being "I entirely agree." Furthermore, trust in institutions (e.g., governmental bodies, insurance firms, etc.) was assessed on a 6-point scale ranging from 1 (I don't trust them at all) to 6 (I completely trust them). Cronbach's Alpha was derived for reliability analysis. The scale of "encounters with privacy violations" fell short of satisfactory dependability (.7) and was removed from further consideration.

Selection of Information Types

This study is done on the hypothesis proposed by (Markos, Milne, & Peltier, 2017) in a research paper. This study employs the same data types as other studies to do a descriptive comparison of Delhi users with users from the United States, Brazil, and Germany. Finally, the researcher examined the data types and updated them in order to select appropriate items for Delhi participants. This analysis estimates which type of information corresponds to Delhi's laws and culture with globally.

The researchers (Markos, Milne, & Peltier, 2017) did qualitative research to examine the narrative coherence of the data types and to identify additional sensitive information types. Following a brief introduction to the subject, participants pondered what data they share whenever they use the internet or use smart gadgets. Second, all of the information kinds analyzed was provided in the form of an online questionnaire, and participants were asked to evaluate their sensitivity and score them on a 6-point Likert scale. Furthermore, some of the items were revealed to be incomprehensible to Delhi online users. Additional elements were omitted due to translation issues as well as significant disparities in the importance of certain information categories between cultures (for example, the security number, as this ID is not prevalent in Delhi). To allow for comparability, the final list includes 39 information categories that are identical to those found in the (Markos, Milne, & Peltier, Information Sensitivity and Willingness to Provide Continua: A Comparative Privacy Study of the United States and Brazil, 2017) study.

The final section of the questionnaire assessed participants' privacy disposition, experiences with privacy infractions, and risk proclivity. Table 1 has a list of the things. All items were graded with the help of a 6-point Likert scale, with 1 being "I do not agree at all" and 6 beings "I entirely agree." Furthermore, trust in organizations (e.g., government units, insurers, etc.) was graded on a six-point Likert scale ranging from 1 (I don't trust them at all) to 6 (I absolutely trust them) (I completely trust them). Cronbach's Alpha was derived for reliability analysis.

Statistical Analysis

The comparison of Delhi results with that of (Markos, Milne, & Peltier, Information Sensitivity and Willingness to Provide Continua: A Comparative Privacy Study of the United States and Brazil, 2017) is descriptive. The rankings of the data categories are evaluated using rank-order correlation. Instead of utilizing the ranks, simply put sensitivity as a rank to contribute to the various lists. Hierarchical cluster analysis is used to categorize data types depending on their perceived sensitivity. Regression studies are used to investigate the impact of user characteristics on the impression of sensitivity (method: enter). For all analyses, the level of significance was fixed at 5%.

RESULTS

This section summarizes the descriptive findings of Delhi Internet users' perceptions of information sensitivity and their attitude toward privacy. Secondly, it compares Delhi results to American, Brazilian, and German results and outcomes. Furthermore,

Table 1. Items under different constructs

Constructs	Mean	S.D
Disposition to Value Privacy		
Compared to others, I am more eager to share my personal information with companies online	2.89	1.788
I am interested in preserving my privacy online	4.18	1.643
Compared to others, I tend to be more concerned about threats to my personal privacy.	4.08	1.598
Risk Propensity		
I am not inclined to take a risk with matters of my personal data or privacy online.	3.90	1.609
Privacy Violation Experience		
I have had bad experiences with regard to my online privacy.	3.36	1.380
I experienced misuse of data from friends or family.	3.21	1.535
Trust in Institutions		
I trust government institutions to use my private data	3.36	1.520
I trust private non-governmental institutions to use my private data	3.05	1.561

this part also examines the sensitivity results, emphasizes their characteristics, and identifies factors that affect the sensitivity of Internet users in Delhi.

Information Sensitivity of Internet Users in Delhi

The results of the study show the rank–order of each information type with respect to the average sensitivity ratings based on survey results. The rank–order is ranked from highest to lowest sensitivity degrees based on an average value (M) of Internet users. As a result, M = 9.64 was assigned to the Password, giving it the highest sensitivity. Then, each Biometric and Financial information with M = 9.23 and M = 9.01, respectively, with some fluctuation. Religion, and Occupation, on the other hand, were less sensitive, with M = 3.2, M =4.12, and M =2.27, respectively.

According to our statistics, Internet users in Delhi have a very different perception of information sensitivity. Internet users in Delhi demonstrated high levels of sensitivity for each of the 39 values shared by all nations, including passwords, fingerprints, digital signatures, passport numbers, credit scores, economic level, and political affiliation. They were less sensitive than their counterparts in the United

States, Brazil, and Germany in seven items: license plate number, ZIP code, mother's maiden name, place of birth, etc.

Delhi, Brazil, and Germany had the highest password sensitivity scores of 9.67, 9.2, and 9.34, respectively. The social security number is the most sensitive form given by American consumers (9.6). Users in Delhi are clearly more sensitive to verification information (passwords, fingerprints, digital signatures, and passport numbers) than users in other nations. Furthermore, when comparing Delhi users to other countries, the political affiliation category shows the largest variation.

Based on the values, the correlation for information sensitivity reveals a strong similarity of $r = 0.97$ between Delhi and Germany, $r = 0.81$ between Delhi and the USA, and $r = 0.77$ between Delhi and Brazil. In particular, several distinctions can be drawn between Delhi users and those from other nations. The biggest disparity between Delhi and Brazil users was in law enforcement, where they differed by 7.9 and 3.8 points, respectively. The most noticeable variation between Delhi and American users was in the mother's maiden name, which differed by 4.2 and 8.1, respectively. The largest difference between Delhi and Germany users was in private phone numbers, which differed by 6.1 and 7.6 points, respectively.

Influences on Perceived Sensitivity

Aside from cross-national comparisons, research has attempted to measure the various user characteristics in order to investigate their impact on individual perceptions of sensitivity. The privacy disposition had a large positive influence on all data kinds, indicating that those who respect their privacy viewed most information to be far more sensitive. Risk propensity was found to have an impact on all data kinds, however, it was most noticeable in the intermediate sensitive cluster. A higher risk proclivity, as expected, resulted in a lower perceived sensitivity.

Users who trust institutions view extremely sensitive material as more sensitive, while the trust index has no effect on other info clusters. Age had a slight influence on how sensitive information was perceived but not on how other data categories were regarded. With the exception of the least sensitive information, a higher level of education increases sensitivity. Gender does not have a substantial influence on perceived sensitivity. Personal factors under examination account for only a small variability.

The final section of the questionnaire assesses Delhi users' attitudes toward a variety of privacy concerns, including disposition to privacy, proclivity to take risks, privacy breach experience, and trust in institutions. Participants place a high emphasis on maintaining their privacy (M = 3.78, SD = 1.48). In terms of risk-taking proclivity, they are more likely to risk releasing personal info (M = 6.18, SD = 1.49). In terms of their experiences with internet privacy intrusions, several participants reported a negative or misleading experience (M = 2.01, SD = 1.84). Finally, participants show a difference in trust in institutions based on their type.

Discussion

The purpose of this study was to investigate the views of information sensitivity in a limited portion of India by focusing on online consumers in Delhi as a case study. The researchers compared the results to other countries, specifically the United States, Brazil, and Germany. Based on the findings, the researchers deduced/discovered various parallels and contrasts between Delhi users and Americans, Brazilians, and Germans. In general, Delhi users indicated lower averages in sensitivity to these categories when compared to other nations. Furthermore, these sorts of information that don't have any danger instances were taken into account; these data types are not processed for any security objectives in Delhi.

This study discovered minor differences in the sense of information sensitivity among Internet users in Delhi, the United States, Brazil, and Germany. Nonetheless, our findings revealed commonalities in the global model of information sensitivity perception. Internet users in Delhi had similar perceptions to those in Germany, but they differed the most from those in Brazil. Apart from personally identifiable information, Delhi Internet users had lesser sensitivity levels as compared to that of the US and Germany, but higher sensitivity in the case Brazil.

LIMITATIONS AND FUTURE RESEARCH DIRECTIONS

Until now, the sensitivity impressions presented in this research have been limited to situational evaluation of various data kinds. The future steps will be to investigate info sensitivity in various contexts (for example, medical services, IT) in order to assess the contextual impact. In addition, the participants' prior emotional state or current framing of a scenario may contribute to systematic variance in the data. An emotional stimulus could be utilized before the empirical measurement of reported sensitivity and privacy perceptions to manipulate emotional states. Another limitation of the study is the time constraint. The study was carried out over a couple of months. A longer duration would have given researchers more time to explore more on the topic and present an in-depth picture. Also, the study was conducted only in Delhi state. If the researcher broadens the sample target and conducts the study on the whole of India instead of focusing on one state then it can give a more accurate presentation of all the samples and better results in the comparison section of the study.

Because of future demographic issues, it is crucial to understand why age and generation present unique difficulties to appropriate internet activities. When examining a similar study, the impact of users' ages on privacy views and actions produced a mixed picture. The researchers found no age impact on sensitivity perceptions in this study. One might assume that older internet users have acceptable and sufficient understanding regarding data sensitivity due to their long experience and a greater degree of awareness as a result of regular media exposure to the topic. Children and teenagers should be included in future research as vulnerable internet and media users in terms of attitudes toward information sensitivity.

Over a variety of time frames, it is possible to see patterns of long-term change and, in doing so, create a dynamic segmentation. Future research should focus on studying the key variables across a large period of time, say 5-10 years to see the evolution in the changing priorities of internet consumers across a nation or nations.

CONCLUSION

The research's objective is to assess the attitude of internet users toward information sensitivity and online privacy. Researchers utilized an online questionnaire, examined, and compared the results of 385 Delhi participants with that of American, Brazilian, and German users. According to the findings, there are minor disparities in the impression of information sensitivity among Internet users in Delhi, the United States, Brazil, and Germany.

Nonetheless, the rank–order of data demonstrates that nations are similar. This research focused on a critical area of the world. In general, Asian countries, notably India, have been overlooked in such studies. As a result, this research leads to a better understanding of the international perspective of information sensitivity. This research adds to the area of information privacy, sensitivity, and cybersecurity by providing perceptions of a subcontinent (India) that differs from the typical research articles of Western counterparts.

REFERENCES

Anica, I. D., Škareb, V., & Milakovićc, I. K. (2019). The determinants and effects of online privacy concerns in the context of ecommerce. *Electronic Commerce Research and Applications*, 36.

Ashworth, L., & Free, C. (2006). Marketing Dataveillance and Digital Privacy: Using Theories of Justice to Understand Consumer's online Privacy Concerns. *Journal of Business Ethics*, 67(2), 107–123. doi:10.100710551-006-9007-7

Bandyopadhyay, S. (2011). Online Privacy Concerns Of Indian Consumers. *International Business & Economics Research Journal, 10*(2).

Bansal, G., Zahedi, F. M., & Gefen, D. (2010). The impact of personal dispositions on information sensitivity, privacy concern and trust in disclosing health information online. *Decision Support Systems, 49*(2), 138–150. doi:10.1016/j.dss.2010.01.010

Belanger, F., Hiller, J. S., & Smith, W. J. (2002). Trustworthiness in electronic commerce: The role of privacy, security, and site attributes. *The Journal of Strategic Information Systems, 11*(3-4), 245–270. doi:10.1016/S0963-8687(02)00018-5

Buchanan, T., Paine, C., Joinson, A. N., & Reips, U. D. (2007). Development of Measures of Online Privacy Concern and Protection for use on the internet. *Journal of the American Society for Information Science and Technology, 58*(2), 157–165. doi:10.1002/asi.20459

Castañeda, J. A., & Montoro, F. J. (2007). The effect of internet general privacy concern on customer behaviour. *Electronic Commerce Research, 7*(2), 117–141. doi:10.100710660-007-9000-y

De', R., Pandey, N., & Pal, A. (2020). Impact of digital surge during Covid-19 pandemic: A viewpoint on research and practice. *International Journal of Information Management.*

Kansal, P. (2014). Online privacy concerns and consumer reactions: Insights for future strategies. *Journal of Indian Business Research, 6*(3), 190–212.

Liu, C., Marchewkab, J. T., Luc, J., & Yu, C. S. (2004). Beyond concern- a privacy trust behavioral intention model of electronic commerce. *Information & Management, 42*(2), 289–304.

Malheiros, M., Preibusch, S., & Sasse, M. A. (2013). "Fairly truthful": The impact of perceived effort, fairness, relevance, and sensitivity on personal data disclosure. *LNSC, 7904*, 250–266.

Malhotra, N. K., Kim, S. S., & Agarwal, J. (2004). Internet User's Information Privacy Concerns (IUIPC): The Construct. the scale, and a Casual Model. *Information Systems Research, 15*(4), 336–355.

Markos, E., Milne, G. R., & Peltier, J. W. (2017). Information Sensitivity and Willingness to Provide Continua: A Comparative Privacy Study of the United States and Brazil. *Journal of Public Policy & Marketing, 36*(1), 79–96.

Mekovec, R. (2010). Online privacy: Overview and preliminary research. *Journal of Information and Organizational Sciences, 34*(2).

Miyazaki, A. D., & Fernandez, A. (2001). Consumer perceptions of privacy and security risks for online shopping. *The Journal of Consumer Affairs*, *35*(1), 27–44.

Norberg, P. A., Horne, D. R., & Horne, D. A. (2007). The privay paradox: Personal information disclosure intentions versus behaviours. *The Journal of Consumer Affairs*, *41*(1), 100–126.

Ortlieb, M., & Garner, R. (2016). *Sensitivity of personal data items in different online contexts*. Information Technology.

Raja, A. G. (2016). *Online privacy and security concerns of consumers*. Information & Computer Security.

Raja, A. G. (2016). Online privacy and security concerns of consumers. *Information & Computer Security*, *24*(4), 348–371.

Romansky, R. P., & Noninska, I. S. (2020). Challenges of the digital age for privacy and personal data protection. *Mathematical Biosciences and Engineering*, *17*(5), 5288–5303.

Schomakersa, E. M., Lidyniaa, C., Mullmannb, D., & Zieflea, M. (2019). Internet users' perceptions of information sensitivity – insights from Germany. *International Journal of Information Management*, *46*, 142–150.

Sheehan, K. B., & Hoy, M. G. (2000). Dimensions of privacy Concern among online consumers. *Journal of Public Policy & Marketing*, *19*(1), 62–73.

Wang, C., Zhang, N., & Wang, C. (2021). Managing privacy in the digital economy. *Fundamental Research*, *1*(5), 543–551.

Wirth, J., Maier, C., Laumer, S., & Weitzel, T. (2019). Perceived information sensitivity and interdependent privacy protection: A quantitative study. *Electronic Markets*, *29*, 359–378.

Yang, F., & Wang, S. (2014). Student's perception towards personal information and privacy disclosure in e-learning. *The Turkish Online Journal of Educational Technology*, *13*(1), 207–216.

ADDITIONAL READING

Changa, Y., Wongb, S. F., Libaque-Saenz, C. F., & Leed, H. (2018). The role of privacy policy on consumers' perceived privacy. *Government Information Quarterly*, *35*(3), 445–459. doi:10.1016/j.giq.2018.04.002

Dinev, T., & Hart, P. (2006). Privacy Concerns and Levels of Information Exchange: An Empirical Investigation of Intended e-Services Use. *e-Service Journal, 4*(3), 25–59. doi:10.2979/esj.2006.4.3.25

Markos, E., Labrecque, L. I., & Milne, G. R. (2018). A New Information Lens: The Self-concept and Exchange Context as a Means to Understand Information Sensitivity of Anonymous and Personal Identifying Information. *Journal of Interactive Marketing, 42*, 46–62. doi:10.1016/j.intmar.2018.01.004

Milne, G. R., Pettinico, G., Hajjat, F. M., & Markos, E. (2017). Information Sensitivity Typology: Mapping the Degree and Type of Risk Consumers Perceive in Personal Data Sharing. *The Journal of Consumer Affairs, 51*(1).

Tolsdorf, J., Reinhardt, D., & Iacono, L. L. (2022). Employees' privacy perceptions: Exploring the dimensionality and antecedents of personal data sensitivity and willingness to disclose. *Proceedings on Privacy Enhancing Technologies, 2022*(2), 68–94. doi:10.2478/popets-2022-0036

Yang, S., & Wang, K. (2009). The Influence of Information Sensitivity Compensation on Privacy Concern and Behavioral Intention. *The Data Base for Advances in Information Systems, 40*(1), 38–51. doi:10.1145/1496930.1496937

APPENDIX

Constructs	Mean	S.D
Disposition to Value Privacy		
Compared to others, I am more eager to share my personal information with companies online	2.89	1.788
I am interested in preserving my privacy online	4.18	1.643
Compared to others, I tend to be more concerned about threats to my personal privacy.	4.08	1.598
Risk Propensity		
I am not inclined to take a risk with matters of my personal data or privacy online.	3.90	1.609
Privacy Violation Experience		
I have had bad experiences with regard to my online privacy.	3.36	1.380
I experienced misuse of data from friends or family.	3.21	1.535
Trust in Institutions		
I trust government institutions to use my private data	3.36	1.520
I trust private non-governmental institutions to use my private data	3.05	1.561

Compilation of References

He, Z., Huang, J., & Zhou, J. (2020). Open banking: credit market competition when borrowers own the data (No. w28118). National Bureau of Economic Research.

Petrović, M. (2020). PSD2 influence on digital banking transformation-Banks' perspective. *Journal of Process Management. New Technologies, 8*(4).

Scraping. (n.d.). *Open Banking, APIs, and Liability Issues*. Academic Press.

Gozman, D., Hedman, J., & Olsen, K. S. (2018). *Open banking: emergent roles, risks & opportunities*. Academic Press.

Lynn, T., Rosati, P., & Cummins, M. (2020). Exploring open banking and banking-as-a-platform: Opportunities and risks for emerging markets. In *Entrepreneurial finance in emerging markets* (pp. 319–334). Palgrave Macmillan. doi:10.1007/978-3-030-46220-8_20

Datwani, L., & Raman, A. (2020). *India's New Approach to Personal Data Sharing*. Document de travail. Washington, DC: CGAP. https://www. cgap. org/research/publication/indiasnew-approach-personal-data-sharing

Stiefmueller, C. M. (2020, July). Open Banking and PSD 2: The Promise of Transforming Banking by 'Empowering Customers'. In *International Conference on Applied Human Factors and Ergonomics* (pp. 299-305). Springer. 10.1007/978-3-030-51057-2_41

Mohammed, D. (2015). Cybersecurity compliance in the financial sector. *Journal of Internet Banking and Commerce, 20*(1), 1–11.

Pazarbasioglu, C., Mora, A. G., Uttamchandani, M., Natarajan, H., Feyen, E., & Saal, M. (2020). *Digital financial services*. World Bank.

Nicholls, C. C. (2019). Open banking and the rise of FinTech: Innovative finance and functional regulation. *Banking & Finance Law Review, 35*(1), 121–151.

Baret, S., Celner, A., O'Reilly, M., & Shilling, M. (2020). COVID-19 potential implications for the banking and capital markets sector. *Maintaining Business And Operational Resilience, 11*(8), 74–88.

Dong, C., Wang, Z., Chen, S., & Xiang, Y. (2020, September). BBM: A Blockchain-Based Model for Open Banking via Self-sovereign Identity. In *International Conference on Blockchain* (pp. 61-75). Springer. 10.1007/978-3-030-59638-5_5

Huang K. Madnick S. (2020). Cyber securing cross-border financial services: calling for a financial cybersecurity action task force. Available at SSRN 3544325.

Omarini, A. E. (2018). *Banks and FinTechs: How to develop a digital open banking approach for the bank's future.* Academic Press.

Wewege, L., Lee, J., & Thomsett, M. C. (2020). Disruptions and Digital Banking Trends. *Journal of Applied Finance and Banking, 10*(6), 15–56.

Kulkarni, M., & Patil, K. (2020, March). Block Chain Technology Adoption for Banking Services-Model based on Technology-Organization-Environment theory. In *Proceedings of the International Conference on Innovative Computing & Communications (ICICC).* 10.2139srn.3563101

Laplante, P., & Kshetri, N. (2021). Open Banking: Definition and Description. *Computer, 54*(10), 122–128. doi:10.1109/MC.2021.3055909

Hsiao, Y. (2021). *Opportunity Exploration and Evaluation: in the Trend of Open Banking.* Academic Press.

Hassani, H., Huang, X., & Silva, E. (2018). Digitalisation and big data mining in banking. *Big Data and Cognitive Computing, 2*(3), 18. doi:10.3390/bdcc2030018

Zhang, Q., Zhu, J., & Ding, Q. (2019, October). OBBC: A blockchain-based data sharing scheme for open banking. In *CCF China Blockchain Conference* (pp. 1-16). Springer.

Thomas, R., & Chatterjee, A. (2017). Unified payment interface (UPI): A catalyst tool supporting digitalization–utility, prospects & issues. *International Journal of Innovative Research and Advanced Studies, 4*(2), 192–195.

Puppala, V. K. (n.d.). *Digital technology–The 4th industrial revolution & beyond.* Academic Press.

Premchand, A., & Choudhry, A. (2018, February). Open Banking & APIs for Transformation in Banking. In *2018 International Conference on Communication, Computing and Internet of Things (IC3IoT)* (pp. 25-29). IEEE. 10.1109/IC3IoT.2018.8668107

Zachariadis, M., & Ozcan, P. (2017). *The API economy and digital transformation in financial services: The case of open banking.* Academic Press.

Brodsky, L., & Oakes, L. (2017). Data sharing and open banking. McKinsey & Company.

Mansfield-Devine, S. (2016). Open banking: Opportunity and danger. *Computer Fraud & Security, 2016*(10), 8–13. doi:10.1016/S1361-3723(16)30080-X

Drigă, I., & Isac, C. (2014). E-banking services–features, challenges and benefits. *Annals of the University of Petrosani. Economics, 14*, 49–58.

Abdullaziz, O. I., Wang, L. C., & Chen, Y. J. (2019). HiAuth: Hidden Authentication for Protecting Software Defined Networks. *IEEE eTransactions on Network and Service Management*, *16*(2), 618–631. doi:10.1109/TNSM.2019.2909116

Agrawal, R., & Prabakaran, S. (2020). Big data in digital healthcare: Lessons learnt and recommendations for general practice. *Heredity*, *124*(4), 525–534. doi:10.103841437-020-0303-2 PMID:32139886

Ahad, A., Tahir, M., Aman Sheikh, M., Ahmed, K. I., Mughees, A., & Numani, A. (2020). Technologies trend towards 5G network for smart health-care using IoT: A review. *Sensors (Basel)*, *20*(14), 4047. doi:10.339020144047 PMID:32708139

Ahmadi, H., Arji, G., Shahmoradi, L., Safdari, R., Nilashi, M., & Alizadeh, M. (2019). The application of internet of things in healthcare: A systematic literature review and classification. *Universal Access in the Information Society*, *18*(4), 837–869. doi:10.100710209-018-0618-4

Ahmed, M., Amster, D., Barette, M., Cross, T., & Heron, G. (2008). Emerging Cyber Threats Report for 2009. Georgia Tech Information Security Centre.

Ajayi, E. F. G. (2016). Challenges to Enforcement of Cyber Crime Laws and Policy. *Journal of Internet and Information Systems.*, *6*(1), 1–12. doi:10.5897/JIIS2015.0089

Al Duhaidahawi. (2020). Analysing the effects of FinTech variables on cybersecurity: Evidence form Iraqi Banks. *International Journal of Research in Business and Social Science*, *9*(6), 123–133.

Aladaileh, M. A., Anbar, M., Hasbullah, I. H., Chong, Y. W., & Sanjalawe, Y. K. (2020). Detection Techniques of Distributed Denial of Service Attacks on Software-Defined Networking Controller–A Review. *IEEE Access: Practical Innovations, Open Solutions*, *8*, 143985–143995. doi:10.1109/ACCESS.2020.3013998

Alansari, M. M., Aljazzaf, Z. M., & Safraz, M. (2019). On Cyber Crimes and Cyber Security. In M. Sarfraz (Ed.), *Developments in Information Security and Cybernetic Wars* (pp. 1–41). IGI Global. doi:10.4018/978-1-5225-8304-2.ch001

Alberts, C., & Dorofee, A. (2002). *Managing information security risks: the OCTAVE Approach.* Addison Wesley.

Al-Issa, Y., Ottom, M. A., & Tamrawi, A. (2019). eHealth cloud security challenges: A survey. *Journal of Healthcare Engineering*. PMID:31565209

Al-Sharafi, M. A., Arshah, R. A., Abu-shanab, E., & Elayah, N. (2020). The Effect of Security and Privacy Perceptions on Customers Trust to Accept Internet Banking Services, An Extension of TAM. *Journal of Engineering and Applied Sciences, 10.* doi:10.3923/jeasci.2016.545

Alshra'a, A. S., & Seitz, J. (2019). Using INSPECTOR Device to Stop Packet Injection Attack in SDN. *IEEE Communications Letters*, *23*(7), 1174–1177. doi:10.1109/LCOMM.2019.2896928

Alsmadi, I. (2019). *The NICE cyber security framework: Cyber security intelligence and analytics.* Springer. doi:10.1007/978-3-030-02360-7

Ambohara, M., & Koien, G. M. (2015). Cyber Security and the Internet of Things: Vulnerabilities, Threats, Intruders and Attacks. *Journal of Cyber Security.*, *4*, 65–88. doi:10.13052/jcsm2245-1439.414

Anica, I. D., Škareb, V., & Milakovićc, I. K. (2019). The determinants and effects of online privacy concerns in the context of ecommerce. *Electronic Commerce Research and Applications*, 36.

Ashraf & Majid. (2021). Central Bank Risk Management, Fintech and Cybersecurity. *International Monetary Fund Working Papers, 2021*(105), 6-55.

Ashworth, L., & Free, C. (2006). Marketing Dataveillance and Digital Privacy: Using Theories of Justice to Understand Consumer's online Privacy Concerns. *Journal of Business Ethics*, *67*(2), 107–123. doi:10.100710551-006-9007-7

Bandyopadhyay, S. (2011). Online Privacy Concerns Of Indian Consumers. *International Business & Economics Research Journal, 10*(2).

Bandyopadhyay, D., & Sen, J. (2011). Internet of Things: Applications and Challenges in Technology and Standardization. *Wireless Personal Communications*, *58*(1), 49–69. doi:10.100711277-011-0288-5

Bandyopadhyay, S., Sengupta, M., Maiti, S., & Dutta, S. (2011). Role of middleware for internet of things: A study. *International Journal of Computer Science & Engineering Survey, 2*(3), 94–105. doi:10.5121/ijcses.2011.2307

Bansal, G., Zahedi, F. M., & Gefen, D. (2010). The impact of personal dispositions on information sensitivity, privacy concern and trust in disclosing health information online. *Decision Support Systems*, *49*(2), 138–150. doi:10.1016/j.dss.2010.01.010

Belanger, F., Hiller, J. S., & Smith, W. J. (2002). Trustworthiness in electronic commerce: The role of privacy, security, and site attributes. *The Journal of Strategic Information Systems*, *11*(3-4), 245–270. doi:10.1016/S0963-8687(02)00018-5

Benazir, R., Oeshwik, A., & Shireen, S. (2021). Fintech in Bangladesh: Ecosystem, Opportunities and Challenges. *International Journal of Business and Technopreneurship*, *11*, 73–90.

Bernik, I. (2014). Cyberwarfare. *Cybercrime and Cyberwarfare*, 57-140.

Bertino, E., Kantarcioglu, M., Akcora, C. G., Samtani, S., Mittal, S., & Gupta, M. (2021, April). AI for Security and Security for AI. In *Proceedings of the Eleventh ACM Conference on Data and Application Security and Privacy* (pp. 333-334). 10.1145/3422337.3450357

Bettini, C., & Riboni, D. (2015). Privacy protection in pervasive systems: State of the art and technical challenges. *Pervasive and Mobile Computing*, *17*, 159–174. doi:10.1016/j.pmcj.2014.09.010

Boerman, S. C., Kruikemeier, S., & Zuiderveen Borgesius, F. J. (2021). Exploring motivations for online privacy protection behavior: Insights from panel data. *Communication Research*, *48*(7), 953–977. doi:10.1177/0093650218800915

Brooks, M., & Yang, B. (2015, September). A Man-in-the-Middle attack against OpenDayLight SDN controller. *Proceedings of the 4th Annual ACM Conference on Research in Information Technology.* 10.1145/2808062.2808073

Buchanan, T., Paine, C., Joinson, A. N., & Reips, U. D. (2007). Development of Measures of Online Privacy Concern and Protection for use on the internet. *Journal of the American Society for Information Science and Technology, 58*(2), 157–165. doi:10.1002/asi.20459

Bultum. (2017). *Adoption of Electronic Banking System in Ethiopia Banking Industry: Barriers and Driver.* Academic Press.

Burt, S., & Sparks, L. (2003). E-commerce and the retail process. A review. *Journal of Retailing and Consumer Services, 10*(5), 275–286. doi:10.1016/S0969-6989(02)00062-0

Callen-Naviglia, J., & James, J. (2018). *Fintech, regtech and the IMP.* Academic Press.

Camqc, N. (2008). *Emerging Trends in Cyber Crime. In 13*[th] *Annual Conference. New Technologies in Crime and Prosecution Challenge and Opportunities. International Association of Prosecutors.* http://www.odpp.nsw.gov.ahe/default-source/speeches.by.nicholas.cowdery/ emerging-transformation-cyber-crime.pdf

Castañeda, J. A., & Montoro, F. J. (2007). The effect of internet general privacy concern on customer behaviour. *Electronic Commerce Research, 7*(2), 117–141. doi:10.100710660-007-9000-y

CCDCOE. (n.d.). *The NATO Cooperative Cyber Defence Centre of Excellence is a multinational and Interdisciplinary Cyber Defence Hub.* Retrieved from https://ccdcoe.org/ https://ccdcoe.org › organisations › apec

Chang, W., Chung, W., Chen, H., & Chou, S. (2003). An International Perspective on Fighting Cyber Crime. *ISI Proceedings of the 1*[st] *NSF/NIJ Conference on Intelligence and Security Informatics,* 379-384.

Chen, D., & Zhao, H. (2012, March). Data security and privacy protection issues in cloud computing. In *2012 International Conference on Computer Science and Electronics Engineering* (Vol. 1, pp. 647-651). IEEE. 10.1109/ICCSEE.2012.193

Cheng, M., Crow, M., & Erbacher, R. F. (2013, January). Vulnerability analysis of a smart grid with monitoring and control system. In *Proceedings of the Eighth Annual Cyber Security and Information Intelligence Research Workshop* (pp. 1-4). 10.1145/2459976.2460042

Cline, R. J., & Haynes, K. M. (2001). Consumer health information seeking on the Internet: The state of the art. *Health Education Research, 16*(6), 671–692. doi:10.1093/her/16.6.671 PMID:11780707

Comer, D., & Rastegarnia, A. (2019). Externalization of Packet Processing in Software Defined Networking. *IEEE Networking Letters, 1*(3), 124–127. doi:10.1109/LNET.2019.2918155

Cybenko, G., & Hallman, R. (2021). Resilient distributed adaptive cyber-defense using block-chain. *Game Theory and Machine Learning for Cyber Security, 22*, 485–498. doi:10.1002/9781119723950.ch23

Cybercrime. (2020). https://www.techopedia.com/definition/2387/cybercrime

De', R., Pandey, N., & Pal, A. (2020). Impact of digital surge during Covid-19 pandemic: A viewpoint on research and practice. *International Journal of Information Management.*

Deloitte & Indian Chamber of Commerce. (2017). *Disruptions in Retail through Digital Transformation Reimagining the Store of the Future.* Author.

Deng, S., Gao, X., Lu, Z., & Gao, X. (2018). Packet Injection Attack and Its Defense in Software-Defined Networks. *IEEE Transactions on Information Forensics and Security, 13*(3), 695–705. doi:10.1109/TIFS.2017.2765506

Dinh, H. T., Lee, C., Niyato, D., & Wang, P. (2013). A survey of mobile cloud computing: Architecture, applications, and approaches. *Wireless Communications and Mobile Computing, 13*(18), 1611. doi:10.1002/wcm.1203

Dong, S., & Sarem, M. (2020). DDoS Attack Detection Method Based on Improved KNN With the Degree of DDoS Attack in Software-Defined Networks. *IEEE Access: Practical Innovations, Open Solutions, 8*, 5039–5048. doi:10.1109/ACCESS.2019.2963077

Dreamgrow Report. (2021). *The 15 Biggest Social Media Sites and Apps.* Available at: https://www.dreamgrow.com/top-15-most-popular-social-networking-sites/

Drury, G. (2008). Opinion piece. Social media: Should marketers engage and how can it be done effectively? *Journal of Direct, Data and Digital Marketing Practice, 9*(3), 274–277. doi:10.1057/palgrave.dddmp.4350096

Duggal, R., Brindle, I., & Bagenal, J. (2018). Digital healthcare: Regulating the revolution. *BMJ (Clinical Research Ed.), 360*. PMID:29335296

Dumortier, J., & Goemans, C. (2004). Legal challenges for privacy protection and identity management. *Nato Science Series Sub Series III Computer And Systems Sciences, 193*, 191–212.

Edwards, L. (2004). Reconstructing consumer privacy protection on-line: A modest proposal. *International Review of Law Computers & Technology, 18*(3), 313–344. doi:10.1080/1360086042000276762

Eom, T., Hong, J. B., An, S., Park, J. S., & Kim, D. S. (2019). A Systematic Approach to Threat Modeling and Security Analysis for Software Defined Networking. *IEEE Access: Practical Innovations, Open Solutions, 7*, 137432–137445. doi:10.1109/ACCESS.2019.2940039

Ervural, B. C., & Ervural, B. (2018). Overview of Cyber Security in the Industry 4.0 Era. In *Industry 4.0: Managing The Digital Transformation. Springer Series in Advanced Manufacturing.* Springer. doi:10.1007/978-3-319-57870-5_16

Feng, D., Min, Z., & Yu, L. (2014). Big Data Security and Privacy Protection. *Chinese Journal of Computers*, *37*(1), 246–258.

Gai, K., Qiu, M., & Sun, X. (2018). A survey on FinTech. *Journal of Network and Computer Applications*, *103*, 262–273.

Gao, S., Peng, Z., Xiao, B., Hu, A., Song, Y., & Ren, K. (2020). Detection and Mitigation of DoS Attacks in Software Defined Networks. *IEEE/ACM Transactions on Networking*, *28*(3), 1419–1433. doi:10.1109/TNET.2020.2983976

Gordon, L., & Loeb, M. (2002). The economics of information security investment. *ACM Transactions on Information and System Security*, *5*(4), 438–457. doi:10.1145/581271.581274

Gubbi, J., Buyya, R., Marusic, S., & Palaniswami, M. (2013). Internet of things (IoT): A vision, architectural elements, and future directions. *Future Generation Computer Systems*, *29*(7), 1645–1660. doi:10.1016/j.future.2013.01.010

Gupta, B. B., Perez, G. M., Agrawal, D. P., & Gupta, D. (2021). Handbook of Computer Networks and Cyber Security: Principles and Paradigms. In Software-Defined Network (SDN) Data Plane Security: Issues, Solutions, and Future Directions (pp. 341–387). Springer.

Haider, S., Akhunzada, A., Mustafa, I., Patel, T. B., Fernandez, A., Choo, K. K. R., & Iqbal, J. (2020). A Deep CNN Ensemble Framework for Efficient DDoS Attack Detection in Software Defined Networks. *IEEE Access: Practical Innovations, Open Solutions*, *8*, 53972–53983. doi:10.1109/ACCESS.2020.2976908

Hoo, K. S. (2000). *How much is enough? A risk management approach to computer security*. Retrieved October 25, 2006. Available at: http://iis-db.stanford.edu/pubs/11900/soohoo.pdf

HowardP. N.GulyasO. (2014). *Data breaches in Europe: Reported breaches of compromised personal records in europe, 2005-2014*. Available at SSRN 2554352. doi:10.2139/ssrn.2554352

Hua, J., Zhou, Z., & Zhong, S. (2021). Flow Misleading: Worm-Hole Attack in Software-Defined Networking via Building In-Band Covert Channel. *IEEE Transactions on Information Forensics and Security*, *16*, 1029–1043. doi:10.1109/TIFS.2020.3013093

Huo, H. (2016). Exploration of Security and Privacy Protection Technology in the Big Data Era. *Cyber Security Technology and Applications*, *11*(5), 79–88.

Imran, M., Durad, M. H., Khan, F. A., & Abbas, H. (2020). DAISY: A Detection and Mitigation System Against Denial-of-Service Attacks in Software-Defined Networks. *IEEE Systems Journal*, *14*(2), 1933–1944. doi:10.1109/JSYST.2019.2927223

Jain, P., Gyanchandani, M., & Khare, N. (2016). Big data privacy: A technological perspective and review. *Journal of Big Data*, *3*(1), 25. Advance online publication. doi:10.118640537-016-0059-y

Jaishankar, K. (2020). Cyber Victimology: A New Sub-Discipline of the Twenty-First Century Victimology. In An International Perspective on Contemporary Developments in Victimology (pp. 3-19). Springer.

Jasper, S. E. (2017). US cyber threat intelligence sharing frameworks. *International Journal of Intelligence and CounterIntelligence, 30*(1), 53–65. doi:10.1080/08850607.2016.1230701

Jayalath & Premaratne. (2021). Analysis of Key Digital Technology Infrastructure and Cyber Security Consideration Factors for Fintech Companies. *International Journal of Research Publications (IJRP), 84*(1), 128-135. doi:. doi:10.47119/IJRP100841920212246

Jolly, V. (n.d.). The Influence of Internet Banking on the Efficiency and Cost Savings for Bank's Customers International. *Journal of Social Sciences and Management, 3*(3), 163–170. doi:10.3126/ijssm.v3i3.157

Jones, P. (1985). The Spread of Article Numbering and Retail Scanning in Europe. *Service Industries Journal, 5*(3), 273–279. doi:10.1080/02642068500000042

Joshi, Y., & Singh, A. (2013). A Study on Cyber Crime and Security Scenario in India. *International Journal of Engineering and Management Research., 3*(3), 13–18.

Juneja, A., Juneja, S. V., Bali, V., Jain, & Upadhyay, H. (2021). Artificial intelligence and cyber security: Current trends and future prospects. *The Smart Cyber Ecosystem for Sustainable Development, 27*, 431–441. doi:10.1002/9781119761655.ch22

Kang, J. (1998). Information Privacy in Cyberspace Transactions. *Stan. Law Review, 1193*, 1198.

Kansal, P. (2014). Online privacy concerns and consumer reactions: Insights for future strategies. *Journal of Indian Business Research, 6*(3), 190–212.

Kaplan, A. M. (2012). If you love something, let it go mobile. Mobile marketing and mobile social media 4x4. *Business Horizons, 55*(2), 129–139. doi:10.1016/j.bushor.2011.10.009

Kareem, H. M., Duhaidahawi, A., Zhang, J., Abdulreza, M. S., & Sebai, M. (2020). An efficient model for financial risks assessment based on artificial neural networks; Evidence from Iraqi Banks (2004-2017). *Journal of Southwest Jiaotong University, 55*(3). Advance online publication. doi:10.35741/issn.0258-2724.55.3.8

Khan, M. A., & Malaika, M. (2021). *Central Bank Risk Management, Fintech, and Cybersecurity.* International Monetary Fund.

Khrais, L. T. (2019). Highlighting the Vulnerabilities of Online Banking System. *Journal of Internet Banking and Commerce, 20*(3).

Kim, S., Yoon, S., Narantuya, J., & Lim, H. (2020). Secure Collecting, Optimizing, and Deploying of Firewall Rules in Software-Defined Networks. *IEEE Access: Practical Innovations, Open Solutions, 8*, 15166–15177. doi:10.1109/ACCESS.2020.2967503

Kim, Y., Park, Y.-J., Choi, J., & Yeon, J. (2015). An Empirical Study on the Adoption of "Fintech" Service: Focused on Mobile Payment Services. December. *Advanced Science and Technology Letters, 114*(26), 136–140. doi:10.14257/astl.2015.114.26

Kizza, J. M. (2013). *Guide to Computer Network Security*. Springer. doi:10.1007/978-1-4471-4543-1

Kleemans, E. R., & Stol, W. P. (2016). Cybercriminal Networks, Social Ties and Online Forums: Social Ties Versus Digital Ties Within Phishing and Malware Networks. *British Journal of Criminology*, 1–19. doi:10.1093/bjc/azw009

Konstantin, B. (2017). Phishing Threat Avoidance Behavior, an Empirical Investigation. *Computers in Human Behavior*, *60*, 185–197. https://doi.org/10.1016/j.chb

Krausz, M., & Walker, J. (2013). *The true cost of information security breaches and cybercrime*. IT Governance Publishing.

Lee, W. W., Zankl, W., & Chang, H. (2016). An ethical approach to data privacy protection. *Isaca Journal*.

Li, S., Da Xu, L., & Zhao, S. (2018). 5G Internet of Things: A survey. *Journal of Industrial Information Integration*, *10*, 1–9. doi:10.1016/j.jii.2018.01.005

Liu, C., Marchewkab, J. T., Luc, J., & Yu, C. S. (2004). Beyond concern- a privacy trust behavioral intention model of electronic commerce. *Information & Management*, *42*(2), 289–304.

Malheiros, M., Preibusch, S., & Sasse, M. A. (2013). "Fairly truthful": The impact of perceived effort, fairness, relevance, and sensitivity on personal data disclosure. *LNSC*, *7904*, 250–266.

Malhotra, N. K., Kim, S. S., & Agarwal, J. (2004). Internet User's Information Privacy Concerns (IUIPC): The Construct. the scale, and a Casual Model. *Information Systems Research*, *15*(4), 336–355.

Markos, E., Milne, G. R., & Peltier, J. W. (2017). Information Sensitivity and Willingness to Provide Continua: A Comparative Privacy Study of the United States and Brazil. *Journal of Public Policy & Marketing*, *36*(1), 79–96.

Mathew, A. (2021). Artificial intelligence for offence and defense-the future of cyber security. *Educational Research*, *3*(3), 159–163.

Mekovec, R. (2010). Online privacy: Overview and preliminary research. *Journal of Information and Organizational Sciences*, *34*(2).

Milena, V. (2020). Fintech and Financial Stability Potential Influence of FinTech on Financial Stability, Risks and Benefits. *Journal of Central Banking Theory and Practice*, *9*(2), 43–66.

Misra, G., Kumar, V., Agarwal, A., & Agarwal, K. (2016). Internet of things (IOT)–a technological analysis and survey on vision, concepts, challenges, innovation directions, technologies, and applications (an upcoming or future generation computer communication system technology). *American Journal of Electrical and Electronic Engineering*, *4*(1), 23–32.

Miyazaki, A. D., & Fernandez, A. (2001). Consumer perceptions of privacy and security risks for online shopping. *The Journal of Consumer Affairs*, *35*(1), 27–44.

Moran, A. (2020). Cyber security. In *International Security Studies* (pp. 299–311). Routledge.

Muthuppalaniappan, M., & Stevenson, K. (2021). Healthcare cyber-attacks and the COVID-19 pandemic: an urgent threat to global health. *International Journal for Quality in Health Care, 33*(1).

Najaf, K., Mostafiz, M. I., & Najaf, R. (2021). Fintech firms and banks sustainability: Why cybersecurity risk matters? *International Journal of Financial Engineering*, *8*(02), 2150019. doi:10.1142/S2424786321500195

National Crime Records Bureau. (n.d.a). Retrieved from https://ncrb.gov.in/en/Crime-in-India-2020

National Crime Records Bureau. (n.d.b). Retrieved from https://ncrb.gov.in/en/Crime-in-India-2019

National Crime Records Bureau. (n.d.c). Retrieved from https://ncrb.gov.in/en/Crime-in-India-2018

National Crime Records Bureau. (n.d.d). Retrieved from https://ncrb.gov.in/en/Crime-in-India-2017

National Crime Records Bureau. (n.d.e). Retrieved from https://ncrb.gov.in/en/Crime-in-India-2016

Ng & Kwok. (2017). Emergence of Fintech and cybersecurity in a global financial centre: Strategic approach by a regulator. *Journal of Financial Regulation and Compliance*.

Ng, A. W., & Kwok, B. K. (2017). Emergence of Fintech and cybersecurity in a global financial centre: Strategic approach by a regulator. *Journal of Financial Regulation and Compliance*.

Norberg, P. A., Horne, D. R., & Horne, D. A. (2007). The privay paradox: Personal information disclosure intentions versus behaviours. *The Journal of Consumer Affairs*, *41*(1), 100–126.

Oomen, I., & Leenes, R. (2008). Privacy risk perceptions and privacy protection strategies. In *Policies and research in identity management* (pp. 121–138). Springer. doi:10.1007/978-0-387-77996-6_10

Ortlieb, M., & Garner, R. (2016). *Sensitivity of personal data items in different online contexts*. Information Technology.

Patel, K. K., & Patel, S. M. (2016). Internet of things-IOT: definition, characteristics, architecture, enabling technologies, application & future challenges. *International Journal of Engineering Science and Computing, 6*(5).

Peng, L., & Fang, W. (2015). Heterogeneity of Inferring Reputation of Cooperative Behaviors for the Prisoners' Dilemma Game. *Physica A*, *433*, 367–378. doi:10.1016/j.physa.2015.03.053

Peotta & Holtz. (n.d.). A formal Classification of Internet Banking Attacks and Vulnerabilities. *International Journal of Computer Science and Information Technology, 3*(1).

Peters, G. W., Panayi, E., & Chapelle, A. (2015). Trends in Crypto-Currencies and Blockchain Technologies: A Monetary Theory and Regulation Perspective. SSRN *Electronic Journal, 3*(3). doi:10.2139/ssrn.2646618

Phan, T. V., Nguyen, T. G., Dao, N. N., Huong, T. T., Thanh, N. H., & Bauschert, T. (2020). DeepGuard: Efficient Anomaly Detection in SDN With Fine-Grained Traffic Flow Monitoring. *IEEE eTransactions on Network and Service Management, 17*(3), 1349–1362. doi:10.1109/TNSM.2020.3004415

Philippon, T. (2016). The Fintech Opportunity. *National Bureau Of Economic Research, 8*(3), 6–10. https://www.nber.org/papers/w22476

Qureshi, K. I., Wang, L., Sun, L., Zhu, C., & Shu, L. (2020). A Review on Design and Implementation of Software-Defined WLANs. *IEEE Systems Journal, 14*(2), 2601–2614. doi:10.1109/JSYST.2019.2960400

Raja, A. G. (2016). Online privacy and security concerns of consumers. *Information & Computer Security, 24*(4), 348–371.

Raja, A. G. (2016). *Online privacy and security concerns of consumers.* Information & Computer Security.

Rasool, R. U., Ashraf, U., Ahmed, K., Wang, H., Rafique, W., & Anwar, Z. (2019). Cyberpulse: A Machine Learning Based Link Flooding Attack Mitigation System for Software Defined Networks. *IEEE Access: Practical Innovations, Open Solutions, 7*, 34885–34899. doi:10.1109/ACCESS.2019.2904236

Reba. (2018). *State of Cyber Security in Ethiopia.* Ethiopian Telecommunications Agency, Standards and Inspection Department, Standards Division.

Roberts, N., & Grover, V. (2012). Leveraging Information Technology infrastructure to facilitate a firm's customer agility and competitive activity: An empirical investigation. *Journal of Management Information Systems, 28*(4), 231–270. doi:10.2753/MIS0742-1222280409

Romanosky, S., & Acquisti, A. (2009). Privacy costs and personal data protection: Economic and legal perspectives. *Berkeley Technology Law Journal, 24*, 1061.

Romansky, R. P., & Noninska, I. S. (2020). Challenges of the digital age for privacy and personal data protection. *Mathematical Biosciences and Engineering, 17*(5), 5288–5303.

Safeena, R., & Hema, D., & Abdullah. (2019). Customer Perspectives on E-Business Value, Case Study on Internet Banking. *Journal of Internet Banking & Commerce, 15*, 1–8.

Sahay, S. K., Goel, N., Jadliwala, M., & Upadhyaya, S. (2021). Advances in secure knowledge management in the artificial intelligence era. *Information Systems Frontiers, 23*(4), 807–810. doi:10.100710796-021-10179-9

Sallam, A., Refaey, A., & Shami, A. (2019). On the Security of SDN: A Completed Secure and Scalable Framework Using the Software-Defined Perimeter. *IEEE Access: Practical Innovations, Open Solutions, 7*, 146577–146587. doi:10.1109/ACCESS.2019.2939780

Salman, O., Elhajj, I., Kayssi, A., & Chehab, A. (2015). Edge computing enabling the internet of things. *2015 IEEE 2nd World Forum on Internet of Things (WF-IoT)*, 603–608. 10.1109/WF-IoT.2015.7389122

Samuel, K. O., & Osman, W. R. (2014). Cyber Technology Attack of the Contemporary Information Technology Age: Issues, Consequences and Panacea. *International Journal of Computer Science and Mobile Computing.*, *3*(5), 1082–1090.

Sarma, M., Matheus, T., & Senaratne, C. (2021). Artificial intelligence and cyber security: a new pathway for growth in emerging economies via the knowledge economy. In *Business Practices* (pp. 51–67). Growth and Economic Policy in Emerging Markets.

Scaranti, G. F., Carvalho, L. F., Barbon, S., & Proenca, M. L. (2020). Artificial Immune Systems and Fuzzy Logic to Detect Flooding Attacks in Software-Defined Networks. *IEEE Access: Practical Innovations, Open Solutions*, *8*, 100172–100184. doi:10.1109/ACCESS.2020.2997939

Schilit, B., Hong, J., & Gruteser, M. (2003). Wireless location privacy protection. *Computer*, *36*(12), 135–137. doi:10.1109/MC.2003.1250896

Schomakersa, E. M., Lidyniaa, C., Mullmannb, D., & Zieflea, M. (2019). Internet users' perceptions of information sensitivity – insights from Germany. *International Journal of Information Management*, *46*, 142–150.

Schueffel, P. (2016). Taming the beast: A scientific definition of fintech. *Journal of Innovation Management*, *4*(4), 32–54.

Seema, P. S., Nandini, S., & And Sowmiya, M. (2018). Overview of Cyber Security. *International Journal of Advanced Research in Computer and Communication Engineering*, *7*(11), 125–128. doi:10.17148/IJARCCE.2018.71127

Senthilkumar, S. A., Rai, B. K., Meshram, A. A., Gunasekaran, A., & Chandrakumarmangalam, S. (2018). Big data in healthcare management: A review of literature. *American Journal of Theoretical and Applied Business*, *4*(2), 57–69. doi:10.11648/j.ajtab.20180402.14

Sethi, P., & Sarangi, S. R. (2017). Internet of things: Architectures, protocols, and applications. *Journal of Electrical and Computer Engineering*, *2017*, 9324035. doi:10.1155/2017/9324035

Shah, S. S. H., Xinping, X., Khan, M. A., & Harjan, S. A. (2018). Investor and manager overconfidence bias and firm value: Micro-level evidence from the Pakistan equity market. *International Journal of Economics and Financial Issues*, *8*(5), 190.

Shah, S., Diwan, S., Kohan, L., Rosenblum, D., Gharibo, C., Soin, A., ... Provenzano, D. A. (2020). The technological impact of COVID-19 on the future of education and health care delivery. *Pain Physician*, *4S*(23), S367–S380. doi:10.36076/ppj.2020/23/S367 PMID:32942794

Shapiro, J. S., Mostashari, F., Hripcsak, G., Soulakis, N., & Kuperman, G. (2011). Using health information exchange to improve public health. *American Journal of Public Health*, *101*(4), 616–623. doi:10.2105/AJPH.2008.158980 PMID:21330598

Sharma, M. (2016). Issue and Legal Consequences. *International Journal of Scientific and Engineering Research, 7*(12), 168–172.

Sheehan, K. B., & Hoy, M. G. (2000). Dimensions of privacy Concern among online consumers. *Journal of Public Policy & Marketing, 19*(1), 62–73.

Shen, Y. (2019, July). An Empirical Study on the Influential Factors of User Loyalty in Digital Fitness Community. In *International Conference on Human-Computer Interaction* (pp. 550-559). Springer. 10.1007/978-3-030-22219-2_40

Shin, S. Y. (2021). Privacy protection and data utilization. *Healthcare Informatics Research, 27*(1), 1–2. doi:10.4258/hir.2021.27.1.1 PMID:33611870

Shin, S., & Gu, G. (2013). Attacking software-defined networks. *Proceedings of the Second ACM SIGCOMM Workshop on Hot Topics in Software Defined Networking - HotSDN '13.* 10.1145/2491185.2491220

Singh, N., & Singh, A. K. (2018). Data privacy protection mechanisms in cloud. *Data Science and Engineering, 3*(1), 24–39. doi:10.100741019-017-0046-0

Smys, S. (2020). A survey on internet of things (IoT) based smart systems. *Journal of ISMAC, 2*(4), 181–189. doi:10.36548/jismac.2020.4.001

Stawowski. (n.d.). *Client side Vulnerability Assessment.* Retrieved from http://www.clico.pl/services/Clientside_Vulnerab ility_Assessment.pdf

Stratton, C., Kadakia, S., Balikuddembe, J. K., Peterson, M., Hajjioui, A., Cooper, R., Hong, B.-Y., Pandiyan, U., Muñoz-Velasco, L. P., Joseph, J., Krassioukov, A., Tripathi, D. R., & Tuakli-Wosornu, Y. A. (2020). Access denied: The shortage of digitized fitness resources for people with disabilities. *Disability and Rehabilitation*, 1–3. doi:10.1080/09638288.2020.1854 873 PMID:33305961

Tan, L., Pan, Y., Wu, J., Zhou, J., Jiang, H., & Deng, Y. (2020). A New Framework for DDoS Attack Detection and Defense in SDN Environment. *IEEE Access: Practical Innovations, Open Solutions, 8*, 161908–161919. doi:10.1109/ACCESS.2020.3021435

Tarjan, L., Šenk, I., Tegeltija, S., Stankovski, S., & Ostojic, G. (2014). A readability analysis for QR code application in a traceability system. *Computers and Electronics in Agriculture, 109*, 1–11. doi:10.1016/j.compag.2014.08.015

Taylor, M., Reillya, D., & Wren, C. (2020). Internet of things support for marketing activities. *Journal of Strategic Marketing, 28*(2), 149–160. doi:10.1080/0965254X.2018.1493523

The Indian Evidence Act,1872(Act I of 1872)

The Indian Penal Code,1860 (Act 45 of 1860)

The Information Technology Act,2000(Act 45 of 1860)

The Negotiable Instruments Act,1881(Act 16 0f 1881)

The use of Artificial Intelligence and Cyber security. (n.d.). www.computer.org/publications/tech-news/trends/the-use-of-artificial-intelligence-in-cybersecurity

Thorsten & Weigold. (n.d.). *Secure Internet Banking Authentication*. Academic Press.

Thyagarajan, C., Suresh, S., Sathish, N., & Suthir, S. (2020). A typical analysis and survey on healthcare cyber security. *Int. Journal of Scientific & Technology Research*, *9*(3), 3267–3270.

Tr, R. (2021). Internet of Things (IoT) and Cyber Physical Systems (CPS) for Smart Applications. *International Journal of Sensors, Wireless Communications and Control*, *11*(3), 262–262. doi:10.2174/221032791103210310141755

Tsai, F. S., & Chan, K. L. (2007, April). Detecting cyber security threats in weblogs using probabilistic models. In *Pacific-Asia Workshop on Intelligence and Security Informatics* (pp. 46-57). Springer. 10.1007/978-3-540-71549-8_4

Tully, J., Selzer, J., Phillips, J. P., O'Connor, P., & Dameff, C. (2020). Healthcare challenges in the era of cybersecurity. *Health Security*, *18*(3), 228–231. doi:10.1089/hs.2019.0123 PMID:32559153

Vande Putte, D., & Verhelst, M. (2014). Cybercrime: Can a standard risk analysis help in the challenges facing business continuity managers? *Journal of Business Continuity & Emergency Planning*, *7*(2), 126–137. PMID:24457324

Varadharajan, V., & Tupakula, U. (2020). Counteracting Attacks From Malicious End Hosts in Software Defined Networks. *IEEE eTransactions on Network and Service Management*, *17*(1), 160–174. doi:10.1109/TNSM.2019.2931294

Vázquez, D. F., Acosta, O. P., Spirito, C., Brown, S., & Reid, E. (2012, June). Conceptual framework for cyber defense information sharing within trust relationships. In *2012 4th International Conference on Cyber Conflict (CYCON 2012)* (pp. 1-17). IEEE.

Vermesan, O., Friess, P., & Guillemin, P. (2011). Internet of things strategic research roadmap. *Global Technological and Societal Trends*, *1*, 9–52.

Wang, C., Zhang, N., & Wang, C. (2021). Managing privacy in the digital economy. *Fundamental Research*, *1*(5), 543–551.

Wang, J., Tan, Y., Liu, J., & Zhang, Y. (2020). Topology Poisoning Attack in SDN-Enabled Vehicular Edge Network. *IEEE Internet of Things Journal*, *7*(10), 9563–9574. doi:10.1109/JIOT.2020.2984088

Wang, Y., Hu, T., Tang, G., Xie, J., & Lu, J. (2019). SGS: Safe-Guard Scheme for Protecting Control Plane Against DDoS Attacks in Software-Defined Networking. *IEEE Access: Practical Innovations, Open Solutions*, *7*, 34699–34710. doi:10.1109/ACCESS.2019.2895092

Wei, K., Jian, W., & Kui, R. (2016). A Survey of Big Data Security Protection Technology. *Journal of Network and Information Security*, *2*(4).

Wirth, J., Maier, C., Laumer, S., & Weitzel, T. (2019). Perceived information sensitivity and interdependent privacy protection: A quantitative study. *Electronic Markets, 29,* 359–378.

Wong, D., Kuen, H., Loh, C., & Randall, B. (2015). *To trust or not to trust, the consumers dilemma with e-banking.* Academic Press.

Wüeest. (2015). *Threats to Online Banking, Symantec Security Response.* Academic Press.

Xu, Y., Sun, H., Xiang, F., & Sun, Z. (2019). Efficient DDoS Detection Based on K-FKNN in Software Defined Networks. *IEEE Access: Practical Innovations, Open Solutions, 7,* 160536–160545. doi:10.1109/ACCESS.2019.2950945

Yan, F. (2016). Big Data Security and Privacy Protection. *Electronic Technology and Software Engineering,* (1), 227.

Yang, F., & Wang, S. (2014). Student's perception towards personal information and privacy disclosure in e-learning. *The Turkish Online Journal of Educational Technology, 13*(1), 207–216.

Yang, P., Xiong, N., & Ren, J. (2020). Data security and privacy protection for cloud storage: A survey. *IEEE Access: Practical Innovations, Open Solutions, 8,* 131723–131740. doi:10.1109/ACCESS.2020.3009876

Yan, Z., Zhang, P., & Vasilakos, A. V. (2014). A survey on trust management for internet of things. *Journal of Network and Computer Applications, 42,* 120–134. doi:10.1016/j.jnca.2014.01.014

Yeole, A. S., & Kalbande, D. R. (2016, March). Use of Internet of Things (IoT) in healthcare: A survey. In *Proceedings of the ACM Symposium on Women in Research 2016* (pp. 71-76). 10.1145/2909067.2909079

Ying, L. (2016). Research on Big Data Security and Privacy Protection. *Information Communication,* (1), 162–163.

Yoon, S., Cho, J. H., Kim, D. S., Moore, T. J., Free-Nelson, F., & Lim, H. (2020). Attack Graph-Based Moving Target Defense in Software-Defined Networks. *IEEE eTransactions on Network and Service Management, 17*(3), 1653–1668. doi:10.1109/TNSM.2020.2987085

Yuehong, Y. I. N., Zeng, Y., Chen, X., & Fan, Y. (2016). The internet of things in healthcare: An overview. *Journal of Industrial Information Integration, 1,* 3–13. doi:10.1016/j.jii.2016.03.004

Zeng, D., Guo, S., & Cheng, Z. (2011). The web of things: A survey. *Journal of Communication, 6*(6), 424–438.

Zhang, D. (2018, October). Big data security and privacy protection. In *8th International Conference on Management and Computer Science (ICMCS 2018)* (Vol. 77, pp. 275-278). Atlantis Press.

Zhang, P., Zhang, F., Xu, S., Yang, Z., Li, H., Li, Q., Wang, H., Shen, C., & Hu, C. (2021). Network-Wide Forwarding Anomaly Detection and Localization in Software Defined Networks. *IEEE/ACM Transactions on Networking, 29*(1), 332–345. doi:10.1109/TNET.2020.3033588

Zhijun, W., Qing, X., Jingjie, W., Meng, Y., & Liang, L. (2020). Low-Rate DDoS Attack Detection Based on Factorization Machine in Software Defined Network. *IEEE Access: Practical Innovations, Open Solutions, 8,* 17404–17418. doi:10.1109/ACCESS.2020.2967478

About the Contributors

Sukanta Kumar Baral has his M. Com, PGDBA, LL. B, MBA and Ph.D. (Awarded in the year 1999) from Utkal University, Bhubaneswar, Orissa. He has authored 18 books with most current, comprehensive and state-of-art analysis to fulfil the need of Commerce & Management students, professionals and executives working in related fields. He has been honoured with 17 prestigious National and International Awards. He has been associated as the Life Member of 24 prestigious Indian Organisations and as an active academician, he has been closely associated with several Indian and foreign Universities. He is the Chief Editor of the 'Splint International Journal of Professionals', a Quarterly Published International Journal, ISSN 2349 – 6045 (P) 2583-3661 (O), abstracted and indexed @ ProQuest, USA, J-Gate, Indian Citation Index & International Scientific Indexing since 2013. He has contributed 137 Research Articles in different referred National and International Journals to his credit and working as Professor, Department of Commerce, Faculty of Commerce & Management at Indira Gandhi National Tribal University (A Central University of Govt. of India), Amarkantak, Madhya Pradesh, India.

Richa Goel is Assistant Professor-Economics and International Business at Amity International Business School, Amity University Noida. She is a Ph.D. in Management and has a journey of almost 18 years in academic and consistently striving to create a challenging and engaging learning environment where students become life-long scholars and learners. Imparting lectures using different teaching strategies, she is an avid teacher, researcher, and mentor. She has to her credit a number of publications in reputed national and international journals accompanied with participation in conferences. She is serving as a member of review committee for conferences journals and acting as Lead Editor of Annual International Referred Journal and Research Coordinator with Amity International Business School. Her area of interest includes Economics, Business Law, Human Resource Management and Diversity Management.

* * *

Avishak Bala, BBA from North South University in Finance and Accounting Major, is an Entrepreneur, Artist and a Sports Person. During his university life, he was involved with a lots of extracurricular activities. He is a lifetime Core Member and a Former Music Co-ordinator of North South University Shangskritik Shangatha (NSUSS). Also, he has been the Music Coordinator of North South University's Annual Cultural Evening (ACE) for three consecutive years. In 2017, he initially entered into the garments business. Also gradually started restaurant business with his friends. However, he successfully managed all these activities along with the academic pressure. Moreover, Avishak Bala performed indifferent voluntary activities in The US Embassy (The American Centre Dhaka), The EMK Centre and North South University Language Club and got the Appreciation Certificate. Currently, he is working with a UK based MNC (Quantanite).

Aswani Kumar Cherukuri is a Professor at Vellore Institute of Technology (VIT), India. His research interests include information security and machine learning. Dr. Ch. Aswani Kumar earned the Young Scientist Fellowship from Tamilnadu State Council for Science and Technology and was awarded the Inspiring Teacher Award from The Indian Express (India's leading English daily newspaper). He has worked on various research projects funded by the Government of India's Department of Science and Technology, Department of Atomic Energy, and the Ministry of Human Resources Development. Dr. Ch. Aswani Kumar has published more than 150 refereed research articles in various national/international journals and conferences and is an editorial board member for several international journals. He is a Senior Member and distinguished speaker of the Association for Computing Machinery (ACM), a member of the Institute of Electrical and Electronics Engineers (IEEE), and Vice-Chair of the IEEE Taskforce on Educational Data Mining. Dr. Ch. Aswani Kumar earned a PhD in informational retrieval, data mining, and soft-computing techniques from VIT.

Shivani Choudhary, born and raised in Delhi, has done her post-graduation from Amity University, Noida; specializing in Master of Arts in Business Economics. She has done her undergraduate in Economics, from Jamia Millia Islamia under the aegis of Delhi's Central University. Her research interest areas are Industry 4.0, cryptocurrency, cybersecurity and human resource. Prior to this, she has presented her research work in the 5th International Hybrid Conference: Harnessing Innovation, Technology and Society 5.0 hosted by Amity School of Economics, Amity University. She aims to nurture the academic and research curiosity, resilience in herself and those around her; and believes in undertaking a harmonious blend of human touch and data driven methodology for scientific research in upcoming technological fields.

Sunita Rani Das is working as Assistant Director in the Monetary Policy Department of Bangladesh Bank, Head Office.

Ayon Dutta, MBA(DU), BBA(DU), is a Banker, Economic Thinker, Auditor and Journal Editor. Of his 5 years of Banking career, he has been working as Credit Analyst of Bank Asia Limited since 2018 in Bangladesh. He is also worked as Assistant Manager (Audit) of Bangladesh Overseas Employment and Services Limited. Ayon Dutta has been occupying himself in Journal Writing nationally 2019. He is also served as a coordinator in the organization Somajer Jonne Jagoron (Sojja) and also served as a teacher in the institution named Shapnoroth between 2014 and 2016. He is a debater, economic thinker, Member of WF fund management Committee in Barapukuria Coal Mine School. He is also served as an Accounts and Finance Executive in the Travel based Platform "Travelindream.com". He is awarded with DBBL merit scholarship award, PB merit scholarship award, Board Merit Scholarship Award 2010, Anirbaan Srutilekhok Sommanona 2016 and honored by DC for Scientific project Exhibition.

Nabila Fahria is working as a Deputy Director in Monetary Policy Department of Bangladesh Bank since November, 2016. Before joining Bangladesh Bank she worked as a Pricing Specialist in Robi Axiata Limited. She acquired her Bachelor's and Master's degree in economics from North South University and also had working experience as a Teaching Assistant. During her service period in the central bank, she has extensively worked with various secondary data sources and analyzing all the economic indicators in detail. Also working as a team member of Economic Model Forecasting Unit. She has worked on macroeconomic and forecasting model and her current interests are monetary and fiscal policy, financial inclusion, development sector, etc.

Seema Garg is Associate Professor at Amity International Business School, Amity University. She has done her M.Sc , M.Phil from Delhi University, Delhi and Ph.D from Jamia Millia Islamia University, Delhi. Her area of specialisation is Decision Sciences. She has over 19 years experience in academics and teaching. Her publications are in the areas of data Envelopment analysis, Modelling and Efficiency Optimization using Data Envelopment Analysis application of DEA. She has pursued research in truly inter- disciplinary areas. She has to her credits a number of reputed national and international journals. She is the Merit certificate holder from Central Board of secondary education and also recipient of National Scholarship for academic performance. She has also received the Best teacher award from MLA of Delhi.

Partho Ghosh, BBA (North South University), is an Entrepreneur, Auditor, and Economic thinker. He worked as an Auditor at Hope Foundation CCDB for the International Labor Organization during 2014-2017. He is an Entrepreneur and Business figure. Partho Ghosh initially started restaurant business titled Wake 'n' Bite in Kuratoli, Dhaka during his undergraduate life in 2017. He also started selling Garment products and Books as a retailer. He is also expert in online marketing and started an online-based business titled "Hello Online" to serve the people and motivate them to stay at home during the pandemic situation. He is also CEO of family business of sweetmeats and desert named "New Gouronodi Mistanno Bhandar " which is a more than 40 years old business and started online-based services.

Rabinarayan Patnaik, currently working as a Professor in Marketing and Strategic Management at Institute of Management and Information Science (IMIS), was awarded with PhD in Commerce from North Orissa University, India in the year 2012. After being a Bachelor of Engineering in Mining he successfully completed Master of Business Studies from Pune, India. As a Six Sigma Black Belt, each act of his comprises of precision and conciseness. He works very closely and actively as a consultant with various government and non-governmental bodies typically in Technology, Rural and Agricultural Sectors as well as Education. He has authored multiple publications and four number of books to satiate his unending passion towards writing and enriching the lives of others with real time knowledge.

Saila Sarmin Rapti started her career as an Assistant Director in Research Department of Bangladesh Bank in 2016. She received her Master's and Bachelor's degree in Economics from Jahangirnagar University. From the very beginning of her career, she has been actively involved in data analysis of macroeconomic indicators of Bangladesh and SAARC countries. She has gained valuable knowledge by attending in several training programmes on macroeconomic issues in national and international level. Her current areas of research interest are Macroeconomic modeling and forecasting, regional development, financial inclusion, monetary policy analysis etc.

Ramesh Chandra Rath is an eminent professor & academician of an International repute in the field of Management Education (Mkt. &HR) and Clinical Psychology. He has served 24 years of Service in various Government Colleges and Universities of Odisha and abroad. He has obtained his Post Graduate Degree in Clinical Psychology from SCB, Medical College, Cuttack, Affiliated to Utkal University, Vanivihar, Bhubaneswar, and MA in Psychology from Sambalpur University, Concurred his MBA Degree from Delhi University in 1996, Concurred his Ph.D., Degree, from "Birla Institute of Technology, Mesra, Ranchi in 2000 [Green

Marketing & Supply Chain Management] Concurred his Post- Doctorate Degree (D.Litt.) from Patna University Patna, Bihar in the year 2003, Presently, he is working as a Dean (R&D) and Head of the Department of MBA, Guru Gobind Singh Educational Society's Technical Campus, Bokaro steel City,(Jharkhand) India. Dr. Rath has guided Seventeen Ph.D. research scholars from various universities in Odisha and abroad. There are 32 International journals and 38 National Journals with two books of publication to his credit.,

Neeru Sidana has more than 12 years comprehensive teaching experience in academic sector, she is dynamic & laborious personality, a shining star in her career so far and has left good benchmarks to be achieved. Currently associated with Amity School of Economics (ASE), Amity University – Noida. She has worked with leading educational group affiliated with Kurukshetra University. She has also served as Associate Professor – Economics Domain in "Lovely Professional University", Jalandhar-Punjab. Having passion for teaching and training she has participated in more than 50 seminars, workshops, conferences, FDP & MDPs and presented research papers also in national & International repute conferences. She is widely travelled person, her extrovert personality and temperament gives her winning edge.

Tilottama Singh is a certified HR analyst and trained academic, researcher, and trainer with 9 years of experience in the field of Human Resources and Work Dynamics. She is currently employed as an Assistant Professor in Amity University, Noida, UP. Her areas of expertise are: Human Resources & Strategy and her teaching concentration include Human resource, strategy and law. She is also involved in the course and syllabus designing and developing on various Management topics, including analytics, wellbeing and management curriculum. She also serves as the member of AIMA and acts to lead and liaise between the student community and the industry delegates, with a keen interest in training.

Sushant Sinha is an undergraduate student of information technology in Vellore institute of technology, Vellore. His research interests are Security and Software Defined Networks.

Rajeev Srivastava has experience of more than 16 years which include around 12 years in IMS Unison University, Dehradun as Dean IT and Head IT Department and as Head Decision Sciences Department in UPES Dehradun. Expertise in subjects like Data Visualisation using Tableau, Machine Learning using WEKA, Big Data Analytics using MongoDB. Involved in teaching, research and administration for last 16 years. Published more than 30 publications which include Research Papers in Scopus, International and National Journals. Many paper accepted in reputed

Conference like PAN IIM and AMCIS (American conference of Information system). Organized many Conferences, Seminars; FDP's as Coordinator and Chaired many sessions at the Conferences. Reviewer of many International and National Journals. Conducted full day sessions on "ML and IT related issues" in many organisation like OIL Assam, HPCL Pune. Signed MOU with many organizations like Oracle University, NIIT, HPES etc. Completed various certification from Coursera, edX, Google Analytics Academy.

Saurabh Tiwari has more than 14 years of teaching experience in the field of logistics and supply chain management and three years in the manufacturing sector. He has several publications in reputed international journals and completed his Ph.D. in the field of lean manufacturing practices in India. He currently has diversified research interests in transportation, sustainable manufacturing, Industry 4.0, and innovation. He is an Associate Professor in the field of logistics and supply chain management at the School of Business, University of Petroleum and Energy Studies, Dehradun, India.

Index

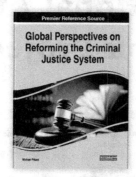

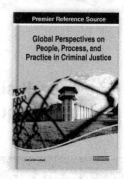

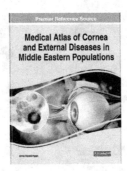
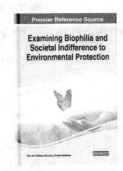
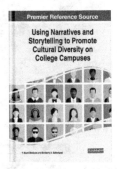

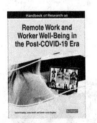

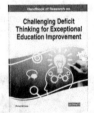

ited States
Publisher Services

Printed in the Un
by Baker & Taylor

Printed in the United States
by Baker & Taylor Publisher Services